CW01072726

CHALK AND CHEESE

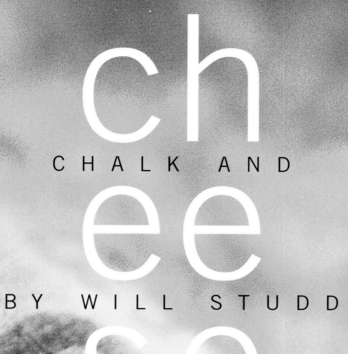

cheese

CHALK AND

BY WILL STUDD

Photography by Adrian Lander

purple egg

First published by Purple Egg in 1999
PO Box 931
South Melbourne
Victoria 3205
Australia

Designed by Ian Scott Design
Co-ordination by Michele Curtis and Allan Campion
Edited by Jenny Lee
Typeset in Trade Gothic by Tony Albers
Printed in Australia by Brown Prior Anderson
Distributed in Australia by Discriptus 03 9482 5995

National Library of Australia Cataloguing-in-Publication data
Studd, Will.
Chalk and Cheese.
Bibliography.
Includes index.
ISBN 0 9586195 0 6.
1. Cheese. 2. Cheese – Australia.
3. Cheese – Varieties. 4. Cheese – Varieties – Australia.
I. Lander, Adrian. II. Title.
637.3

FOR BONNIE, FLEUR, KATE AND SAM

CONTENTS

ACKNOWLEDGEMENTS

This book has been made possible by the continuing encouragement of many people in the cheese industry, both in Australia and overseas. Their commitment to our shared cause of demystifying what real cheese is all about has kept me going, and I have greatly appreciated their help, both direct and indirect.

I am particularly grateful to my wife Bonnie and our children for their patience; to Allan Campion, Michele Curtis and Ian Scott at Purple Egg Publishing for their enthusiasm and commitment to getting it right; to Adrian Lander for his stunning photos; and to Jenny Lee for her editorial skill and perseverance with every detail.

Thanks too to all the people who so generously contributed recipes; Nick Haddow for his unbridled enthusiasm and precious help with some sections; Geoff Jansz for encouraging me to follow my dreams when I first contemplated making the transition from talking about cheese to writing about it; Max Allen for his generosity with the wine and help in tasting it; Max Lake for his contribution to the taste section; my colleagues at Calendar Cheese Company, particularly Sam Hurst, David Herbert and Joe Bradshaw, who kept it growing; my partners in Richmond Hill Café and Larder — Stephanie Alexander, Angela Clemens and Lisa Montague — for their understanding; Maggie Beer for her encouragement and happy smiles; Geoff Slattery for the initial idea; Andrew Wood for his help with the tasting notes; Lorna Garden for her nutritional advice; Captain Chris Blake and Carol for reminding me to sniff the roses occasionally and to dare to try for the top; and especially all those passionate small cheese-makers who work so hard to make it happen, particularly Laurie Jensen and Richard Thomas. May they just get better and better.

PREFACE

My first visit to Australia in 1996 was a real eye-opener for me. I had come to attend an Australian Specialist Cheesemakers' Association meeting in Melbourne, and I travelled with Will Studd through Victoria, visiting cheese-makers from the Western District to Gippsland. What struck me first was the range and quality of cheese now being made around Australia. I tasted many excellent cheeses, and a great diversity of them, from buffalo mozzarella to cow's milk blues; from cheddar-style cheeses to soft and creamy camembert. There was a sense of energy and excitement in the air – excitement that finally cheese-making was experiencing the same burst of creative energy which has become a feature of Australian wine-making and cooking in recent years.

The Australian cheeses themselves were new to me, but the atmosphere was remarkably familiar. In Britain, as in Australia, there is a cheese-making revolution taking place. It is led by people who are fed up with the bland mediocrity of a mass-produced diet. They want to enjoy what they are eating and they want to know something about the people who are producing their food.

Until quite recently, cheese with flavour was hard to come by. Technology ruled. As factories became ever larger, cheese-making changed from a labour-intensive activity to a manufacturing process performed at the touch of a button.

From one perspective the result could be considered 'progress'. Mass-produced cheeses are consistent, innocuous and cheap. People know what to expect from them, and they surprise nobody's tastebuds. For all these reasons they are well suited to the way most food is sold today. No longer is there a knowledgeable person behind the counter to help you find just the thing you are looking for, whether you prefer your cheese punchy and powerful or tenderly mild. When you're on your own in the supermarket, you have to rely on labels to help you make your choice.

A lot of people have had enough of this kind of 'progress'. Cheese eaters, restaurateurs, merchants and shopkeepers have begun to demand food with flavour once more. The result is a powerful revival of the art of cheese-making, an art which we nearly lost in Britain and one which had died out completely in Australia.

One of the things that makes *Chalk and Cheese* very special is the fact that its author really understands cheese and cheese-making. Will Studd illuminates the details which make the difference, whether it's what makes cheeses blue or the difference between modern and traditional brie. It's a great book for anyone, anywhere, who is interested in cheese and good food. *Chalk and Cheese* is an excellent guide to exploring the traditions, stories and flavours that make the world of cheese so rich and varied. I hope you enjoy it.

Randolph Hodgson
London, January 1999

INTRODUCTION

Introduction

I was lucky enough to spend my formative years in a household attuned to the rhythm of the seasons, with good, fresh food to be had in plenty from our own garden. When I was a small boy my family moved from London to the rolling, green Kentish countryside, where my father, a quantity surveyor, had designed and built a house set on several acres of old cherry orchard. All the family worked together to clear away the trees that were past their prime and turn the neglected orchard into a productive garden.

Everyday items that we take for granted today were not easily obtainable then. Their absence always seemed to be blamed on the war, even though it had ended ten years earlier. I can clearly remember tiny bottles of expensive olive oil that could only be bought from the chemist, lemon juice that came from a plastic lemon, and my mother's cherished collection of spices from around the world. Yet we certainly never went hungry, and the kitchen and the garden were the twin hubs of our family life.

Both my father and mother were keen gardeners. With a family that eventually grew to six boys, they had many mouths to feed on a limited income, and it seemed quite natural that we should try to grow most of what we ate, whether it be vegetables, fruit or protein. This experience kindled my interest in gardening and made me aware of the ebb and flow of the seasons and the fluctuating bounties of every harvest. I can recall the excitement of discovering new foods and experimenting with flavours from around the garden, as I would later explore new tastes from around the world.

Tucked away behind the orchard was a huge vegetable garden, meticulously laid out in rows so that it would provide for our needs throughout the year. A separate area contained a soft fruit garden with grapes, currants, berries of all kinds and clumps of rhubarb growing under upturned urns to protect their tender stems from frost. As children we were all kept busy with our designated jobs in the garden. The junior job was emptying the compost bucket; picking a crop was only for those old and sensible enough to know where to stand without crushing the growing plants.

In the spring the orchard was briefly covered with a glorious white mantle that would soon fall and carpet the green grass with a confetti of petals. This was the time for eating our fill of the season's first asparagus and joking about our 'bean thumbs', which were constantly sore from harvesting young broad beans for the freezer. As the season developed, we would dig endless rows of sweet new potatoes and enjoy tender, perfumed raspberries in profusion.

In a good year, summer brought a race with the birds to pick the juicy cherries. The biggest, blackest fruit grew on one particular old tree, and to reach them we had to climb along the creaking boughs, getting covered in purple juice along the way. In years of surplus my mother bottled these cherries in jars of sweet syrup and brought them out for special occasions to serve with clotted cream, which was sent by post from the West Country. Midsummer meant hours on the terrace surrounded by brown onions, shallots and garlic laid out in rows to dry in the sun. We struggled to smile and joke as we peeled the tiny pickling onions, our faces streaked with tears.

Autumn was the season of rain and falling leaves, old-fashioned apples, rock-hard pears, chestnuts and bonfires. Our hands would freeze and the thick Kentish clay would stick to our boots as we worked our way along the rows, wrapping celery with newspaper and string to blanch the stems. After the first frosts of winter the brussels sprouts would crack as you picked them, but they always tasted best in the cold. We also kept chickens for eggs, and in some years turkeys and ducks, which lived in a small mud hut we had all built. There was always plenty of food to eat throughout the year, and plenty of work to do in the garden to keep it coming.

At the age of eight I was sent off to boarding school. It was a crash course in self-reliance. An endless series of overcooked school meals made me all too conscious of the good, fresh food I was missing out on at home. I always looked forward to my mother's homemade fruit cake; I treasured it in my tuckbox and eked it out for as long as possible, which generally was not for long.

It was the poor quality of school meals that inspired my first teenage foray into turning a penny on food. Our boarding house had a boot room, where there was a large china sink and a two-burner gas stove. On reaching a certain grade, at about the age of fifteen, we were allowed to use this facility for making coffee and tea and heating our own meals. One day I had the bright idea of making pancakes as a change from the usual fare of tinned beans or spaghetti on toast. I used the free school milk and scrounged eggs and flour from the old dears working in the kitchen. There was soon a regular evening shift, with hungry boarders lining up to pay for a feed. Unfortunately the housemaster took a dim view of this enterprise, and it did not last long.

After leaving school I enrolled in economics at Leeds University and spent my holidays working in a shop called Justin de Blank in Belgravia, which had a wonderful range of food. Then, at the end of my studies, the mundane world beckoned; I was offered a 'good career job' as an articled clerk for a major London accounting firm. I hated the traditional structure and all it represented. After a year I quit, deciding that specialist food was where my heart and future lay.

My first big break came from a rather mysterious character, known to me only as Mr Vince, who owned a number of smart supermarkets around London and was looking for someone to sublet the delicatessen at the back of his store in Notting Hill Gate. The deli was small and rundown, but I seized on the chance to run my own show. I renamed it Relish and stocked it with the very best of all that could be found in London, including fresh salads, smoked salmon, naturally preserved meats and some of the finest of the world's cheeses. Our facilities were far from luxurious – for a time I matured the brie in a packing-room cupboard – but the formula worked, and within a couple of years I had six outlets in operation around central London.

Marriage and parenthood led me to a little house in the Welsh Harp, which was like living in the country, though very close to London. The house backed on to a park, across which was a cluster of garden allotments. I duly took one up and spent my Saturday mornings yarning about the benefits of blood and bone with the immensely knowledgeable old men who congregated there.

My wife, Bonnie, is an Australian, and we had spent our honeymoon lazing among the turtles at Heron Island. This was the first of several exploratory trips, during which I became increasingly attracted to the uncrowded, easy-going quality of Australian life – and to the prospect of living in a climate where I could grow tomatoes in the open for six months of the year. When I received an offer for my London business, I finally took the plunge. In 1981 we packed up our possessions and moved to Melbourne. My impression was that the cheese available in Australia was very ordinary, and soon I decided that I would try to break the mould. I bought a refrigerated van, employed Jonathan Gunn Russell, an old friend and manager from London, and organised my first air shipment of French and English specialist cheese to Melbourne under the disapproving eye of the quarantine authorities. It was an expensive and risky move, but when the cheese arrived all my doubts evaporated. It tasted really good, and the shipment sold out within a week. It was the beginning of a new business, Butterfields Cheese Factors.

Six months later I had a visit from a couple of young cheese-makers, Laurie Jensen and Richard Thomas, who were seeking advice on how to sell their new 'creamy blue' farm cheese. They feared that the venture was in danger of failing because of established wholesalers' resistance to the price. They gave me a taste, and I felt my prayers had been answered. At last I had found a cheese that had flavour and character and was proudly made in Australia. We named it 'Gippsland Blue', and toasted the birth of Australia's first new farmhouse cheese in decades.

The success of Gippsland Blue marked the beginning of an exciting time. New cheeses began to appear all over the country. Frank Marchand just turned up at the warehouse one day, fresh from the Tasmanian ferry, with a truck full of smelly gruyère. At Timboon, Herman Schultz began to experiment with traditional white-rind cheeses, ripening his first creations in a cardboard box on the veranda. Bill Kirk put King Island on the map with his beautiful King Island Cream, George Ronalds and Laurie Jensen began making triple cream cheese at Jindi, and at Milawa Richard Thomas and David Brown produced Australia's first washed-rind cheese.

The new diversity of Australian cheese-making extended to new sources of milk as well. A Sydney friend tipped me off about a wonderful new goat cheese being made by Gabrielle Kervella in the dry hills near Perth, while closer to home Julie Cameron and Richard Thomas launched the first farmhouse ewe's milk cheese from Meredith Dairy, near Ballarat. When Roger Haldane brought in a herd of dairy buffalo from Italy, the menagerie was finally complete.

I have immensely enjoyed sharing in this process of discovery. Working with these new cheese-makers, I have found I had to seek answers to difficult theoretical questions about the sources of texture and flavour in cheese. I regularly visit Europe and find myself constantly asking questions about what it is that makes the best European cheeses what they are. These are questions that are rarely asked in Europe, where received wisdom and traditional practices are firmly entrenched.

This book is an attempt to share my view on what I have learnt in the cheese game over the years, and on what it is that makes particular cheeses more interesting than others. It is not the only way to look at specialist cheese, nor is it only relevant to what we have achieved in Australia. I hope it will lead to a better understanding of what specialist cheese is about for the future, and an appreciation of just what it is that makes cheese in Australia matter now.

Will Studd
Melbourne, January 1999

origin

ORIGINS

From the Beginning

Cheese is a preserved form of milk, and is one of the oldest manufactured foods. Its origins go back to the dawn of time, when humans first attempted to save surplus seasonal milk for later consumption. Making cheese is based on the natural principles of fermentation, which is used to remove most of the liquid (whey) from the milk, leaving the solids (curds). The most interesting cheeses exhibit a fundamental link between the skills of the farmer, the traditional craft of the cheese-maker and the complex influences of local seasons, soils and geography.

The oldest written record of cheese dates from the fourth millennium BC, when a Sumerian stock-breeder meticulously kept his accounts in cuneiform on clay tablets. Although we do not know the breeder's name, we do know that his herd multiplied fivefold in eight years, and that at the end of the period they were producing enough milk to make 42.5 litres of butter and 63.3 litres of cheese annually.

Cheese was highly valued in many other ancient civilisations. In Egypt, it was included among the supplies buried with the Pharaohs in their magnificent tombs. Ancient Greek literature includes numerous references to cheese-making and to the health-giving properties of cheese. Homer's *Odyssey* describes how Ulysses watches Cyclops, the one-eyed giant, make soft cheese in wicker baskets, and in his other epic poem, the *Iliad*, a warrior is fed goat's cheese to help him recover from the wounds he sustained during the siege of Troy. Cheese occasionally plays a bit part in the Old Testament of the Bible as well; according to the First Book of Samuel, for example, it was on an expedition to deliver cheese and other supplies to his brethren's army that David encountered Goliath.

The beginnings of cheese-making, though, go back long before this. The history of cheese probably began with a fortunate accident as far back as 12000 BC. Historians and archaeologists are still debating where this happened, but it seems likely to have been somewhere in the region

stretching from the Carpathian mountains on the Black Sea, through ancient Turkey and west to modern-day Turkmenistan and Iran. The nomadic people who inhabited this area constantly moved from place to place, stopping only for short periods of time to allow their sheep and goats to graze. Milk would have been an important food, but it was only available during the lactation season in the warmer months.

No one can say for sure how the first cheese was made, but it seems a fair guess that it happened accidentally when milk was stored in a skin bag made from the stomach of a young animal, or perhaps left out in the open in a shallow bowl. In warm weather, or slung over the back of a warm beast, the milk would have naturally fermented, and the whey would have separated from the curds, which were then firmed by the action of natural bacteria or the rennin in the skin bag. People soon realised that the whey made a palatable drink, while the curd could be eaten fresh, or perhaps dried and shaped. These early cheeses would have been rudimentary, soft and fresh, made from goat's or ewe's milk and with a limited shelf life, not unlike some of the fresh cheeses made today.

Somewhere around 6000 BC humans started to cultivate cereal crops and develop basic pasture management techniques. As well as the traditional flocks of roaming sheep and goats, many agricultural peoples began to keep cattle. Of fiery temperament in their wild state, cattle were gradually domesticated by controlled feeding, penning and castration. They required a much larger amount of pasture than sheep or goats, but they had a longer lactation period and produced a greater volume of milk. In particular, they offered a surplus of butterfat, which could easily be collected from on top of the milk. In ancient Greece cow's milk was such a scarce commodity that it was primarily reserved for making butter (*buturon*) or 'cow cheese'.

Cheese gradually became an essential part of the basic daily diet in many countries. The expansion of the Roman Empire from the first century BC helped to spread the knowledge of cheese-making throughout the Mediterranean, Asia Minor and northern Europe. Every Roman legionary was provided with a small cake of salted cheese as part of his daily rations – a convenient food for troops on the move, because it needed no cooking.

Roman writers produced instructional works on agriculture describing the process of cheese-making in some detail. In particular, it is clear that they knew about the use of rennet to harden the curd, the need to press the whey from fresh cheeses to reduce moisture, and the importance of salt to preserve and dry cheese. Larger Roman houses had a separate cheese kitchen, and cheeses were often basted with wine, smoked or dusted with chives and salt before eating.

Goats remained the most important milking animals, while cattle were mainly used as beasts of burden. In Virgil's long didactic poem, the *Georgics*, he bluntly told farmers:

> *Don't follow our forebears' custom, whereby*
> *Mother-cows filled the snowy milk-pails; their young should have all*
> *The benefit of their udders.*

When it came to goats, however, the milk was the main thing:

> *They browse in woods and in Arcadian highlands*
> *On prickly briars and thorns that love the steep,*
> *And of their own accord, leading their kids,*
> *Return at nightfall punctually to stall,*
> *Brushing the threshold with their swollen udders.*
> *So all the more because they less demand*
> *Of human care you'll shield them from the frost*

The collapse of the Roman Empire in 476 AD was followed by a long period of conflict. There were large-scale movements of people from country to country, and some brought new animals with them. The Vikings, for example, introduced the ancestors of the Normandy, Jersey and Guernsey breeds of cattle to northern France and the Channel Islands. During this period, however, many of the skills of cheese-making were lost. Those traditional recipes that were to survive were quietly maintained in remote mountain communities or closely guarded by religious orders, especially the Benedictine and Cistercian monks. The members of religious orders were forbidden to eat meat on fast days, of which there might be as many as a hundred during the year, so cheese was an important alternative source of protein. In their own sequestered world, the cheese-making monks began a culinary revolution by pioneering the use of moulds to ripen soft cheese. It was in the abbeys of France around 800 AD that the Holy Roman Emperor Charlemagne first experienced the delights of roquefort and brie.

Outside the monasteries, dairying was widely regarded as women's work and was not valued highly. The word 'dairy' itself comes from the Middle English word 'dey', meaning a female servant. Most of the cheese eaten in medieval times was simple fresh curd, made in small quantities and consumed close to its point of production. For banquets it might be flavoured with bacon, deep-fried in lard and dusted with sugar, in keeping with the eclectic medieval taste.

WHAT'S IN A NAME?

The European words for cheese fall into two families. The first of these originated from the ancient Greek term for the box (*phormos*) used to strain the whey from the curd. This gave rise to the Latin *forma*, from which came the medieval French word *fromage* and Italian *formaggio*.

The second group came from *caseus*, the Latin word for cheese, which eventually became *Käse* in German, *kaas* in Dutch, *queso* in Spanish and cheese in English.

Meanwhile, in the mountains of Europe, a different tradition was beginning to evolve. From about the sixth century onwards, small farmers pooled their summer milk to make large cheeses that could be stored underground in cellars or caves and slowly matured to a hard, quite dry consistency. The result was a range of long-lived cheeses – the ancestors of gruyère, emmental and parmigiano reggiano – which not only sustained marginal farming communities through the long alpine winter but also functioned as a medium of exchange with the outside world – in twentieth-century terms, a cash crop.

In fact, there were many parts of Europe where cheese was as good as cash. The explosion of trade during the Renaissance, which began in Italy around 1300, outran the supply of coin, and hard cheeses, being relatively portable, high-value items, were used as substitutes. Peasants were often required to pay tithes to their landlords partly in butter and cheese, an imposition that was widely resented. According to Maguelonne Toussaint-Samat in her *History of Food,* the tenant farmers of fifteenth-century Savoy were in the habit of making cheese from a secret second milking, which they did not declare to their landlords. This cheese became known as reblochon, from the French *reblocher,* 'to milk again'.

Each region developed its own traditions and made its own distinctive cheeses according to climatic conditions, local needs and the types of animals raised. In the steep, dry hills of Greece, for example, cheese was mainly made from goat's and ewe's milk, whereas in northern parts of Europe cow's milk became more widely used. Like the alpine herders with their co-operatives, the villagers of seventeenth-century England had 'cheddar clubs', where small farmers pooled their milk to make large wheels of cheddar. The farmers' contributions were carefully recorded, and their share of the proceeds was based on the amount of milk they had provided.

With the Industrial Revolution, the making of cheese began to be transformed. By the 1850s many American dairies had adopted a 'factory' system, in which farmers contracted to provide milk to centralised, modern processing facilities. Europe soon followed; France's first industrial dairy was opened in Normandy in 1875. Over the next hundred years, small-scale local production increasingly gave way to large complexes manufacturing huge quantities of cheese to be sold in the burgeoning cities of Europe and America. The introduction of sophisticated and dependable cheese-making technology, fast and reliable transport facilities, refrigeration and large pooled milk supplies marked the beginning of the end for many small specialist cheese producers. The new colonies of Australia, New Zealand and Canada were to lead this transformation, establishing large factories to export low-cost cheese and butter in bulk to Mother England.

Cheese in Australia

When the First Fleet landed in Sydney Cove on 26 January 1788, they brought with them five cows and two bulls – humped Zebus, an Indian breed that was thought to suit the warm climate of the new colony. It soon became obvious that the land around Sydney Harbour was unsuitable for grazing, so the precious herd was moved inland to Parramatta in search of greener pastures. Within a few weeks they had escaped. It was seven years before their progeny were discovered far away, on the banks of the Nepean River, at a place that is still known as Cow Pastures.

Despite this setback, the colony continued to import cattle from India and England at considerable expense. Herd numbers rose to more than a thousand by 1800, but many of these animals were draught oxen, of no use for dairying. The settlement struggled to provide for itself in the early years, and there was a general shortage of dairy products, as of most basic foods. Farmhouse cheese and butter commanded extraordinarily high prices in the Sydney and Parramatta markets. This was an entrepreneurial opportunity too good to be missed by the small minority of colonists who could afford to import cattle on their own account. Foremost among them were John Macarthur, who set up a dairy on his farm at Parramatta, and Dr John Harris, who built Sydney's first commercial dairy in 1805 on his land at Ultimo.

From 1813, when white settlement spread west of the Great Dividing Range, cattle were widely used to open up new country because they handled the native scrub better than sheep. Cattle numbers increased rapidly in the rich new pastures of the south-east, but the main emphasis was on meat production. The small population, slow transport and poor storage facilities made commercial dairying impracticable beyond the fringes of the towns. There was no refrigeration, and fresh milk quickly went off in the Australian heat. The new immigrants followed the old traditions they had brought from Britain. Butter and cheese were made on the farms in small batches during the spring and summer flush, then drenched with salt and other preservatives to prevent spoiling.

The foundations of an Australian cheese industry were laid in the 1820s. In Tasmania, the Van Diemen's Land Company equipped itself with a cheese room and began producing cheese in commercial quantities, while in New South Wales the farmers of the Illawarra district, south of Sydney, carried their butter and cheese along rough bush tracks to the sea, where sailing vessels picked it up for carriage to city markets. With the advent of regular coastal shipping services, dairying gradually expanded along the southern coast of New South Wales as far as the rich Bega region. By the 1830s, small quantities of dairy products were even being exported.

In the area around Melbourne, dairy farming began with the first permanent white settlement. John Fawkner brought two cows and two calves with him on the schooner *Enterprize* when he arrived from Tasmania in 1835. Within a year the Port Phillip District had 155 cattle. As the settlement expanded, the herds grew rapidly, reaching 347,000 by 1850. Dairying also prospered in South Australia, the other new colony established in the 1830s. In 1844, only eight years after South Australia was founded, local farmers were exporting cheese to Tasmania.

Distance remained a major obstacle to the growth of dairying, but local demand was strong. Cheese, in particular, commanded a premium because it was so scarce. In the mid-1840s Henry Angel, who owned Uardry station in the eastern Riverina, found it a paying proposition to load a cart with a ton of cheese (well-salted, no doubt!) and carry it overland to Sydney, more than 400 miles away.

The pace of change accelerated in the 1850s, when the gold rushes brought hundreds of thousands of hopeful immigrants to Australia. The rise of the goldfields and the rapid growth of the towns transformed the market for dairy foods in the eastern colonies. At the beginning of the gold rush, farms went untended as farmers and farm labourers joined the exodus to the goldfields. The diaries of early gold diggers indicate that dairy products were not part of their staple diet. Even basic provisions often ran short, and cheese was considered a rare luxury. It was only after the first chaotic rush was over that farmers and merchants began to take full advantage of the opportunities offered by the diggers' presence. Unable to grow their own food, the gold diggers formed a huge new market for locally produced provisions. The number of cattle in Australia doubled – from about 2 million to 4 million – between 1851 and 1861.

When the easily won surface gold petered out, many former diggers began to look for alternative ways of making a living in Australia. The obvious opportunity lay in the great tracts of land suitable for agriculture, but there was an obstacle: much of the best country had already been taken up by wealthy woolgrowers, who held it under pastoral leases. In Victoria and New South Wales, displaced miners mounted a long-running political campaign to 'unlock the lands' and open them up for small-scale farming. As a result of these pressures, governments in both colonies passed Land Acts in the early 1860s allowing would-be farmers to take up small blocks of land on time payment. These selectors, as they were known, often bought blocks close to the inland towns and used them for dairying. By the end of the nineteenth century, even the remote communities of western New South Wales and Queensland could enjoy the luxury of fresh milk and butter, though cheese remained a rarity.

Larger-scale cheese production was dominated by wealthy landowners who could afford the high cost of importing stud animals and buying modern equipment. From about 1865 onwards there was growing interest in the American factory system. John Orlebar established the earliest cheese-making venture of this kind in the late 1860s at Tooram in western Victoria, buying his milk on contract from local farmers. Elsewhere large landowners set up cheese and butter factories on estates farmed by tenants or sharefarmers. Among them was Robert Tooth of Kameruka, on the south coast of New South Wales, who imported Jersey cattle for his tenant farmers in the 1860s and used the surplus milk to make cheddars and edam-style cheeses.

In the late 1880s, when low wheat prices threatened many small farmers with ruin, the Victorian Department of Agriculture set out to encourage them to diversify into dairying. Extension officers were sent out to spread the gospel, and the government built a model dairy factory to help farmers familiarise themselves with modern methods. The government also paid a bounty on butter exports and bought a freezing works at Newport in Melbourne to store export butter. The extension officers promoted the use of new machines such as the Laval cream separator and mechanical butter churns. Milking machines were another novelty. Thomas Mitchell, father of Dame Nellie Melba, installed Victoria's first such machine on his Lilydale farm in 1888, but for many years cows continued to be mostly milked by hand. From the early 1890s butter factories also installed equipment to test butterfat levels and began to pay farmers according to butterfat content rather than the volume of milk. Though the farmers complained mightily, the new devices put paid to the age-old practice of watering the milk and gave producers a greater incentive to improve their herds by selective breeding.

Dairy farming was slower to develop outside New South Wales and Victoria. The climate of inland Queensland and South Australia was too dry for dairying, and the local market was small. In Queensland dairying was mainly confined to the Darling Downs and Moreton districts until about 1900, while in South Australia it was limited to the south-eastern coastal regions. Though north-eastern Tasmania was rich dairy country, its producers were cut off from mainland markets by the treacherous Bass Strait. The development of dairy farming in Western Australia was impeded by low soil fertility, remoteness from markets and the high costs of clearing hardwood forests.

Since rural Australia could produce far more foodstuffs than the colonies' relatively small population could consume, access to overseas markets was the key to the expansion of Australian agriculture. At the same time the Industrial Revolution in the northern hemisphere had led to the growth of large cities and an increasing demand for cheap processed foods.

COWS NEED GLASSES

One of the few drawbacks in keeping cows in Australian conditions is their long-sightedness, which makes them scared of anything they cannot recognise – particularly koalas, of all things.

Wheat and wool could be carried to Europe by sea without deteriorating badly, but perishable foods such as meat and cheese required new techniques. Many of the early shipments of salted butter and cheese spoiled during the long sea voyages. Attempts to export butter to London during the 1860s were a disaster; by the time it arrived, the butter was only fit to be used as axle grease.

Nevertheless, the nineteenth century was a melting pot of new ideas and technologies, and the obstacles to exporting perishable goods from Australia were gradually overcome. Great strides were made in transport from the 1870s on. All the eastern colonies built extensive railway systems, bringing urban and overseas markets within the reach of an increasingly prosperous farming community. At the same time, the use of steamships brought a new speed and reliability to international trade.

Refrigeration technology also improved rapidly. A Geelong journalist, James Harrison, designed a machine for manufacturing block ice on a commercial scale in 1851. Over the following decades, engineers and amateur inventors worried away at the problem of designing refrigeration equipment capable of handling large quantities of perishable goods at sea.

In 1857 Augustus Morris, a Victorian Member of Parliament, unsuccessfully tried to persuade local stock-owners to offer £100,000 as a prize for anyone who devised a freezing chamber that would allow meat to be exported to England. Some years later Morris met up with an engineer, E. D. Nicolle, who produced a set of drawings for such a refrigeration chamber. The idea was taken up by Thomas Sutcliffe Mort, a Sydney merchant who owned the rich Bodalla dairy estate on the south coast of New South Wales. Nicolle's machine had a successful trial on land in September 1867, but it proved unreliable at sea. Its main use turned out to be for refrigerated rail transport, which at least allowed Mort to ship Bodalla produce to Sydney, where his Fresh Food and Ice Company was soon able to boast daily deliveries of milk, cream, ice and butter to all parts of the city and suburbs. Mort eventually financed the first successful shipment of frozen meat to London in 1880. The real breakthrough, though, came in the early twentieth century, when it became possible to fit ships with chilling chambers. Chilled foodstuffs arrived at market in better condition than frozen goods, and commanded commensurately higher prices.

Once the problems of distance had been overcome, the new Australian dairy industry had significant cost advantages over competitors in the northern hemisphere. Land in Australia was relatively cheap, pastures grew for most of the year on the eastern coastal fringe, and in most districts cattle could safely be left out in the paddocks over winter, whereas in Europe and North America dairy farmers had to provide sheds and stall-feed cattle throughout the colder months.

The manufacture of dairy products became increasingly tailored to export requirements. Cheeses had to store well for the long journey, and preferably be of a type that was familiar to overseas buyers. Britain was the main export market for Australian agricultural products, so producers concentrated on making cheddar, condensed milk and bulk butter. These commodity types still dominate Australian dairy exports today.

The requirements of large-scale production also influenced the structure of the industry. By the 1880s most of the large tenanted estates had been broken up and dairying had become the province of small farmers, none of whom individually had the capital to establish a factory, nor the output to keep it going. To overcome this problem, farmers established co-operatives to finance the construction of factories and pooled their milk to permit bulk production. The first of these co-operative factories was the aptly named Pioneer Butter Factory, which opened near Kiama in New South Wales in 1884. In Victoria the government offered farmers subsidies to establish similar ventures. The first of many Victorian co-operatives was opened at Cobden in 1888, and Queensland farmers followed suit in 1901. The co-operatives gave farmers access to lower-cost production methods, central distribution and ultimately export markets.

Large-scale production required new techniques. Pasteurisation was introduced in the factories, and new kinds of packaging were adopted. Butter was treated with sulphite preservatives and exported in tins or boxes. Cheese was also tinned for export, but in much smaller quantities. Even during the First World War, when overseas sales of cheese boomed, butter still accounted for the bulk of Australia's dairy exports.

The production of bulk cheddar for export had a huge influence on Australian consumers' tastes and their perceptions of cheese. Mass-produced commodity cheese displaced specialist cheeses produced on small farms, so that for most of the twentieth century cheese in Australia meant low-cost bulk cheddar. Above all, it meant Kraft cheese. This new form of processed cheese was developed by James Kraft in the USA in 1903. Its main commercial advantage was that it could be transported without refrigeration. In the mid-1920s the Australian cheese manufacturer Fred Walker employed Cyril Callister, best known as the the inventor of Vegemite, to develop a method of producing processed cheese that would meet Kraft's licensing requirements. They were successful, and in 1926 Walker acquired the licence to make Kraft cheese in Australia.

Kraft's famous blue-and-yellow packets were a brilliant marketing move, as was the decision to label the new cheese 'cheddar' rather than 'processed cheese'. Australian consumers have been confused about what 'real' cheddar is ever since. To distinguish their cheeses from the ubiquitous Kraft, other producers resorted to labelling their natural cheddar 'tasty cheese'.

Whatever the merits of its product, Kraft claimed credit for a rapid increase in Australian cheese consumption, which almost quadrupled over the next fifty years. Exports of Kraft also helped the Australian dairy industry to establish an international reputation as a leader in the mass production of industrial cheese. The emphasis on bulk production, however, came at the expense of variety.

In 1973 Britain's entry to the European Economic Community ended Australia's preferential access to its main traditional market for dairy products. The Australian dairy industry responded to the challenge with alacrity. Confounding the doomsayers, Australian exporters cultivated new markets that more than made up for the decline of exports to Britain. As part of this strategy, the emphasis in export development shifted from butter to cheese. Until the early 1970s export earnings from butter were at least twice those from cheese, but in 1977 the value of cheese exports outstripped that of butter for the first time. Since then, cheese export volumes and earnings have continued to rise rapidly.

Australia has managed to remain competitive in the world market by continuing to develop new, efficient techniques for the mass production of bulk commodity cheese, butter and milk powder. Australia now produces more than 9 million litres of milk annually, of which 5.6 million litres (62 per cent) come from Victoria. More than 49 per cent of the total volume of cow's milk is exported. While Australia produces just 2 per cent of the world's milk, it holds almost 10 per cent of the world's export markets.

Down on the farm, the dairy industry in the past few decades has seen a rapid rise in productivity, coupled with an equally rapid decline in the number of holdings. According to the Australian Dairy Corporation, the average annual yield of milk per cow has risen from 2750 litres in 1975 to 4744 in 1998, while the number of dairy farms has declined from about 30,000 to 14,000. Over the same period the average number of cows per farm has almost doubled, from 77 to 149.

Until quite recently Australia's low-cost industrial production, the tyranny of distance, quarantine restrictions and protective trade policy all conspired to create barriers to a culture of specialist cheese-making and an appreciation of specialist cheese. It was not until the late 1960s that immigration from Europe and an appreciation of Australia's new multicultural diversity changed our perception of food and broadened our palates – including our knowledge of cheese.

The first cheese-makers to break the mould were small-scale Italian and Greek producers who set up dairies in most of the major cities to supply their own communities with fresh stretched cheeses, feta and ricotta. This movement began with the arrival of Italian immigrants in the

1930s, and gained momentum with the mass migration after the Second World War. Among the first of these cheese-makers was Natale Italiano, founder of the Perfect Cheese Company, who started out selling his products from door to door around Carlton and North Melbourne. Unable to obtain the goat's and ewe's milk from which many of these cheeses were traditionally made, the new producers were often forced to adapt to the use of cow's milk.

Then, in the early 1980s, a new generation of young cheese-makers began to create original Australian specialist cheeses on the farm. These pioneers have travelled, studied and tasted the benchmark cheeses of Europe, and have adapted some of the classic techniques to Australian conditions, while also inventing new methods unfettered by the restrictions of tradition. Their commitment has led to the development of a new interest and national pride in specialist cheeses with a distinctive flavour and unique Australian character. Although this new industry is still small in proportion to the overall market, it is growing as our collective tastes become more sophisticated.

Australia now makes cheeses to suit almost every palate. The range of specialist cheeses is wide, from the mild and delicate to the rich and buttery, from the strong and stinking to the fruity or sharp or salty. Textures are equally diverse, from soft and delicate to hard and crumbly.

Demand for these boutique cheeses has grown rapidly, and many new producers have become established. It is important that these tentative steps are encouraged and that as consumers we also learn how to recognise what is good. The sheer range of choice can be confusing until you realise that different cheeses have particular characteristics that enable them to be classified into general groups, and are at their peak at different times. Enjoyment of good cheese is not a question of pulling a block of plastic-wrapped 'tasty' from the supermarket shelf. It does require a little thought and common sense: an understanding of seasonality, what general characteristics to look for, how to store cheese, and what other foods and wines will best complement different kinds of cheese.

When you eat a piece of cheese, you are participating in an ancient ritual, consuming a natural food created thousands of years ago and still appreciated today.

MILK

Milk

There are ever so many different varieties of cheese, made in every civilized and some uncivilized lands, wherever grass grows and is grazed. The fundamental causes of differences in cheese are differences in the quality of milk from which cheese is made and differences in methods of cheese making.

André L. Simon, *A Concise Encyclopedia of Gastronomy*

All cheese has its origins in milk, and can only be as good as the basic ingredient it starts with. Turning milk into cheese by fermentation is a relatively simple process in theory, but in practice cheese-making is quite complicated because it is affected by so many different factors. Milk is a delicate and complex liquid with a composition that is constantly changing. To produce consistently high-quality cheese, makers have to recognise these changes and adapt their methods accordingly. The fundamental challenge for the cheese-maker wanting to make a consistently good cheese all year round is to modify the milk composition without making a cheese that has lost all its character.

The milk used in large cheese factories is collected from a number of different farms and mixed together in bulk tankers. Usually it is standardised by altering fat and protein levels before being used to make cheese. There is no room for even small quality variations, and the cheese ends up uniform and predictable.

In contrast, smaller specialist cheese-makers use milk from a limited number of sources, or even from a single farm. The milk therefore has unique and special flavours, reflecting the local pastures, the prevailing weather conditions and the composition of the herd or flock. These cheeses often change in character from day to day and season to season.

Selection and Processing

While there are endless variations in milk composition and hundreds of different cheeses, the nature of the curd suitable for a particular type of cheese is broadly determined by the concentration of the milk solids, the level of acidity, the extent of fermentation and how much moisture is retained in the cheese. The solids in milk are a combination of milk sugar (lactose), fats (fatty acids), proteins and salts. In cheese-making two of the most important factors are the levels of fat and protein, which are the essential constituents of cheese.

Fat

The fat in milk is held in suspension in minute globules. It is a complex mixture of compounds called glycerides, and also contains fat-soluble vitamins, including vitamin A.

Traditionally the level of fat is altered to influence the density and texture of different kinds of cheese. To make hard cheeses, for example, the fat level of the milk is commonly lowered either by skimming or by adding skim milk, while for soft cheeses the fat level is often increased by adding cream. Cream not only alters the flavour of cheese but also affects its texture. Historically, cream has commanded a premium in Europe but has been cheaper in Australia, where there is a surplus of butterfat. Quite a lot of Australian specialist cheeses use milk rich in cream, which gives them a mild or even bland flavour and creamy texture. By contrast, some harder traditional European cheeses such as grana padano and farmhouse cheddar are made using a lower-fat or skimmed milk.

Protein

Most of the protein in milk is casein, which binds together to form the curd structure. Casein can hold moisture like a sponge. It will shrink and expel moisture in response to changes in temperature and acidity, and this is how moisture is expelled during cheese-making. During maturation, casein is broken down by enzymes and bacteria, and the breakdown products are responsible for some of the flavour of the cheese.

Protein levels in milk can be altered using ultra-filtration or micro-filtration techniques, which concentrate the protein in milk solids. A basic form of micro-filtration probably originated with the Egyptians, but the development of ultra-filtration in the late 1960s has had important implications for many larger-scale producers of specialist cheese. In the ultra-filtration process, milk is forced through a series of membranes to extract the protein, producing a preparation called retentate.

Cow's milk cheeses made using retentate often have an unusual soft, silky, almost viscous texture and a thick, creamy but short flavour. The equipment for ultra-filtration is expensive, and the process is seldom used in small operations, where variation is part of what makes the cheese interesting. In Europe, however, ultra-filtration technology has become increasingly popular for making industrial soft cheeses, and is partly responsible for the stability and relatively small seasonal quality variation in these types.

Milk also contains lactose, a sugar that is unique to milk. Lactose is water-soluble, and 90 per cent is lost in the whey. Lactose provides food for the bacteria that produce lactic acid during the fermentation process.

Minerals and trace elements are present in milk in very small amounts, but they play a vital role in cheese-making. If the levels are too low or too high, the curd will not form properly and the whey will not be expelled. The most important minerals are calcium and phosphorus.

Milk Processing

During pasteurisation, milk constituents such as protein and lactose are greatly modified and others such as vitamins, bacteria and enzymes are almost destroyed. The higher the processing temperature, the more the components are denatured and the less remains of the milk's natural flavour and character. Some smaller cheese-makers use the prolonged-heating, lower-temperature method known as batch pasteurisation, because they claim it leaves more of the milk's flavour and only destroys 10 per cent of the water-soluble vitamins.

MILK PROCESSING
METHODS

Pasteurisation

The most common methods of pasteurisation are:

- Rapid heating of milk for 15–40 seconds at 71–74°C.
- Batch heating for 30 minutes at 62–65°C.

Pasteurised milk will keep for four to five days.

UHT Treatment

Ultra Heat Treated milk is heated for 2–10 seconds at 130–150°C. This destroys up to 99 per cent of the vitamins. The resulting product will keep for up to six months. UHT milk is not used in specialist cheese-making except as a clean base milk for growing moulds and cultures.

Sterilisation

Milk is heated for 15–30 minutes at 121°C. This destroys 99 per cent of vitamins. The resulting product will keep for three or four months.

Homogenisation

This involves the use of pressure to break up the natural globules of fat and distribute them more uniformly, preventing the cream in cow's milk from rising to the surface.

The spirit of a country, if it is to be true to itself, needs continually to draw great breaths of inspiration from simple realities of the country: from the smell of its soil, the pattern of its fields, the beauty of its scenery and from the men and women who dwell and toil in the rural areas.

Sir George Stapledon

Pasture and Soil

With its huge geographical size and wide climatic range, Australia offers a variety of regional conditions that suit particular types of dairy animals. Most of the dairying regions are along the southern seaboard, and each offers its own range of micro-climates and seasonal variations.

The seasonal change of pasture in the paddocks is one of the most important influences on the quality and character of Australian cheese. The best milk for cheese is widely agreed to come from a diet of fresh natural balanced pastures. Hay is not quite as good, and silage can affect the milk's flavour and maturation.

There's more to pasture than just grass, though. Soil, minerals, land management and even the particular herbage species growing in a paddock produce subtle regional variations. Many of Australia's richest soils are in the drier areas of the continent. The coastal soils tend to have been leached of minerals, especially in the north. The exceptions are the rich volcanic soils of southern Victoria and south-eastern South Australia, and the alluvial plains along the coastal rivers of New South Wales and Tasmania. Not surprisingly, dairying tends to be concentrated in these better-favoured districts.

Pasture management practices also have a strong influence on milk characteristics. Pastures that are regularly ploughed up and resown or constantly bombarded with fertilisers and herbicides offer much less complexity and variety than older untouched natural pastures. Organic or biodynamic pastures preserve the *terroir* of local milk quality. Milk flavour is affected by the seasonal flowering of a particular herbage, or the flush of native wildflowers and grasses at certain times of the year.

The quality of the milk produced directly reflects the local pasture and soil conditions. Each and every paddock is different, with a changing quality and character of feed, and hence of milk and cheese. Pasture quality also affects various types of cheeses differently. It does not always follow that the greenest pasture or richest milk makes the best cheese.

In the northern hemisphere, dairy animals spend the long, cold winter indoors, housed in comfortable sheds and pampered with fresh feed supplemented by nourishing hay, silage and maize. This controlled diet produces a consistent milk yield and helps to make milk and cheese quality dependable.

In Australia, by contrast, winters are relatively mild, and most dairy animals spend their lives outside in the paddocks with a diet that is almost always grass. As a result, Australian specialist cheese is more susceptible to seasonal changes in quality. Animals that graze on open pasture produce good milk during the mild spring and autumn when grass is growing, but production falls sharply when the cold winds blow across the muddy ground in midwinter, or when the February sun is blazing down on bare, dry paddocks. This cycle of abundance and shortage makes it difficult to produce specialist cheese of a consistent quality throughout the year.

On the other hand, the controlled diet fed to European animals eliminates some of the highs of milk and cheese quality as well as the lows. Care has to be taken that consistency is achieved without losing some of the desirable extremes of character associated with a truly seasonal milk supply. Ironically, the benefits of seasonal variety are what make many Australian specialist cheeses so appealingly different, but this same variability limits their potential market acceptance.

Occasionally, particularly in winter, there is not enough quality milk to meet specialist cheese-makers' standards. The struggling cheese-maker then faces an invidious choice between halting production and running out of cheese to sell, or taking the risk of making mediocre cheese from poor-quality milk.

Climate and Seasonality

The Australian continent encompasses a range of climates that suit particular breeds and types of milking animals. Each State has a different regional climate. The dominant influence on the northern half of the continent is the summer monsoon, which brings heavy rain from the north and peters out as it moves inland. In the south, the monsoon is moderated by the influence of south-westerly winds bringing winter rain from the Indian and Southern Oceans. In Victoria and Tasmania the rainfall is spread fairly evenly across the year, but Western Australia and South Australia have strong winter rainfall peaks and dry summers. These broad patterns are moderated by other influences, including local variations in geography.

Different dairy animals adapt well to different climatic patterns. Cows and to a certain extent buffalo prefer improved pasture with good rainfall and rich soil. In parts of southern Australia there is adequate feed for these animals all year, either grown naturally or under irrigation. Compared with cows, sheep prefer to graze on drier open grassland and survive much harsher conditions where the vegetation is dry and sparse in summer. They have adapted well to the open grasslands found in drier parts of Victoria's Western District and across much of the Australian inland. Goats' browsing habits distinguish them from other dairy animals. They flourish in areas with a dry, warm Mediterranean climate such as the hills north of Perth or the sparse country outside Adelaide. Some farmers have adapted goats to colder, wetter regions by breeding, or by providing shelter during winter.

There are wide variations within regions, though, and many milking animals have adapted to apparently inhospitable localities and still produce excellent milk and cheese.

The Peak Growing Periods

There are three special periods in the year when good pasture growth and season combine to produce the best milk for making particular types of cheese. Each seasonal peak provides special qualities and complex flavour characteristics, and offers different benefits to various cheese types. These periods are when some of the best cheeses are made. The timing varies from State to State, with the western States starting up to a month earlier than those in the east.

September: The first growth of spring grass
In early spring, when conditions begin to warm in the paddocks, there is expectancy and excitement in the air. The new spring growth of tender green grass shoots acts as a stimulant to milk production, and cows, goats and ewes begin a brand-new natural lactation season. Spring is the time to look out for fresh cheeses made from this sweet milk, particularly delicate fromage frais or goat's cheese. These soft, unpressed cheeses should have a light perfume and delicate flavour, and are best consumed within days. Cheeses made from spring milk are often high in moisture, and hard cheeses made now tend to be thin-bodied but quick to mature.

October–December: The flowering season
Late spring to early summer is when the pastures are at their most lush and grasses and clovers begin to flower in the paddocks. The warmer weather and good feed conditions mean healthy and contented animals. Mild weather and rich grazing on a wide variety of herbage at this time of year produce complex and consistent milk – and lots of it.

This is the peak of milk volume and is the best time for making virtually all types of specialist cheese, from the softer varieties to the semi-hard and hard types. In particular, it is the peak time for making cheddar and the harder varieties, which will appear in the stores from six to twelve months later. For blue cheese, the peak period extends from late spring to early summer, and these cheeses appear in the stores between January and early March. Flowering clovers can inhibit the maturation of soft blue cheeses made at the end of this period.

March–April: The last growth of autumn grass
Autumn sees the greening of the brown summer paddocks and an end to supplementary feeding with silage and hay. Tender grass shoots sprout again with the cool autumn rain. This second growth of grass means a new period of fresh feed for several months before the cold sets in. If it rains on schedule, the farmers talk of 'grass growing in your pocket'.

At this time of year the milk is low in volume but high in fat, protein and calcium, because the second growth of grass has less feed value than spring grass and seasonal lactation is coming to an end. This is the ideal time for making surface-ripened cheeses, particularly white and washed-rinds.

As a general rule, milk and specialist cheeses will be at their best if they are made when fresh grass is growing. To select cheeses in peak condition means taking a little time to think about when they were made, but the reward is worth the effort.

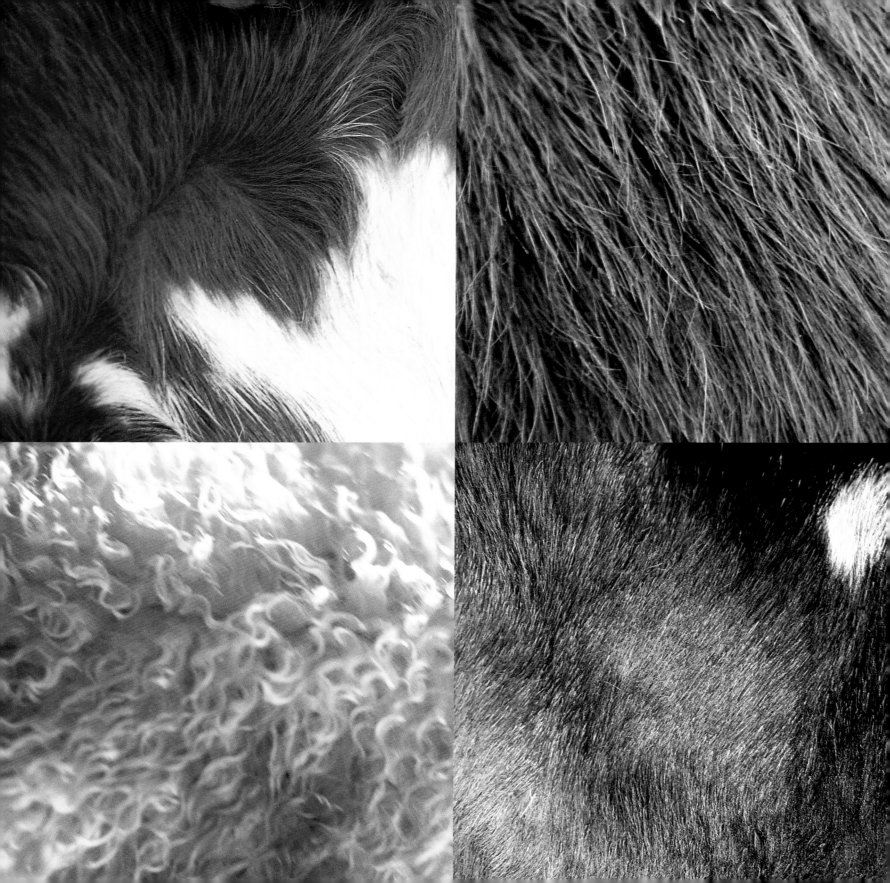

Animal Species and Breeds

One of the challenges of dairy farming is to achieve the best balance of returns from the land on a sustainable basis, and the choice of animal plays an important part in this. Different species and breeds of animals produce different kinds of milk, which have a substantial influence on the character and flavour of cheese.

Cow's milk is most widely used for making cheese in Australia, but all lactating animals produce milk that can be turned into cheese. A large part of the world uses the milk of goats, ewes or buffalo, and in some remote regions camels, llamas, mares and yaks.

As their first food, mammals all respond best to milk provided by their mothers. This milk contains all the substances a newborn baby needs to survive this critical period of its life, to boost its immune defences and grow rapidly. Raw milk contains vital substances, including highly beneficial fatty acids, lactose, minerals such as phosphorus, calcium, potassium and magnesium, and vitamins A, D, E, K, B_1, B_2, B_3, B_5 and B_{12}. The protein in milk is easily digestible, rich in essential amino acids and ranks second only to egg white in terms of nutritional value.

The balance of nutrients in different milks varies according to the needs of each type of animal, to ensure a combination that is readily assimilated by the young of that particular species. Sheep, for example, are small, fat animals and require rich, fatty milk to grow quickly, whereas goats carry little body fat and require milk that is easily digested to provide instant energy.

The properties of milk vary considerably, depending not only on the species of animal milked but also on the different breeds within each species. Every breed produces a different quantity of milk with quite different characteristics. The selection of milk determines the yield of cheese as well as fat and protein ratios, which influence cheese texture and flavour.

Average Milk Composition (%)

Component	Cow	Goat	Ewe	Buffalo
Fat	4.2	3.6	7.0	7.7
Protein	3.5	3.2	5.6	4.5
Lactose	4.9	4.7	4.7	5.0
Salts	0.8	0.8	0.9	0.9

Different milks are suited to making different cheese varieties, and many of the classic European cheeses are based on particular species and breeds of milking animals. Cheddar is best made with cow's milk, for example, and mozzarella from buffalo milk. The requirements of specialist cheese-making have ensured the survival of many low-yield animal breeds, such as the ewes whose milk is used to make roquefort. A similar level of specialisation is gradually developing in Australia as the cheese industry becomes more sophisticated.

Lactose Intolerance

All milk contains lactose, which is a natural sugar. When humans consume milk the lactose is broken down in the small intestine into other sugars – glucose and galactose – under the action of an enzyme called lactase. Most mammals stop producing this lactase enzyme when they are weaned from their mothers. Humans are unique in this respect, because they generally continue to produce lactase throughout their lives and as a consequence can continue to digest milk products.

Lactose intolerance occurs when people do not produce the lactase enzyme, and can lead to a wide range of disorders and allergies. Lactose intolerance can be a permanent condition and is often found in cultures that do not have a history of drinking milk products. It is particularly common among people originating from Asia or Africa.

Lactose-intolerant people cannot drink animals' milk in any quantity without experiencing problems. Generally they can tolerate ordinary unadulterated milk better than boosted modern low-fat milks. This is because full-cream milk is digested more slowly than boosted milks, which often have skim milk powder added and are digested faster.

Contrary to popular belief, lactose intolerance does not mean giving up all cheese. Most of the lactose is in the whey, which is drained off during cheese-making. People with lactose intolerance should avoid ricotta, which is made from whey, and fresh cheeses where the whey is partially retained.

Cows

Cow's milk was not the raw ingredient of the very earliest cheeses, but it is by far the most popular milk for cheese in Western countries today. Because of their large size, volatile temperament and huge feed requirements, cows were the last animals to be domesticated, but thousands of years of selective breeding have transformed them into calm, quite predictable animals, and under the right conditions they yield the largest quantity of milk of any lactating animals. A reasonable milker will produce about twenty litres of milk per day.

Breeds

In Europe specific regions and cheeses have long been associated with particular breeds of cows, but in the comparatively short history of dairy farming in Australia there have been many experiments to establish which breeds are best adapted to particular regions and will produce milk that best meets market requirements.

Friesian

Instantly recognisable, the black-and-white Friesian (sometimes known as the Holstein) is the most popular breed of cow milked in Australia. Originating from the Friesland province of Holland, they are the largest of all the dairy cows. They were heavily promoted by Australian dairy authorities from the 1950s because of the large volume of milk they produce per hectare. Farmers regard them as the best in the business for liquid milk and bulk cheddar, but volume and quality do not sit well together. Friesian milk has a comparatively low butterfat content, and is not necessarily the best for producing a distinct character and flavour in certain cheeses, particularly in cream-enriched soft types.

Jersey

The lovely Jersey originates from the Channel Islands and northern France. These brown cows are well known for producing rich, golden milk, high in butterfat, though they yield a smaller volume of milk than Friesians. Jersey milk is excellent for making butter, soft, creamy cheeses and rich, fresh cream, but it is difficult to use for hard cheeses because it has large fat globules, which resist coagulation and can easily be lost in the whey. Jerseys were the leading breed of milking cow in Australia until the 1950s, but were widely replaced by Friesians because of the rising demand for bulk milk and hard commodity cheese.

Ayrshire

The hardy red-and-white Ayrshire breed was developed in Scotland in the latter part of the eighteenth century and was introduced to Victoria's Western District in the 1840s. For many years Ayrshire cows made up most of the Australian dairy herd. Their milk, which has relatively small fat globules, was considered ideal for the hard, English-style cheeses that dominated the local industry. In recent times Ayrshires have been interbred with other types, particularly Jerseys, and the breed has virtually disappeared as a source of milk for specialist cheese.

Other breeds

Other breeds milked in Australia include Dairy Shorthorns, Guernseys and Illawarra Shorthorns, as well as Brahmans in subtropical and tropical areas. I am unaware of any specialist cheese being made using milk from these breeds at present.

Goats

The goat is a fascinating beast that has been milked since nomadic times. Goat's milk probably provided the original base for all cheese-making. Yet, despite centuries of domestication, goats are demanding to look after. They are intelligent, affectionate but troublesome beasts, and can be destructive if not well managed. They are among the few lactating animals that have continued to survive in the wild. The simple but subtle varieties of cheeses produced with goat's milk are an unfailing source of interest.

Making cheese from goat's milk is a relatively new industry in Australia. In the nineteenth century miners, small farmers and even city-dwellers kept goats for milk and meat when there was not enough pasture to maintain cattle. Many of these goats later escaped into the bush, where they have become serious pests. There are an estimated 150,000 wild goats roaming Australia, some of which are periodically rounded up and exported to Asia for breeding purposes.

It is more expensive to produce cheese from goat's milk than from cow's milk. Dairy goats produce far less milk than cows. The average yield per goat is about three or four litres per day, and the yield of milk solids per litre is also lower than in other milks. Ten litres of goat's milk are required to make a kilogram of cheese. On the other hand, goats are remarkably efficient. In proportion to her body weight, a goat will produce approximately four times as much milk as a sheep and three times as much as a cow. Milk production is extremely seasonal. Goats' short hair, thin skin and small quantities of additional fat provide little insulation, so their lactation is sensitive to cool weather, feed quality and even the number of daylight hours. Elaborate and expensive measures such as the provision of cold-weather shelters are necessary to change the goat's natural milk production cycle.

Unlike most milking animals, goats are browsers, not grazers; that is, they do not flourish on a diet consisting only of green pasture, but prefer to nibble just the tops of the grasses and will quite happily seek out other nutrients from tree foliage, bark and succulent plants. Though they have a reputation for being destructive and chewing away at anything, in fact they are highly selective. Often they can be found climbing trees to obtain the additional nutrients and minerals they need to supplement their diet. These nutrients often need to be provided through supplementary feeding in the farm situation.

Special Qualities

Goat's milk is very delicate, and demands careful handling. It is also volatile and easily tainted with other flavours. Tainting may be caused by poor feed control or the presence of a courting buck in the flock. One of the commonest problems with goat's cheese is a strong 'bucky' flavour, which is extremely off-putting. This strong flavour indicates that poor-quality milk has been used.

The very best cheeses are always made daily, using milk less than twenty-four hours old. The small size of the flocks and the limited volume they produce make it difficult for Australian goat cheese-makers to maintain an adequate daily supply to fill a vat and make cheese economically. Larger farms and increased demand have seen milk volumes and quality improve dramatically in recent years.

The first goat known to have visited Australia came on the Endeavour with Captain Cook. Sailing ships often travelled with a goat to provide milk for the officers and senior crew. Cook's goat went around the world twice on two separate voyages before finally being put out to grass near Gravesend – a place aptly named, as she died within months of returning to land.

NANNY GOATS

In Victorian England wealthy families employed women as wet nurses to breastfeed their children, leaving the wet nurses' own children with no mother's milk. Goat's milk was used as a substitute. This led to the use of the term 'nanny goats', and gave goat's milk a reputation as the food of the poor.

Goat's milk lends itself well to the production of fresh, young, slightly acid cheese types. Although these are the most popular forms of goat's cheese, some of the more mature varieties harden to develop a sensational lingering piquancy, a condensed strength that is an acquired taste.

Goat's milk is naturally homogenised and pure white in colour. Carotene, which gives a yellowish colour to cow's milk, is converted directly into vitamin A by the goat's metabolism. The fatty acids in goat's milk include caproic, caprylic and capric acids, all of which are named after *caper*, the Latin term for billy-goat. Contrary to many myths, goat's milk is quite rich, with an average fat content almost one-and-a-half times that of cow's milk, but the fat globules are only one-fifth the size of those in cow's milk. The protein in goat's milk is also more finely divided than in cow's milk, so that goat's milk curd is much finer and more easily digestible.

Goat's milk is sometimes used by people who are allergic to cow's milk. It is considered free from many of the pathogens that affect cow's milk, and is legally sold in its raw form in Western Australia and New South Wales.

Breeds

As is the case with other lactating animals, the quality of goat's milk varies from breed to breed. The goats milked in Australia are often crossbred flocks that have been produced after experience of local conditions, creating milk with a unique regional character.

Saanen

These large, pure white or cream-coloured goats of Swiss origin arrived in Australia with the early settlers. They are the most common short-haired breed and can be kept in large flocks. They are usually calm and good-natured.

Australian Saanens have frequently set new world records for milk production, and average 4.5 to 5.5 litres daily. Their milk is low in protein solids.

Toggenburg

One of the oldest Swiss brown breeds, with white facial stripes and white-ringed ears, these goats arrived in Australia in 1947. They are more independent and strong-willed than other breeds, making them suitable for free-range grazing. They produce a good volume of milk with average butterfat.

British Alpine

Originally bred in Britain from Swiss Alpine goats and first imported to Australia in 1959, this breed has black-and-white markings similar to Toggenburgs. British Alpines are tall, elegant, highly active and suited to free-range conditions. They produce a high milk volume with above-average butterfat.

Anglo-Nubian

These exotic-looking goats have distinctive long floppy ears, regal noses and curious-shaped faces. The Anglo-Nubians in Australia descend from a group of five imported in 1954. The breed was developed in Britain by crossing native goats with Nubians imported from India, North Africa and the Middle East. Affectionate and with a vocal bark, Anglo-Nubians give less milk than the other three breeds, but their milk is high in solids, butterfat and protein. They are also bred for their meat.

Ewes

Ewes have been used for milking and cheese-making for almost as long as goats. Nomadic tribes in the Middle East were the first to domesticate flocks of sheep and use their milk to make fresh yoghurt and salted cheeses such as labna and feta.

Ewe's milk has been used to make cheese for centuries in Europe, and was the original milk of many old recipes. Classic benchmark cheeses such as roquefort in France, manchego in Spain and pecorino romano in Italy are made of ewe's milk and come from regions where the landscape is unsuited to cows or goats.

Sheep are ideal for Australia's hot, dry conditions. Although they are grazing animals, they can survive in regions where little grass grows, and are far less demanding to look after than goats. Australia has at least ten times as many sheep as people, and the nation was once said to 'ride on the sheep's back'.

Historically, however, sheep in Australia have been grown exclusively for wool and meat. When the idea of milking sheep was initially raised in the early 1970s, many farmers greeted the suggestion with incredulity. As food writer Cherry Ripe described it in *Goodbye Culinary Cringe*:

> *When Jim Konas approached the Victorian Dairy Board a few years ago for any information they had on milking sheep, they laughed out loud. 'How are you gonna catch the bastards? They're wild,' was the response of one of the board's experts.*

More recently, the growing interest in specialist cheese and the falling demand for wool have combined to spur interest in milking ewes. This exciting development has not occurred without considerable effort, hardship and visionary thinking by some committed farmers. One major challenge has been to adapt the Australian broadacre system of sheep grazing to provide a milking flock that is well fed and always close to the milking shed rather than being spread across thousands of hectares.

Ewe's milk is far richer in milk solids than cow's or goat's milk, and far less milk is required to produce the same weight of cheese, but the downside is that each ewe produces only a tiny volume of milk. Milking ewes is a labour-intensive business. The best ewes produce only one or two litres of milk per day, and it takes an average of four litres to produce one kilogram of cheese.
To produce enough milk for cheese-making, even in limited volume, it is therefore necessary to milk a large number of ewes.

Ewe's milk is also extremely seasonal and susceptible to changes in quality. Each ewe lactates for only two or three months. This is the shortest lactation period of any commercially milked animal, and occurs naturally in early spring and autumn, when the grass is greenest and fresh herbage and clovers are present. Many of the classic European cheese-makers only make ewe's milk cheese for six months of the year because of these seasonal attributes. In Australia farmers have experimented with irrigated pastures and intensive farming in sheds in order to achieve a more consistent year-round supply of milk, but the results have been mixed.

Special Qualities

As long as ewe's milk is kept refrigerated it holds its texture and flavour well for several days without spoiling. This has important implications for cheese-making. While fresh milk may only be available in small daily quantities, it can be held and used when there is sufficient to fill a vat. The milk does not taint easily, but old or poor-quality milk can produce cheeses with horrible soapy 'lanolin' or rancid lamb flavours.

Ewe's milk is pure white in colour and, like goat's milk, contains no carotene. As ewe's milk cheeses age, they develop a distinctive translucent off-white ivory colour. The milk is thick and viscous and has more so-called goat fatty acids (caproic, caprylic and capric) than cow's milk. This produces a different flavour in the cheeses, which are often made in a style that uses stronger flavours to balance the richness of the milk.

Ewe's milk is well suited to mature cheese types with a comparatively high salt content such as blue cheese, feta and pecorino, and to making fresh cheeses and yoghurt, where the high acidity balances the rich, silky texture of the milk. It contains almost twice as much protein and calcium as cow's milk, but it also contains almost twice as much fat. The fat is naturally homogenised into much smaller fat globules, making it easy to digest.

Breeds

Until recently there were no suitable dairy sheep from which to select a milking flock in Australia, and imports of appropriate breeds were banned because of concerns about disease. The ewes milked in Australia have mainly been selected from strains originally bred for wool – Border Leicesters, Merinos, White Suffolks, Dorsets and Romneys. Building a flock has been a hit-and-miss affair, with farmers individually selecting the ewes for their milk yield – usually about one litre per day. The results have been uneven, with highly variable volumes and fat and protein ratios.

A change in quarantine regulations in 1996 saw the introduction from New Zealand of two dairy breeds that will yield significantly more milk than existing breeds. When these are crossbred with local sheep they are likely to change the size and prospects of the industry dramatically.

Awassi
This breed originated in the Middle East and was bred for meat and milk by the nomadic Bedouin. It is noted for its fat tail, which can reach a weight of twenty kilograms and is used to store energy in desert conditions. Its milk is high in volume, butterfat and solids. A dairy flock of Awassi – Australia's first – can be found near Cowra in New South Wales.

East Friesland
Originally from the same part of northern Europe as Friesian cows, this distinguished breed has much longer legs and whiter wool than most Australian sheep. Tails are often left on, and the breed has been used extensively in Britain and New Zealand for high-volume milk production with consistent butterfat levels. A good milking ewe can produce up to four litres of milk a day.

Buffalo

Buffalo are extraordinarily big, lumbering, hairy beasts, often quite timid and wary of humans, although they have been known to become very tame and affectionate. In Asia and parts of Italy, they have been widely used to plough wet, marshy soils because of their enormous muscle strength and large hooves, which do not easily sink into the ground.

Buffalo have been bred for milk production for at least 3000 years in many parts of the world, particularly India and South-east Asia, where the buffalo is well suited to the hot, wet climatic conditions. Dairy buffalo were probably first introduced to Europe by Arab traders via Sicily during the sixth century AD.

Buffalo kept as dairy animals are milked once or twice a day. In southern Italy buffalo milk is used to make authentic mozzarella, while in much of Asia the milk is a staple used for yoghurt and soft, fresh cheese types.

Early settlers in northern Australia originally introduced water buffalo as draught animals to cope with the wet tropical conditions. Many escaped and became serious pests, destroying the bush and carrying disease. Now that diseases such as brucellosis have been eradicated there have been a number of attempts to milk these animals, but they have proved quite unsuitable for milking. Their yields are low, primarily because of the breed, but also because buffalo cows have a strong maternal instinct and will give milk only if their young are near by. Buffalo are genetically different from cows by one chromosome, and the two species cannot be interbred.

Special Qualities

Buffalo cows produce between five and seven litres of milk per day on average, but will lactate for eleven months of the year. This is the longest lactation period of any dairy animal. The milk is naturally homogenised, exceptionally rich in fat, protein, calcium and vitamin A, and has a high ratio of solids. It is sold at a premium and produces a good yield of cheese.

Buffalo milk is pure porcelain white in colour and contains no carotene. The basic biochemistry and high lactose levels make this milk most suitable for producing soft fresh cheeses. Buffalo milk has an unforgettable mossy perfume.

Breeds

Fifty-five Mediterranean dairy buffalo cows and two bulls from Campania in southern Italy were introduced to Purrumbete homestead in Victoria's Western District in 1996. In the following year they were joined by fifty animals from a smaller breed known as Murrah, which originates from India and has been bred in Bulgaria for the past thirty years.

Purrumbete is now home to Australia's first dairy buffalo herd. This is an important milestone for Australian specialist cheese, and represents the last piece of the jigsaw in terms of the range of milk types available for cheese-making on a commercial scale.

ng

MAKING

Cheese is a fermented food, which is a gentle way of saying that it is produced by allowing milk to decompose a little – allowing microbes to work on it to change its nature. To our preservative-laden age this may seem like an off-putting idea – but not all decomposition is a bad thing. Most people don't have too much trouble with the notion of decomposed grapes and are even prepared to pay a lot of money for the result, if the wine is particularly special. The idea is to harness the decomposition, to control it in order to come up with something that tastes good, and that's exactly how cheese is produced.

Randolph Hodgson

Skill. Passion. Intuition. These are the three talents that a specialist cheese-maker needs. It is the cheese-maker who turns good milk into great cheese. There is a huge difference between the traditional 'art' of making cheese on a small scale and the 'science' of modern dairy technology, where every stage in the process is defined and the slightest deviation from a standard is considered a fault.

Making cheese on a small scale gives cheese-makers much closer control over the quality of the milk used, but also requires them to adjust methods constantly in response to changing conditions. Specialist cheese-making is much more than a science: it is a skilled craft that requires experience, judgement, a natural empathy with the raw materials and an appreciation of the final product. Because of the many variables, each individual cheese batch is different, a unique example of the cheese-maker's craft. The art of the cheese-maker is to manipulate the natural process in a desired direction, then leave nature to do the rest.

The Basics

To make cheese is to control the natural souring process of milk. The separation of the liquid (whey) leaves behind a concentration of milk solids (curds) containing proteins (casein), sugars, calcium, fat, minerals and vitamins. The fermentation principle depends on the conversion of natural milk sugars (lactose) into lactic acid. The acid development is essential for the preservation of the curd. When all the sugars have been broken down into lactic acid there is nothing left for unwanted bacteria to feed on, so that the remaining curd is stable.

There are as many different ways of making cheese as there are different types, but they have the following basic steps in common:

Milk Preparation

Fresh quality milk is selected and sometimes standardised by the addition or removal of cream. It is then warmed or pasteurised and brought to a temperature at which a starter will work most efficiently.

Addition of Starters

Selected strains of bacteria (known as starter culture) are added to the warm milk. In pasteurised milk these replace the natural bacteria destroyed by heat treatment. The bacteria in the starter culture feed on the lactose, which gives them energy to produce lactic acid. The acid in turn initiates the process of coagulating the curd.

One of the most important quality controls in cheese-making is the timing and close control of the lactic acid-producing bacteria. If there is too little acidity, the cheese remains too moist and will not keep. If there is too much, the cheese will tend to be dry, chalky and flavourless.

Lactic starters are sometimes the only coagulants used in fresh, delicate, young 'lactic' cheese types that require a lot of moisture, but for all other cheese types an additional coagulant is required to improve the control of the process.

Coagulation

Rennet, containing an enzyme called rennin, is added to coagulate the liquid milk into a firm mass. Rennet was originally made from the stomachs of milking animals, but many modern preparations are made in laboratories (see p. 55).

Coagulation is the basis of all cheese-making. While lactic coagulation caused by the starter forms crumbly, porous curds, the enzyme activity of the rennet forms firm, dense, elastic curds. By controlling the balance between these two processes, the cheese-maker can manipulate the extent of coagulation to form semi-soft curds with a texture similar to tofu or junket.

Cutting the Curds

The coagulated mass of curds is held together in a gel-like suspension topped with thin liquid whey. The whey is then encouraged to escape by cutting the curd into pieces, usually with a series of thin crossed wires like the strings of a tennis racquet.

The type of cheese being made determines how finely the curds are cut. The more the curds are cut, the more surface area is presented to allow the whey to escape and the drier the remaining curd. The more whey is left in the curd, the shorter the shelf life of the cheese.

Soft cheeses depend on a certain level of retained moisture and require careful curd handling to ensure that the delicate curds are not broken. Semi-soft cheeses do not require quite the same level of care, and curds are cut more frequently to enable more whey to run off. In harder cheeses the curd is finely cut and sometimes cooked to produce a dense texture that will keep for a long time.

In some cheese-making the whey is then drained off, while in others it is left to aid in acid development or to provide a liquid base in which to heat the curds.

Stirring and Heating

The temperature at which the curds are held also determines the cheese type. The curds contract when heated, expelling further whey and lactose.

Usually soft cheeses are made with a gentle heat, and the curd is cut in large pieces to retain moisture. In harder cheese types the curds are heated or scalded in whey, hot water or a combination of both.

Draining and Hooping

The curds are transferred to draining moulds or perforated hoops. These determine the size and shape of the finished cheese. The hoops are regularly turned to encourage the whey to drain evenly from the curds.

Pressing

Semi-hard and hard-cooked cheeses are then pressed for varying lengths of time and at different pressures to expel still more whey and to form the curd particles into a compact shape. Cheddar, for example, is pressed for up to eighteen hours at a pressure of eighty pounds per square inch. The pressing time depends on how dry the curd needs to be. The larger the cheese, the longer it will take to reduce the moisture level.

Salting

Salt is important in all cheese-making. It is used to halt the action of lactic bacteria, so controlling texture and maturation. It also dries the curd by drawing out more whey, enhances the flavour and preserves the surface against unwanted bacteria and moulds. How much salt is used and when it is added depends on the cheese type. Salt may be added to the cut curds, or the fresh cheese may be immersed in brine, or the rind may be dry-salted.

The ideal salt concentration is between 1 and 3 per cent. Oversalting can make the texture too dry and prevent the flavour from maturing, but if there is too little salt the cheese will taste bland and may not keep.

Maturation

Maturation is the crucial phase where each cheese develops its individual character. Maturation of specialist cheeses with a natural rind requires a carefully controlled environment with regulated temperature and humidity. It is essential to create just the right maturation conditions to develop the cheese's full flavour potential.

Caring for a cheese until it has achieved a superb flavour requires patience, and also the skill to select the right cheeses to start with. Good cheese deserves real care. In Europe the best cheeses are often cared for by specialist retailers or wholesalers, known in France as *affineurs*, who have purpose-built facilities to cure and mature cheeses under controlled temperature and humidity conditions. Sometimes maturation is undertaken on behalf of cheese-makers who have limited facilities of their own, particularly for harder, longer-maturing cheeses.

Farmhouse to Factory

Farmhouse Cheese

Specialist cheese made only by hand
on the farm with only milk produced on
that farm, so that the cheese reflects
the specific local character of one farm
and one herd.

Artisan Cheese

Specialist cheese made by hand rather
than machine, using milk collected
from a specific region. These cheeses
are made by small dairies, and are also
sometimes made on a larger scale.

Industrial Cheese

Cheese made in large volume using
mechanised methods and bulk milk
collected from many different farms
spread over a wide region.

Starters

Left in a warm place to sour naturally, raw milk curdles, and the coagulated curd can then be used to produce a young, acidic, fresh cheese. When milk is pasteurised, however, the naturally occurring flora and bacteria that are responsible for starting this action are destroyed, and have to be replaced with controlled cultures or 'starters'. These are added after pasteurisation, and are carefully developed for specific cheese types, usually in European laboratories.

Starter cultures are used to initiate the fermentation of milk, which dictates the flavour and texture of the mature cheese. This process results in the formation of lactic acid, which serves the following purposes:

- aiding coagulation
- encouraging the expulsion of moisture from the curd
- inhibiting the growth of pathogens, and
- contributing to the flavour.

In earlier times, cheeses were started with the sour whey from the previous day's cheese-making. These starters contained a mixture of unknown bacteria unique to each individual dairy. They were not dependable, and produced cheeses of highly variable quality.

During the 1880s, following Louis Pasteur's discovery of pasteurisation, scientific work by Christian Hansen's laboratories in Denmark led to the development of controlled starter cultures. These were supplied to larger cheese-makers, but their composition and performance were still mixed. Better controls were developed in the 1930s, after the invention of the electron microscope, when New Zealand scientists used bacteriophages – viruses that attack and destroy particular kinds of bacterial cells – to produce single-strain starters.

Modern starter cultures are usually supplied frozen and can be a selected single strain or mixed, depending on the conditions and the particular cheeses made.

Starters fall into two main groups:

- *mesophilic starters* work best at medium temperatures; the optimum is 37°C
- *thermophilic starters* work under higher temperature conditions; the optimum is 60°C.

Rennet and Other Coagulants

Animal Rennet

Rennet has been used for many centuries in cheese-making to help improve the natural clotting process of milk. It contains an enzyme – chymosin or rennin – that breaks down the milk protein. A very small amount of rennet will set a large vat of milk: one part of rennin can coagulate 15,000 parts of milk.

Animal rennet is extracted from the lining of the fourth stomach (known as the vells) of young calves, lambs or kids. The first commercial rennet preparations appeared in 1874. Most traditional cheese-makers still swear by this type of rennet because they believe it makes the best cheese true to type and provides a good maturation quality.

Vegetable Rennet

Some cheeses are deliberately made with rennet substitutes produced from moulds or plant material. In the past small cheese-makers in remote regions of Europe used a wide range of plants as coagulants, including artichokes, butterwort, thistles, nettles, safflower, melon and fig leaves, and a plant known as Our Lady's Bedstraw. These plant extracts, however, often produce a bitter flavour and can be inconsistent in strength. As a result, larger cheese-makers usually regard these old methods as too risky for commercial use.

Microbial Rennet

In the 1970s, as world cheese production increased and supplies of animal rennet ran short, a new vegetarian or 'microbial' rennet was developed. The active element of this preparation is an enzyme extracted from moulds (*Rhizomucor meihei* and *Rhizomucor pusillus*). Approved as suitable for vegetarians, microbial rennet sometimes produces bitter flavours in mature cheeses, and the yields can be lower in hard cheese because it creates firmer curds.

Fermentation-Produced Chymosin (FPC)

Advances in genetic engineering during the late 1980s made it possible to develop rennet substitutes using chymosin produced by genetically encoded micro-organisms. This substitute was originally produced by using genetic material extracted from calf stomach cells as a template, then biosynthesising it by cell division. It is claimed that this process has ended the cheese industry's dependence on the slaughter of calves for producing rennet. FPC is also cheaper and much more reliable than animal rennet.

Most small cheese-makers in Australia use FPC. Some of these cheeses are marketed as containing non-animal rennet, or labelled as 'suitable for vegetarians'. The manufacturer and regulatory authorities claim that FPC does not contain residual organisms or DNA fragments from the host animal, but vegetarians attracted to the idea should understand that the very process of of producing milk for cheese-making requires many calves, kids and lambs to be culled.

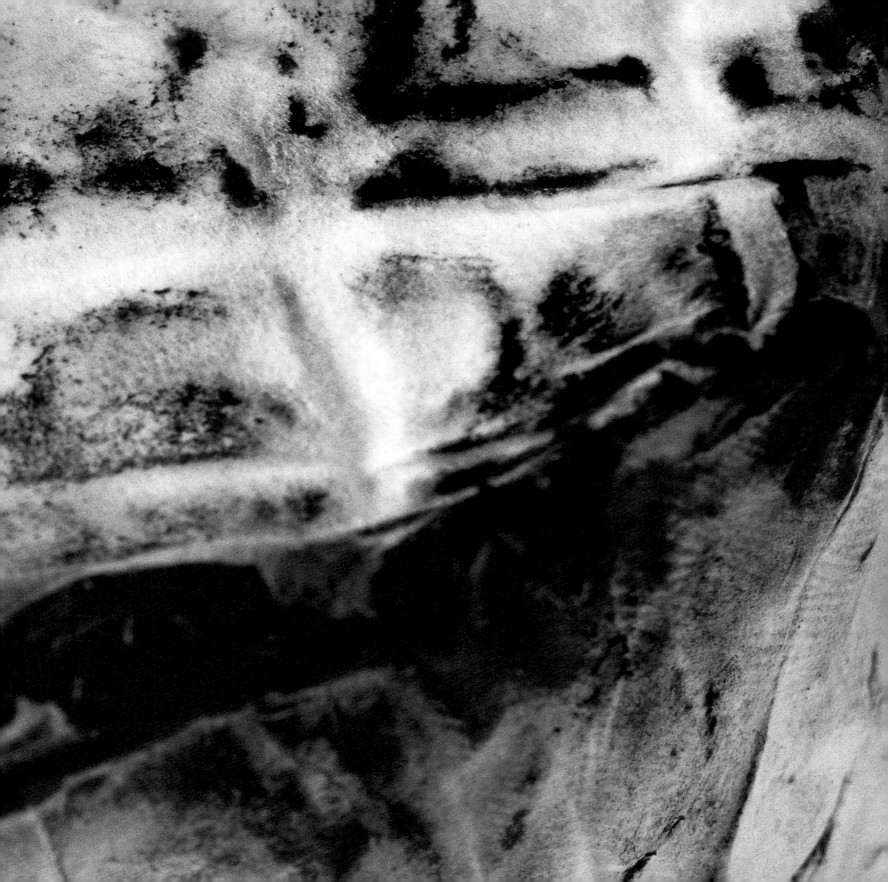

The Rind

*The flavour and aroma of hermetically sealed cheeses cannot be expected to be
the same as traditional cheese.*

R. Scott, *Cheesemaking Practice*

Natural cheese is an organic, living food. Whenever a natural rind is used to protect
and mature a cheese, it provides an essential clue to its identity, and to what flavour
and texture you can expect to find underneath.

The moist curds produced in the early stages of cheese-making will soon spoil unless
they are salted and protected from unwanted contamination. The traditional way to
preserve cheese has been to encourage a natural protective covering to grow on
the outer surface; this is the rind, nature's 'packaging'. As well as offering protection
from unwanted contamination, a natural rind sets up a complex relationship between
the surface activity on the cheese and what is happening inside.

Every naturally ripened cheese has a living covering that needs just the right conditions to survive. The individual character and flavour of a cheese type are produced by the millions of bacteria and their enzymes within the cheese mass, interacting with the yeasts, moulds and bacteria growing on the cheese surface. A natural-rind cheese is one of the most prolific sources of bacteria in any food known to humankind. Despite this slightly disconcerting fact, traditional cheese has also proved to be one of our safest foods.

Many smaller Australian cheese-makers use natural rinds that preserve the identity and unique flavours of their cheeses. These natural coverings are a world apart from the industrial packaging in which most Australian cheese is sold. With the exception of fresh cheeses, the presence of a natural rind is a basic identifying characteristic of a real specialist cheese.

Natural rinds fall into two broad groups:

- *active microbial rinds* such as yeasts, moulds and bacteria
- *inert natural coverings* such as ash or charcoal, salt, cloth, lard and oils.

Active Microbial Rinds

Yeast

All mould-ripened cheeses use yeasts at some stage of their development. Yeasts are important because of their symbiotic relationship with the successful development of moulds and bacteria on all surface-ripened cheeses.

Yeasts appear on the surface of all these cheeses first and reduce the surface acidity, creating better conditions for the growth of moulds and aerobic bacteria. They also play a part in the chemical changes occurring on the surface and contribute to the development of flavour.

Moulds

Moulds are the dominant influence responsible for ripening white-rind and blue cheeses.

Geotrichum
Certain fresh cheeses, especially goat's milk cheeses, are deliberately covered with a mould culture known as geotrichum, which forms a wrinkled skin around the cheese. (The French call this 'toad skin'.) This process encourages the exterior to dry out and the interior to soften, and adds a characteristic flavour.

White
The rind cover in white-rind cheeses is a white mould similar to a type of mushroom culture. All white cheese moulds originate from a mother mould known as *Penicillium camemberti*. Selected moulds are introduced to the milk with the starter, and are usually sprayed on the surface of the drained cheese as well. In traditional surface-ripened cheeses the mould directly influences the texture and flavour of the interior.

Blue

In blue cheese, the ripening does not come from the rind, but from the action of blue-mould cultures inside the cheese. The ancestor of all blue cheese moulds is *Penicillium roqueforti* or *Penicillium glaucum*, which originally was found in humid caves. These moulds are introduced throughout the body of the cheese in the milk or added to the curds before hooping. The cheeses are then spiked with needles, allowing air to reach the aerobic spores inside the cheese and leading to the growth of blue veins from the centre of the cheese towards the outer rind.

Bacteria

The strain of bacteria used in all surface-ripened washed-rind cheeses is known as *Brevibacterium linens*. It is introduced in humid maturing conditions and naturally migrates to the surface of the damp cheese as a result of regular washing. It produces a characteristic orange colour and strong cowyard smell as it softens and flavours the interior of the cheese.

Inert Natural Coverings

Ash

Smothering a fresh cheese in ash or charcoal neutralises the acidity of the surface and so enables a surface mould bloom to grow, altering the maturation characteristics of the interior.

Cloth

Wrapping a cheese in cheesecloth or bandages and covering it with lard provides a semi-permeable rind that allows the cheese to 'breathe'. The cloth allows fresh air to move slowly in and out of the cheese, releasing moisture and fermented gas. The surface of the cloth slowly forms a greyish mould, which has a secondary effect on the flavour of the cheese.

Oils

Large cooked cheeses with smooth rinds are commonly oiled to form a semi-permeable rind. The oil helps to prevent moulds and bacteria growing on the smooth surface of the rind and contributes to the sweet flavour of the cheese underneath.

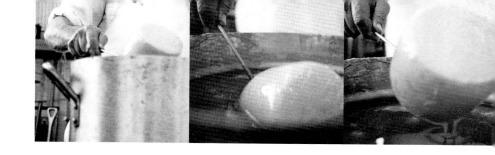

Modern Industrial Packaging

Not all cheese depends on natural rind cover for protection. Modern vacuum packing provides effective rind protection because it suffocates any aerobic organisms on the surface of the cheese. This makes for minimum maintenance in maturation and easy handling but, as with many mass-produced foods, the individual flavour and texture dimensions of the mature cheese are often sacrificed for the sake of consistency.

Vacuum Bags

A false protective rind is created by wrapping the cheese in a plastic bag, which is drawn tight by mechanically sucking all the air out of the bag. The drawback is that this results in a microenvironment where absolutely nothing can grow, good or bad. The advantage of vacuum packing is minimum maintenance, moisture retention and hence predictable, uniform product quality.

Gas Flush

Cheeses may also be protected by being kept in a modified atmosphere of carbon dioxide and nitrogen, which can extend shelf life by a month or more. This method suffocates all cheeses with a rind, but has an advantage over vacuum packing in the case of fresh cheese types, because it avoids sucking out the free moisture.

Wax

Beeswax was once used as a natural covering for cheese, but this is rare today. The waxed cheeses so widely available now have invariably been matured in vacuum, then unwrapped and covered in coloured wax to make them look attractive. This does not re-create the benefits of maturation under a natural rind.

Plasticoat

Some cheeses, particularly washed-curd cheeses, have a thin coating of plasticoat painted on to their smooth rinds. This clear, shiny substance provides an artificial barrier that is also permeable to some degree. The rinds of these cheeses are then easy to wipe and keep clean of any moulds.

TYPES

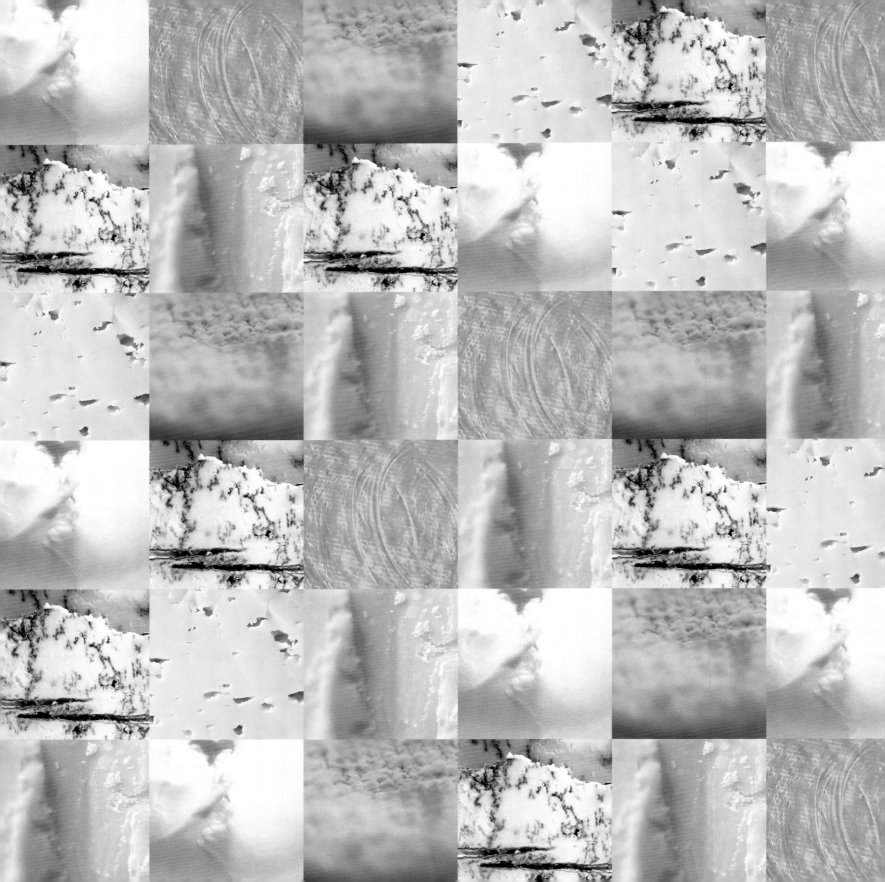

Types

There are many different methods of cheese-making, which produce an almost endless variety of cheeses, from delicate, fresh curds best eaten as soon as possible after they are made to huge wheels of hard cheese that can take years to reach their peak. If the variety is sometimes bewildering, there are some fairly simple rules that will help you to choose and eat each kind of cheese at its best.

Cheeses can be loosely grouped into categories according to their level of moisture and maturity. These categories are arranged here, beginning with the freshest.

Fresh
Uncooked and unripened curd cheeses. The simplest of these are moist, low-salt, short-lived cheeses such as fromage frais and fresh goat cheese, but marinated fresh cheeses and fresh stretched-curd cheeses are also subdivisions within this category.

White
Fresh cheese curds ripened by the introduction of a surface white-mould rind. White-rind cheeses can be further subdivided into traditional and modern types and triple cream cheeses.

Washed
Fresh cheese curds surface-ripened by the introduction of a bacterial culture, then washed to control the growth of bacteria. This group can also be subdivided into modern and traditional types.

Blue
Cheeses made by the addition of a blue-mould culture, which ripens the cheese from the inside out. Blue cheese can be subdivided into groups with three kinds of rind: scraped, natural and white-mould.

Semi-hard
Cheeses in which the curds are preserved by scalding and pressing. This group can be subdivided into cheddar, stirred-curd and mature stretched-curd cheeses.

Hard
Cheeses in which the curd is cooked at high temperature, then pressed heavily and matured for long periods. This category can be subdivided into granular types and smooth-textured cheeses.

Processed
One category of cheese that is not discussed in detail in this book is processed cheese. Almost 40 per cent of all cheese produced in Australia falls into this category. To make processed cheese, blends of surplus cheese are cooked, stabilised and mixed with emulsifiers to form a uniform mass with a semi-soft, pliable texture and mild, predictable flavour. Processed cheeses usually do not require refrigeration.

sh

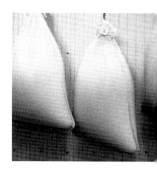

FRESH

Fresh Cheeses
and Other Fresh Dairy Products

Fresh Cheeses

Fresh cheeses are exactly as their name suggests – soft, deliciously moist, naked curds. They are simple cheeses by definition, best eaten as soon as possible after making, and are made from all types of milk. They include delicate cheeses such as fromage frais, fromage blanc, cream cheese and fresh goat's and ewe's curd. Related cheeses include fresh cheeses marinated in brine or oil such as feta, and fresh stretched-curd cheeses such as mozzarella.

The quality of a fresh cheese is determined by the quality of the milk, the type of starter used and the care taken in setting the fragile curds. The object is to retain moisture in the curd, which is sometimes simply set with lactic acid. The more moisture is left in the cheese, the more the curd retains its precious whey and the natural proteins, minerals and, most importantly, the milk sugars that give this type of cheese its special sweetness and subtle character.

Fresh cheeses first became popular in Australia as a result of postwar migration, and were initially based on Italian and Greek varieties. Today these cheeses still appeal as specialist products, but much of their individual character has been lost as a result of the use of co-operative cow's milk and packaging designed for extended shelf life rather than for flavour.

The early 1980s saw a new wave of development begin, with small farmhouse cheese-makers making a range of fresh curd cheeses from goat's and ewe's milk. Among the pioneers of this movement were Gabrielle Kervella, making goat's milk cheeses at Gidgegannup in Western Australia, and Julie Cameron, who began making ewe's milk cheeses at Meredith Dairy, near Ballarat. The type of milk used in fresh cheese has a significant effect on the end result, and the emergence of new producers and the use of new milk types has brought Australia fresh cheeses with a rich diversity of flavours and textures.

Fresh cow's milk cheeses made on the farm can have delicate nuances, and are best eaten when sweet and lactic, still perfumed with a distinctive cowy aroma. Most fresh cow's milk cheeses, however, are made with co-operative milk by large industrial producers and have a thick, creamy texture that is best suited to cooking; when used as eating cheeses they can be dull and cloying on the palate. Fresh cow's milk cheese is often boosted with cream to make cream cheese, and flavoured with herbs and spices to make it more appealing. One of Australia's more disastrous innovations is fruit cheese, a concoction that makes poor use of both cheese and dried fruit.

Goat's milk is perfectly suited to specialist fresh cheese types. A well-made fresh goat's milk cheese has a delicious, mild, creamy flavour with a lingering mouthfeel and a light, refreshing acidity that always demands another try. Fresh goat's milk cheeses represent the most popular type of specialist fresh cheeses, and come in all shapes and sizes such as pyramids, logs and buttons or discs. When aged, goat's milk cheese will harden to a nugget with a dense, strong taste, and is best enjoyed in small quantities.

FROMAGE FRAIS AND FROMAGE BLANC

The most perishable fresh cheese types are fromage frais and fromage blanc. Both are similar high-moisture cheeses with a limited life, best enjoyed within a day or two of making, and can be made from any type of milk.

Fromage frais is made with added salt, which draws out some of the moisture to lift and concentrate the flavour.

Fromage blanc is unsalted, mild and has a more delicate texture and soft mouthfeel.

Meredith Marinated Feta

Ewe's milk is rich and creamy, producing fresh cheeses with a dense, satiny texture and mild savoury flavour, at their best when really fresh and slightly acid. Ewe's milk tends to be well suited to cheeses with some acidity or salt to balance the richness of the milk, and those made with out-of-season milk can develop a lanolin or soapy flavour.

Buffalo milk is highly perfumed but in general has similar characteristics to ewe's milk.

Cheese-makers have long sought ways of extending the short shelf life of fresh cheeses – by scalding them, by pickling or marinating them, by coating them with ash. These methods produce a number of sub-categories of fresh cheese.

Ashed goat cheese

The use of ash as a coating can be traced back to the small farmhouse cheese-makers of France, who preserved their autumn cheeses through the winter months by coating them with *sel noir* (black salt), a mixture of salt and ash made from vine cuttings, or originally charcoal from the fireplace. This ash provided an instant natural rind for protection and neutralised surface acidity, allowing natural moulds to grow. The ash coating allowed the moisture to be drawn out and the curd to mature without the rind becoming rancid or sticky.

Most of the ashed goat's milk cheeses made in Australia are covered in charcoal or vine ash but eaten fresh. In this case the ash coating is cosmetic rather than functional, but the best of these cheeses are well worth maturing for longer periods, and they are not very difficult to look after. Stored in a humid place with a maximum temperature of 7°C for a few weeks, they will develop a blue-grey, mottled rind, condensed, nutty texture and strong, creamy flavour.

MAKING CHEESE AT HOME

(Courtesy of Richard Thomas)

You will need:

2-litre container of pasteurised milk

1 tbsp yoghurt

¼ plain junket tablet, dissolved in warm boiled water

Warm the milk to 20°C by immersing the unopened carton or bottle in hot water, then add the yoghurt and mix it a little. Allow the mix to sit for an hour or so, then add the dissolved junket. Turn the container upside-down a few times to ensure it is well mixed, then allow it to sit overnight. The following morning, empty the curdled milk into a clean tea towel, or even better a new superwipe, and hang it to drain for 12 hours.

With any luck, you now have the simplest form of cottage cheese, which can be used fresh in cheesecakes and dips. Alternatively, you can make it into feta by pressing it under a bowl of water for a day or so, then immersing it in a strong salt solution.

Marinated or pickled cheese

One of the most widely used methods of preserving fresh cheese is to pickle it in a brine solution. The best example of this is feta. In the eastern Mediterranean, where it originated, feta was made from a mixture of ewe's milk and goat's milk and matured in wooden barrels. Each region developed a different recipe, depending on the available milk. The more goat's milk used, the firmer the cheese; the more ewe's milk, the softer and creamier the texture.

The name 'feta' is relatively modern and literally means 'slice' – the form in which it is served. It is one of Australia's most popular cheeses. Modern copies made from cow's milk lack the tang and complexity (and price) of those made using traditional methods. Industrial tinned feta can be kept for long periods and tends to be quite sharp and salty. It is a good idea to rinse feta under cold water to remove excess salt before eating.

Feta is lower in fat than many hard cheeses, and can also be marinated in oil infused with herbs.

Fresh stretched-curd cheeses

Stretched-curd cheeses form a unique category of cheese, sometimes referred to as 'pasta filata' cheese. They can be divided into two sub-types – fresh and hard. Hard stretched-curd cheeses are discussed in the section on semi-hard cheeses (p. 129).

Fresh stretched-curd cheeses are 'intensively worked', requiring careful judgement on the part of the cheese-maker. Temperature is crucial; after draining, the curds are melted in a vat of hot water until they settle to the bottom, and the cheese-maker must know exactly when to begin stretching and pulling this elastic mass. The object is to pull or tear (*mozzare*) a section of the melted cheese so that the outer layer forms a thin skin around the moist stretched curds within. The ball is then placed in a cold brine solution. Each ball contains moist, milky layers of spun curd covered with a thin rind.

Often known as *fiore di latte* (flower of the milk), fresh stretched-curd cheeses are sold uncured, resting in a salty whey brine. The most popular are mozzarella (fist-sized balls) and bocconcini (little mouthfuls). Most of these cheeses are made from cow's milk collected on a co-operative basis. They are either handmade or, in larger operations, stretched and formed by machine. The major attraction of these cheeses is not their flavour, which is mild, lactic and slightly sweet, but their firm, yielding, tender texture, which is ideal for soaking up stronger flavours and also becomes stringy and elastic when cooked. The bigger the ball, the better the texture and the more moisture contained inside the thin skin – an important consideration in the overall flavour profile. It helps to remember that fresh stretched-curd cheeses are best eaten no more than a day old, as is the tradition in Italy.

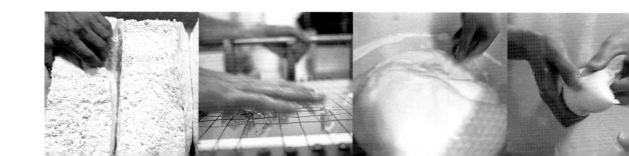

BUFFALO MOZZARELLA

Buffalo mozzarella, although a relative newcomer to Australia, dates back to the sixth century AD in the swampy and malarial areas of southern Italy close to Naples. This pure buffalo milk cheese was once regarded as a food of the poor, but in Italy it is now officially regarded as the only true mozzarella. Although in many other countries the name is applied to cow's milk cheeses, this is misleading, because the authentic *mozzarella di bufala* has far more character and flavour than any made from cow's milk.

The unique qualities of buffalo milk are revealed at their sensual best in a well-made fresh mozzarella. Rich-textured, stringy layers of moist curd, porcelain white in colour, are encased in a distinctive thin, slippery skin, which when cut releases a sweet whey with a perfume that whistles up the back of the nostrils. Once experienced, the fragrance of buffalo milk can never be forgotten.

Purrumbete Buffalo Mozzarella

HOMEMADE YOGHURT

Yoghurt is very simple
to make at home.
You will need:

1 litre milk

2 tablespoons natural
yoghurt or yoghurt starter

Bring the milk almost
to the boil to kill off any
potential bacteria and
denature the protein.

Let it cool to 40°C, add
two tablespoons of live
set yoghurt (or yoghurt
cultures).

Pour into a thermos or
a large pot and incubate
at 35°C overnight.
The yoghurt should
slowly set.

Store at 2–4°C.

Remember to retain
a little of the 'starter'
for next time.

Other Fresh Dairy Products

Yoghurt

Yoghurt is widely seen as a convenient, healthy food, high in protein, low in fat and generally good for you. It is used as a staple in cooking in the Middle East and Asia. Most Australian yoghurt is made from cow's milk, but it is also made from goat's, ewe's and buffalo milk.

Yoghurt is not strictly cheese. It is thickened by a bacterial starter rather than rennet, and the whey is not separated and drained off as in cheese-making, so the fat content of the yoghurt remains the same as that of the milk used to produce it.

Yoghurt has its origins in fermented, slightly alcoholic milk-based drinks, which were popular among the nomadic peoples of Central Asia. In Britain too, the Celts drank brews of curdled milk with beer or cider. During medieval times a 'posset' of curdled milk and hot wine was popular as an aid to digestion, and there were many tales about the mysterious benefits of yoghurt, but how it was made was not commonly understood.

The health benefits of live yoghurt became popularly known from the 1880s through the research of Dr E. Metchnikoff, who linked the longevity of Bulgarian peasants to their consumption of large amounts of sour milk or *yohourth*. Metchnikoff established that the fermented milk encouraged certain bacteria to settle in the intestines, where they increased the availability of proteins, milk sugars and other nutrients such as calcium. This beneficial activity has since been claimed to improve our immune systems, reduce cholesterol and offer an antidote to the side-effects of antibiotics. As a result, live yoghurt has developed a reputation as a wonder food. It is digested quickly (90 per cent within one hour) and is highly beneficial to the digestive system. Most industrial yoghurt, however, has little to do with 'real live yoghurt' and has few benefits to health, despite the marketing hype.

Bacteria in yoghurt

The strains of bacteria used to bring about coagulation in yoghurt have a significant effect on flavour. The standard yoghurt culture is a mixture of two different lactic bacteria:

- *Lactobacillus bulgaricus,* which acidifies the milk by causing lactose to form lactic acid, and gives natural yoghurt a fresh and slightly sour flavour; and

- *Streptococcus thermophilus,* which generates digestible fatty acids and gives the coagulated casein texture and aroma under the influence of gentle warmth.

These cultures combine to produce a balance of acidity, flavour and texture. Different yoghurts use different ratios and variations of these cultures, but their symbiotic action occurs in all real 'live' yoghurts.

There are two clearly identifiable types of yoghurt available commercially:

- *traditional set yoghurt,* which is gently cooked and set in a jar or pot, sometimes with a thin liquid on the top. This is normally 'live'; and

- *stirred yoghurt,* which is agitated into a homogenised mass and often contains stabiliser and additives. Some of these products are not yoghurt at all, but milk thickened with powdered skim milk, stabilised with gelatine and often mixed with fruits and flavouring. Sugar and artificial sweeteners are commonly added, and these products are of questionable nutritional value.

Cultures in yoghurt

Several different starter cultures are commonly used to make yoghurt more easily digestible. These cultures have been developed from bacteria originating in the human gut. The most widely used are bifidobacteria and *Lactobacillus acidophilus.*

It is debatable whether there is any benefit in adding these cultures to stirred yoghurt. Adding them to active yoghurt is counterproductive, because the *L. bulgaricus* quickly reduces *acidophilus* to negligible quantities.

Kefir

This cultured milk product originates from the Caucasus region of Russia. The mountain people of the region have long thought of it as a gift from god; its name means 'good feeling' or 'pleasure'. The cauliflower-like grains of kefir culture were said to have amazing healing powers as far back as the eighth century, and Moslem tribesmen took care to prevent it passing out of their control for fear of losing its healing powers. It was not until 1908 that the culture was first brought to the West, supposedly after an extraordinary saga involving a royal princess, love and deception in the court of the Tzar of Russia.

Kefir is fermented, slightly alcoholic milk containing a slightly different blend of cultures from those used in yoghurt. Its unique flavour is created by the combination of lactobacillus acidification and the alcoholic production of yeast. Some health food stores sell kits for making kefir at home.

Whey Cheeses

During cheese-making, most of the protein, fat and minerals are left in the curd, but some escape with the whey. These can be recovered by reheating the whey and adding a weak acid to coagulate the residual solids, producing low-fat whey cheeses.

Most whey cheeses are sold fresh, and are mild, sweet and fragile, with a short shelf life. The best-known of these is ricotta (meaning re-cooked). Some are pressed and have a longer shelf life; these include ricotta salata, which is traditionally made from ewe's milk, and is firm yet moist and tender with a mild, milky, slightly salty flavour.

Many industrial whey cheeses are bulked out with skim milk to boost the yield. The best cheeses avoid this, because it alters the delicate cheese's flavour, texture and clean, refreshing mouthfeel.

Cream

Cream is the fat that naturally rises to the surface of cow's milk, but is also present in a naturally homogenised form in ewe's, goat's and buffalo milk. One of the main reasons for the historical popularity of cow's milk over other types is that the fat globules in cow milk are far easier to separate into cream.

Cream was traditionally extracted by leaving fresh milk to stand and then skimming the surface, but these days it is removed by centrifugal force in a separator. Pure cream is highly perishable in its natural form, and most industrial dairy companies add a tiny amount of peroxide to extend shelf life; they are not obliged to disclose this on the label.

Cream is sold in various forms, classified according to fat levels and whether it is fresh or soured:

- *reduced fat or light cream* contains 18–25 per cent milk fat, and is ideal for pouring;
- *thickened cream* is 35 per cent milk fat; it is thickened by adding gelatine, and separates easily when cooked;
- *pure whipping cream* contains 35–45 per cent milk fat, and is good for cooking or whipping;
- *rich double cream* contains 48–55 per cent milk fat, making it thick enough to be spooned. This cream has often been scalded, and has a slight caramel sweetness;
- *sour cream* contains 35 per cent milk fat, and is made from cream treated with a bacterial culture that raises its acidity and gives a slightly sour, tangy taste; and
- *crème fraîche* is 48 per cent milk fat and is sometimes sold as sour cream, but is left to mature naturally without any bacterial starters.

Clotted cream

This type of cream was originally made in the south-west of England during the summer, when there was a surplus of rich, creamy milk. Milk was placed in a shallow bowl overnight next to a warm stove. The slow heat caused the cream to rise to the surface and thicken, and also encouraged bacteria to ripen the cream slightly. This left a rippled, chewy skin over a layer of thick cream, which was often substituted for butter.

Today most clotted cream is made by scalding standardised cream and leaving it to cool. Modern clotted cream is thicker than the traditional version.

Mascarpone

Mascarpone is made from cream and originated in Italy during the sixteenth century. It is not a cheese because no starter or rennet is used, nor is it butter because it is not churned. The traditional technique of producing it is relatively simple. The cream is heated to 100°C, then curdled with citric acid and hung to drain in a muslin bag for several days. The result is a rich cream with a smooth texture and slightly tart sweetness.

Butter

Butter was considered a luxury food in ancient times and was basically developed as a way of preserving milk fat for use during the colder seasons. Butter-making is an expensive process. It takes more than twenty litres of milk to make a kilo of butter. To make butter, cream is churned until it releases the butterfat. Almost all butter made in Australia is made in large factories during the seasonal milk flush, and is a by-product of skim milk powder. The exceptions are a few small makers producing limited quantities of farmhouse butter or whey butter.

Butter was the cornerstone of Australian dairy exports for most of the twentieth century. The demand for milk with a high butterfat content was one reason for the popularity of the Jersey and Shorthorn breeds. During the 1970s, however, overproduction in Europe, low international prices and falling domestic consumption led to a decline in the Australian butter industry, and large industrial concerns changed their focus to milk, dried milk powder and cheese.

Australian butter has a distinctive yellow colour and slight green pasture flavour. Because it is made on a seasonal basis, it is often stored frozen in blocks. The sweetness and flavour change depending on how long it has been stored; old butter tastes slightly rancid and cheesy.

The use of butter in cooking has been often been referred to as one of the defining differences between the traditional foods of the warm Mediterranean countries, which naturally used olive oil, and the colder lands of northern Europe, which used butter.

Two main types of butter are sold in Australia:

- *sweet cream butter* is sold either salted or unsalted, and its flavour depends on its age and the quality of the fresh cream used;
- *cultured butter* is made using an active acid culture to ripen the cream, giving the butter a more aromatic flavour and slight sweetness but also a much shorter shelf life.

Buttermilk

Buttermilk is traditionally the liquid released during butter-making, but most commercial buttermilk is made from milk and milk powder. Buttermilk has a higher acid content than skim milk and is more easily digestible. Fermented and thickened with the addition of a starter, it was once used to make whey butter, which often has a slightly cheesy taste from the partially fermented curds.

Tasting Notes

Cabecou

Producer: Woodside Cheesewrights (SA)
Classification: Artisan
Form: 20g disc
Milk: Goat – local farms
Average fat: 30%
Rennet: FP Chymosin
Best season: Autumn
Description: Eaten fresh, these cheeses are tender and delicate, but when aged they have a mottled, mouldy rind and brittle texture with a developed goat flavour and a touch of yeastiness.
Additional notes: The name (literally 'little goat') comes from Quercy and Rouergue in France, where these cheeses are sometimes wrapped in leaves and sprinkled with marc, then further fermented in jars.

Chèvre Button

Producer: Kervella Cheese (WA)
Classification: Farmhouse
Form: 20g disc
Milk: Goat – organic
Average fat: 25%
Rennet: FP Chymosin
Best season: Autumn
Description: Light, sweet and delicate when fresh, these cheeses age over a week or two to develop mottled blue spots and become dry and nutty, with a concentrated, creamy goat flavour and just a hint of the organic pasture.
Additional notes: Chèvre buttons mature well, and are delicious dried and marinated in virgin olive oil with fresh herbs and garlic.

Clyde River Chevrets

Producer: Tasmanian Highland Cheeses (Tas)
Classification: Farmhouse
Form: 50g thick discs, vacuum-packed in twin or six-packs
Milk: Goat
Average fat: 20%
Rennet: FP Chymosin
Best season: Autumn
Description: A firm, slightly salty goat curd cheese with a clean flavour and acid, crumbly texture.
Additional notes: Ideal for grilling.

Faudel Feta in Brine

Producer: Faudel Farmhouse Cheese Company (Vic)
Classification: Farmhouse
Form: Small irregular rectangles in 1.5 or 3.5kg buckets
Milk: Goat
Average fat: 20%
Rennet: FP Chymosin
Best season: Spring & autumn
Description: A dense, creamy curd cheese with a fresh, milky acidity, salty flavour and just a hint of goat.

Fromage Blanc

Producer: Kervella Cheese (WA)
Classification: Farmhouse
Form: 500g tub
Milk: Goat – organic
Average fat: 25%
Rennet: FP Chymosin
Best season: Autumn
Description: This simple fromage blanc is moist, light and fluffy in texture. The flavour is mild and slightly sweet, with a trace of fresh flowers and hay.

Additional notes: The quality of the organic milk used is revealed in the subtle depth of flavour. Ideal for cooking or enjoyed cold with some crusty bread on a warm autumn day.

Fromage de Chèvre

Producer: Faudel Farmhouse Cheese (Vic)
Classification: Farmhouse
Form: 1kg pyramid, vacuum-sealed
Milk: Goat
Average fat: 20%
Rennet: FP Chymosin
Best season: Autumn
Description: A firm, dense, slightly dry curd cheese that has been naturally drained overnight. The mild goat flavour is balanced by a slightly citric tang.
Additional notes: Rod Faudell keeps his goats inside most of the year, hand-feeding them according to European methods. This ensures consistently high-quality milk for cheese-making.

Fromage Frais

Producer: Faudel Farmhouse Cheese Company (Vic)
Classification: Farmhouse
Form: 1.1kg tub & 200g cups
Milk: Goat
Average fat: 16%
Rennet: FP Chymosin
Best season: Spring
Description: A moist, light, delicate curd cheese with a slightly sweet, nutty taste balanced with a gentle, acidic, salty finish.

Additional notes: This simple cheese is best enjoyed as fresh as possible and can be used as a replacement for butter, cream or sour cream.

Gippsland Chèvre

Producer: Tarago River Cheese Company (Vic)
Classification: Artisan
Form: 1.2kg buckets
Milk: Goat – local farm
Average fat: 20%
Rennet: Halal calf
Best season: Spring & autumn
Description: A moist, delicate, slightly coarse-textured fresh chèvre with balanced sweet acidity and mild goat flavour.

Gourmet Feta

Producer: Hellenic Cheese Farm (Vic)
Classification: Artisan
Form: 200g block, vacuum-packed
Milk: Goat – mixed source
Average fat: 20%
Rennet: FP Chymosin
Best season: Spring & summer
Description: A dense, dry, crumbly feta, quite strong, with a sharp, marinated tang.
Additional notes: Also available marinated in oil infused with dried herbs and spices.

Gourmet Feta

Producer: Island Pure (SA)
Classification: Artisan
Form: 300g vacuum-packed
Milk: Ewe – two farms
Average fat: 37%
Rennet: Halal calf
Best season: Spring

Description: Crumbly, mild feta with a clean, creamy aftertaste.
Additional notes: Less salty than conventional feta due to maturation under vacuum.

Gourmet Feta

Producer: Timboon Farmhouse Cheese (Vic)
Classification: Farmhouse
Form: 250g jars & 500g bucket
Milk: Cow – biodynamic
Average fat: 30%
Rennet: Microbial
Description: Smooth cow's milk feta sliced into small discs and submerged in oil flavoured with dried herbs and spices.
Additional notes: Lower in salt than ordinary feta due to preservation in oil. Ideal in the summer for use in fresh salads.

Grabetto

Producer: Yarra Valley Dairy (Vic)
Classification: Artisan
Form: 60g upright cone
Milk: Goat – regional
Average fat: 30%
Rennet: FP Chymosin
Best season: Autumn
Description: Fresh, smooth-textured cheese that develops a strong goat flavour as it ages.
Additional notes: Ideal for grilling when mature.

Haloumi

Producer: Island Pure (SA)
Classification: Artisan – two farms
Form: 300g block, vacuum-packed
Milk: Ewe

Average fat: 37%
Rennet: Halal calf
Best season: Spring
Description: Firm and slightly rubbery with a light yellow colour and a mild, milky flavour with a touch of salt. Sold with or without mint.
Additional notes: One of the classic tests for haloumi made from pure ewe's milk is whether it squeaks when eaten fresh.

Hellenic Chèvre

Producer: Hellenic Cheese Farm (Vic)
Classification: Artisan
Form: 100g & 1.2kg cylindrical logs, vacuum-packed
Milk: Goat – mixed source
Average fat: 20%
Rennet: FP Chymosin
Best season: Spring
Description: A smooth, heavy-textured fresh cheese with mild goaty flavour and a sharp acid tang.
Additional notes: This cheese is available in a variety of flavours: sweet paprika, herbed, ashed and blue.

Herb Torte

Producer: Timboon Farmhouse Cheese (Vic)
Classification: Farmhouse
Form: 140g log in plastic container
Milk: Cow – biodynamic
Average fat: 28%
Rennet: Microbial
Description: Dense cream-enriched cheese rolled in finely diced herbs, garlic and spices.

Jannei Fresh Chèvre

Producer: Jannei Goat Dairy (NSW)
Classification: Farmhouse
Form: 150g, 250g, 500g & 1kg cylindrical logs, vacuum-packed
Milk: Goat
Average fat: 23%
Rennet: FP Chymosin
Best season: Autumn
Description: Soft, dense, creamy-textured cheese with a hint of goat on the finish.
Additional notes: Sold plain or with a dusting of charcoal.

Kervella Fromage Frais

Producer: Kervella Cheese (WA)
Classification: Farmhouse
Form: 120g round
Milk: Goat – organic
Average fat: 21%
Rennet: FP Chymosin
Best season: Spring & autumn
Description: A delicious, moist, fresh cheese with a fine, melting texture and mild, clean, lactic sweetness balanced with just the right level of tartness.

Kervella Pyramid

Producer: Kervella Cheese (WA)
Classification: Farmhouse
Form: 100g pyramids, plain or ashed, cellophane wrap
Milk: Goat – organic
Average fat: 25%
Rennet: FP Chymosin
Best season: Autumn
Description: A moist, rindless fresh cheese with a fine, melting texture and mild, clean, lactic sweetness balanced with just the right level of tartness.

Additional notes: Gabrielle Kervella has been recognised as creating a quality benchmark with this delicious cheese. Her ashed pyramids are usually eaten fresh, but can be left to mature in humid conditions. After a few weeks they develop a nutty, flaky texture and a sweet flavour that lingers at the back of the palate.

Kytren Fresh Chèvre

Producer: Kytren Pure Goats Milk Cheese (WA)
Classification: Farmhouse
Form: 130g pyramids (ashed or plain) & 350g plain logs
Milk: Goat
Average fat: 21%
Rennet: FP Chymosin
Best season: Spring & autumn
Description: Fresh, light and creamy in texture; mild flavour balanced with a hint of acidity.

Meredith Fresh Chèvre Pyramid

Producer: Meredith Dairy (Vic)
Classification: Farmhouse
Form: 180–200g pyramid wrapped in waxed paper
Milk: Goat
Average fat: 25%
Rennet: Calf
Best season: Autumn
Description: Moist, slightly wet texture with a creamy flavour and delicious lemony, salty freshness indicating the high quality of the fresh milk.
Additional notes: Also available as a log, vacuum-packed and wrapped in tissue paper.

Meredith Fromage Blanc

Producer: Meredith Dairy (Vic)
Classification: Farmhouse
Form: 125g plastic containers
Milk: Goat
Average fat: 11.5%
Rennet: Calf
Best season: Spring & autumn
Description: Light and tender, this mild cheese has all the sweetness of fresh milk balanced with a slight, refreshing sourness.
Additional notes: Best eaten fresh to appreciate the subtle complexity and delicate texture.

Meredith Fromage Frais

Producer: Meredith Dairy (Vic)
Classification: Farmhouse
Form: 125g plastic containers
Milk: Goat
Average fat: 11.5%
Rennet: Calf
Best season: Spring & autumn
Description: Fresh, sweet, milky aroma, light and delicate texture with a gentle, acidic flavour and just a hint of sweetness.

Meredith Marinated Feta

Producer: Meredith Dairy (Vic)
Classification: Farmhouse
Form: 325g jars
Milk: Goat
Average fat: 25%
Rennet: Calf
Description: Pieces of soft, creamy curd marinated in blended oil with fresh herbs and garlic.
Additional notes: Developed by Richard Thomas, this cheese is great as a standby for salads or crumbling over steamed vegetables.

Milawa Chèvre

Producer: Milawa Cheese Company (Vic)
Classification: Artisan
Form: 150g & 600g vacuum packs
Milk: Goat – regional
Average fat: 25%
Rennet: Calf
Best season: Spring to autumn
Description: Solid and dry-textured, with a fresh acidity and strong goat flavour.
Additional notes: Also sold ashed with black charcoal dust. The vacuum-packing of this fresh cheese alters the texture of the slowly drained day-old curds. Visitors to the cellar-door facility at the old butter factory have the opportunity to try it unpacked.

Mount Emu Creek Feta

Producer: Mount Emu Creek Dairy (Vic)
Classification: Artisan
Form: 2kg buckets, vacuum-packed
Milk: Ewe – local farms
Average fat: 30%
Rennet: FP Chymosin
Best season: Spring & summer
Description: Made according to the traditional Greek method, this pure ewe's milk feta is naturally white in colour and has a solid, dry, crumbly texture. Rich and creamy but not cloying, it has a rounded aftertaste balanced with a hint of lanolin.

Mount Emu Creek Ricotta

Producer: Mount Emu Creek Dairy (Vic)
Classification: Artisan
Form: 300g & 2kg vacuum-packed
Milk: Ewe – local farms
Average fat: 25%
Rennet: FP Chymosin
Best season: Spring
Description: Made from whey using a traditional method, this low-fat cheese has a dry, satiny texture and mild, sweet, slightly nutty flavour.
Additional notes: Ideal for cooking with added flavours.

Persian Feta

Producer: Yarra Valley Dairy (Vic)
Classification: Farmhouse
Form: 250g tin & 1.5kg tub
Milk: Cow
Average fat: 27%
Rennet: FP Chymosin
Description: Fine-textured, soft feta cheese marinated in oil infused with local pink garlic and herbs and spices.
Additional notes: This marinated cheese was developed from a traditional Persian recipe. A good combination of creamy, slightly sweet, salty cheese, herbs and flavoured oil.

Purrumbete Buffalo Mozzarella

Producer: Purrumbete Buffalo Cheese (Vic)
Classification: Artisan
Form: 50g hand-shaped balls; 1.5kg bucket
Milk: Buffalo – one farm

Average fat: 23%
Rennet: FP Chymosin
Best season: Summer
Description: Hand-stretched, pure porcelain in colour and encased in a thin, shiny skin, this delicate but firm cheese oozes with delicious, creamy, slightly sweet whey. It has a unique aroma and sweet, lactic flavour, with a slightly mossy aftertaste.
Additional notes: Buffalo mozzarella is traditionally served with ripe tomatoes and shredded green basil, seasoned with pepper and drizzled with virgin olive oil – a combination of red, white and green that echoes the colours of the Italian flag. Facita is the same cheese base flattened into a sheet, which can be used as a wrap for fresh ingredients.

Riverina Fresh Pecorino

Producer: Riverina Cheese (NSW)
Classification: Artisan
Form: 1kg wheel, vacuum-packed
Milk: Ewe – regional origin
Average fat: 25%
Rennet: FP Chymosin
Best season: Spring
Description: A semi-hard, smooth-textured fresh cheese with a mild, rounded, slightly salty flavour.
Additional notes: This cheese is made with milk from crossbred Awassi sheep milked at Cowra.

Snowy Mountains Chèvre

Producer: Hobbit Farm (NSW)
Classification: Farmhouse

Form: 700g log, vacuum-packed
Milk: Goat
Average fat: 42%
Rennet: FP Chymosin
Best season: Autumn
Description: Moist and slightly nutty flavour with a mild goaty aftertaste.
Additional notes: The same cheese is also available flavoured with alpine pepper plant, or as a marinated chèvre matured in olive oil, fresh herbs, garlic and sun-dried tomatoes.

Traditional Farmhouse Chèvre

Producer: Tasmanian Highland Cheeses (Tas)
Classification: Farmhouse
Form: 1kg pyramid-shaped log & 250g round log, vacuum-packed
Milk: Goat
Average fat: 25%
Rennet: FP Chymosin
Best season: Spring & autumn
Description: Fine-textured, creamy cheese with a full, rich, clean goat flavour balanced with a mild, lemony tang.
Additional notes: Also sold coated with ash.

Westhaven Fresh Chèvre

Producer: Westhaven Dairy (Tas)
Classification: Artisan
Form: 150g log, vacuum-packed
Milk: Goat – regional
Average fat: 45%
Rennet: FP Chymosin
Best season: Spring & summer
Description: Extruded curd cheese that is gently beaten until smooth and creamy. Mild, slightly lemony and consistent.

Whitelaw

Producer: Top Paddock Cheeses (Vic)
Classification: Farmhouse
Form: 150g & 1kg discs, wrapped in foil-backed paper and vacuum-packed
Milk: Cow – red breed
Average fat: 18%
Rennet: FP Chymosin
Best season: Spring & autumn
Description: Pale yellow in colour with a moist appearance. Mild, sweet, lactic flavour with a fresh, slightly acidic finish.
Additional notes: Can be substituted for quark, fromage blanc or similar cheeses with fresh fruit and in desserts or savoury dishes. Also comes in a herb & garlic flavour.

Woodside Goat Curd

Producer: Woodside Cheesewrights (SA)
Classification: Artisan
Form: 1kg buckets
Milk: Goat – local farms
Average fat: 45%
Rennet: FP Chymosin
Best season: Spring & autumn
Description: A moist, moussey (fluffy) white curd with retained sweetness, a delicate balance of acidity and a mild, clean, creamy finish.
Additional notes: Made almost entirely using lactic coagulation, which takes 24 hours, then carefully hand-ladled and drained to avoid destroying the delicate curd matrix. The same curd is used in Edith's cheese (see p.96).

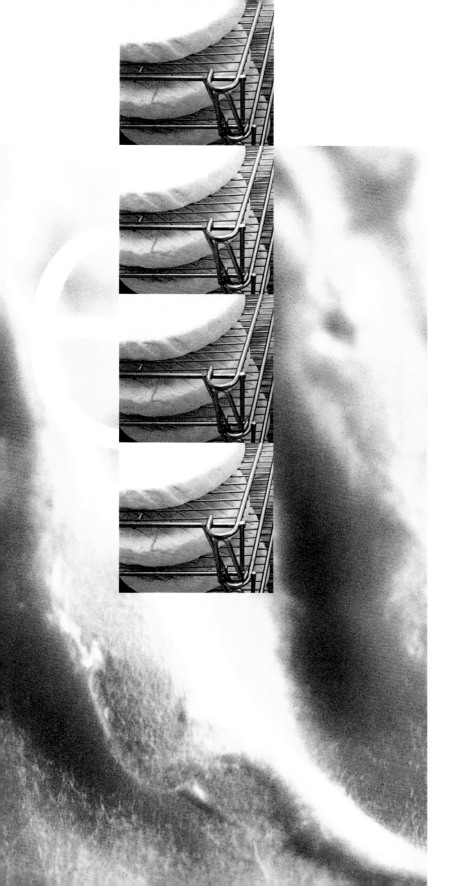

WHITE

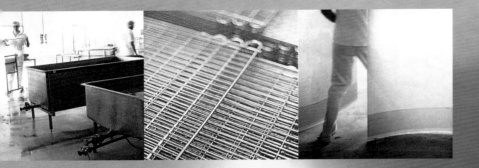

White-rind

Soft, oozing white-rind cheeses are among the most popular types of specialist cheese made in Australia. Virtually all the white-rind cheeses available here until the 1980s were tinned 'camemberts' and 'bries' mass-produced in Europe and stabilised to survive long periods in transit with haphazard refrigeration. These cheeses, which were usually mild and quite firm in texture, have had an enduring influence on Australian consumer tastes. When Australian producers began making their own white-rind cheeses, they faced a market that had already become accustomed to products that were stabilised, easily stored, reliable and bland.

The cultivation of a natural rind of white mould around moist, salted curds represents one of the first steps in preserving fresh cheese. This surface rind extends the life of the fragile curd by acting as a barrier against contamination and moisture loss. The rind also has an important influence on the texture, maturation and flavour development of white-rind cheeses. All types of milk are used to make white-rind cheeses, but cow's milk is the most popular.

White-mould cultures were used in European cheeses long before modern refrigeration. Microflora were encouraged to form on the surface of fresh cheeses spontaneously as part of the maturation process, which took place in cool, damp cellars or caves. The original 'white' rind cheeses are believed to have been grey or even black on the outside. It is only recently that scientists have developed a more dependable range of cultures that give a pure white covering. Many strains of culture are used, but the most popular is a white mould known as *Penicillium candidum*.

These cultures are usually added to the milk after pasteurisation, and a solution is sometimes sprayed on the surface of the fresh cheese after brining. The cheese is then matured in a controlled environment with high humidity. Like mushrooms and other fungi, these hydrophilic (water-loving) white moulds thrive in moist, humid conditions, and as a living culture they need air, though not too much. *P. candidum* grows best at a temperature of 12°C with 95 per cent humidity, and takes a little over a week to cover the exterior of the cheese with a downy white coat.

The starter culture, the handling of the curd, the draining time and ambient temperature are crucial in determining how much acidity a white-mould cheese will develop and how much moisture it will retain. Great care is required to ensure that the curd matrix is broken as little as possible so that the cheese will remain moist. The curd cutting has to be timed carefully to ensure that the curds are not damaged or torn, and the curd must be handled gently when it is transferred into the draining hoops. Small cheese-makers commonly ladle the curd into the hoops by hand. In France this process is known as *moulage à la louche* (literally 'casting with the ladle'), a phrase that can be found on the labels of the best camemberts. The curd is then drained gradually, without added pressure, so that it remains soft and keeps its natural moisture and flavour.

After draining, the fresh formed curd is either sprinkled with dry salt by hand or immersed in a cold brine solution to give it a light coating of salt. The salt seals the outer surface, forming the initial basis of a rind and a clean platform for the white-rind cultures to grow on. At this stage the *Penicillium candidum* is usually sprayed on the surface of the cheese. Care needs to be taken, however, as too much mould can give the cheese a bitter or cardboardy flavour; some cheesemakers find this second mould spraying unnecessary.

The cheeses are then transferred to darkened curing rooms. Access to these rooms is closely controlled to prevent contamination by rogue moulds. Clear signs of the mould start to appear after just a few days, and within five or six days it can grow up to half a centimetre thick. At this point it is silky-soft and has the texture of wet velvet. Like soft snow, it flattens if touched, leaving an indentation in the fluffy white mould.

The smell in the curing rooms is a good indicator of the stage the moulds have reached. Initially, when the bare cheeses enter the room, the smell is sweet and milky. After ten days the smell changes to that of sweet rotting apples, indicating that the cheeses are ready to pack.

After leaving the humid maturing rooms the mould still needs to be protected carefully so that it does not dry out or sweat. This is achieved by wrapping the cheese in a special 'breathing' paper, which acts as a barrier to contamination while the cheese matures and offers a micro-environment to keep the moulds active within. The paper squashes the rampant white-mould bloom flat.

The white rind preserves the cheese for up to three months, and the health of the white mould is always an indicator of the quality and health of the cheese within. The thick bloom of mould dies off after about sixty days. If the cheese is left too long, the interior dries out and the mould discolours to a mottled off-yellow and becomes smelly, often with an ammonia tang.

Types of White-rind Cheese

White-rind cheeses are available in many different textures and flavours, and it can be difficult to choose a cheese that suits your palate. People often complain that a cheese is too bland or too strong, too hard or too runny. To avoid disappointment, it is essential to understand that white-rind cheeses are made by two distinct methods, which produce very different results. These methods can loosely be categorised as 'traditional' and 'modern'.

There is another subcategory of white-rind cheese, which will only be mentioned here in passing. This is known as triple cream cheese, and is made from full-cream milk with further cream added. In form, these cheeses are usually thick discs or squares with a dry, acid centre that only breaks down slowly, rarely softening all the way through. They are best when they have a certain amount of acidity, as otherwise they are too buttery and cloying on the palate.

Traditional
The traditional method of making white-rind cheeses from whole, unstandardised milk dates back more than a thousand years, and was in general use until the 1970s. In this method, the rind not only preserves the curd but also helps the relatively dry, acid interior of the cheese to break down. For this reason, these cheeses are described as 'surface-ripened'.

Curds are formed by the action of mesophilic (medium-temperature) starters, which traditionally were often made from the previous day's whey. These starter cultures are usually slow-acting and gentle on the curd, which can

help to give the ripened cheese a fuller flavour. Their disadvantage is that they take more time, and therefore require more work, than the modern, faster-acting thermophilic starters.

After the curds have formed they are hooped and drained for up to twenty-four hours before brining and spraying with white mould. During the long, gentle draining the curds are encouraged to develop acidity: this is the central difference between the traditional and modern methods of manufacture. When it is young, a traditional cheese has a dry, acidic, chalky texture. The pH is approximately 4.4, and if eaten the cheese would have a dull, dry texture and pronounced acid flavour.

Traditional cheese only matures from the outer rind towards the centre, and there is no way of rushing this process. Under ideal conditions, maturation takes about forty-five days. The surface mould sends root-like filaments into the chalky curd centre, slowly breaking it down to a soft, sticky texture. Flavour and texture vary daily as the cheese matures. There is a critical period of just a few weeks when the inner curds are fully broken down and the cheese is '*à point*' – a perfect balance of soft bulging texture and full flavour – before it becomes overripe.

Traditional white-rind cheeses rarely have a perfect all-white rind. It is quite acceptable to have a wrinkled crust, often mottled with light reddish-brown pigments – a sign that other cultures have been used. It is also acceptable to cut the rind off before eating.

Knowing just when a white-rind cheese is ready to eat requires skill, a little experience and, most importantly, patience. Cut it too early and it will have a chalk line; too late and the mould will have died. The reward for careful maturation, however, is a full individual flavour, rich and mouth-watering, and a sticky, oozing texture with a restless moving edge.

Modern

Modern white-rind cheeses differ from traditional cheeses in that they have a soft texture from the day they leave the maturation room at the dairy. The internal curds are not allowed to develop acidity or a dry, chalky centre.

In the modern method, the curd's natural acid development is stabilised by using thermophilic starters, which only work within a narrow temperature range. Temperature is carefully controlled to regulate the action of the starters until the correct acidity is achieved. The curds are drained swiftly in very warm rooms, then moved to cooler rooms. By the time the cheeses are brined and sprayed with white-mould culture, they have a perfect, creamy centre with no chalk line. Once the white mould has grown to form a rind, the cheese will hold a reasonably stable, soft texture for up to seventy days.

By contrast with the traditional method, the white surface mould has a minimal influence on the internal texture of modern stabilised cheeses; for this reason, they are often sold as 'pre-ripened'. They do not change much over time, which makes them well-behaved and very predictable. The disadvantage is that they tend to be rather insipid in both flavour and texture. To improve the flavour, most cheese-makers add cream to the milk, bringing the fat level to 60 per cent or more. The cheese is then known as double brie. The rind in this type of cheese is carefully designed to add flavour, and should be pure white with a pleasant mushroom taste.

In spite of the carefully controlled conditions in which it is manufactured, modern white-rind cheese is particularly susceptible to seasonal variations in milk quality. Small farmhouse or artisan operations without the technology to standardise the protein content of milk often find it difficult to achieve the crucial stability in the acidification of the curd. This can produce harder, creamy cheeses in spring and soft, runny, unpredictable cheese in late autumn. When poorly stabilised, usually by mistake, these cheeses can have quite an interesting creamy texture and a rich, clotted flavour.

The larger Australian producers mostly make white-rind cheese by the modern method. Stabilised cheeses appeal to retailers and most consumers because they are easy to handle, convenient, require no careful maturing and suit the modern 'fast' lifestyle. Although traditional white-rind cheeses have flavour and personality, they are not easy to mature, and the results are invariably inconsistent.

Because retailers lack the time, the conditions and in all likelihood the knowledge to mature traditional cheeses properly, it is often difficult to find them in good condition. Unless we encourage producers and retailers to appreciate and care for these glorious cheeses, there is a danger that they will disappear altogether.

Brie and Camembert

Brie and camembert were developed a thousand years apart, and take their names from the French localities where they were made. Brie originated in the Ile-de-France in the eighth century AD. It was made in large discs about 35cm in diameter, each weighing 2kg. Camembert is said to have been invented in Normandy during the French Revolution by a woman who was hiding a fugitive priest from Brie. Combining his knowledge of cheese-making with the local method of making washed-rind cheeses, she produced a smaller surface-ripened mould cheese, about 250g in weight. This cheese took the fancy of Napoleon III, who named it after the village of Camembert, where it was first sold.

Apart from the difference in size and origin, genuine brie and camembert have quite different aromas and flavours. Brie has a pervasive fungal smell balanced with a subtle, slightly sweet, milky character. The rind often becomes flecked with light orange and red marks when ripe, and the cheese develops a soft, smooth, buttery texture with a rich, concentrated flavour and just a hint of ammonia.

Camembert is often eaten young in Normandy, with a thick white coat and chalky heart, but as it ripens in the box it develops a smell somewhat akin to cooked cauliflower, and the rind becomes lightly stained with thin, moist orange marks. The texture of a mature camembert is supple, with a creamy, rich moistness to touch. It is thicker in texture than a mature brie, with a slight saltiness and distinctive, long, full flavour on the secondary palate.

In Australia the distinction between these two styles of cheese is not so well defined. Manufacturers often use the same technique and curds for both, and the only real difference becomes the size. This situation highlights the unfortunate tendency to apply irrelevant European names to specialist Australian cheeses. Australian cheeses are unique because the conditions here are unique, and we should follow the lead of European cheese-makers and name cheeses after local places or regions.

Stages of ripeness

Week 1

Week 2

Week 3

Week 4

Week 5

Kangaroo Island Brie

Edith's Cheese

Tasting Notes

Affine

Producer: Kervella Cheese (WA)
Classification: Farmhouse
Form: 100g log & 250g round, paper wrap
Milk: Goat – organic
Average fat: 30%
Rennet: FP Chymosin
Type: Traditional
Best season: Autumn
Description: A thin, white, papery mould covers a firm curd that is sweet and creamy when young but matures to a dense, smooth texture, with a much more concentrated flavour that lingers long on the palate. A perfect balance of condensed, sweet, creamy goat's cheese blended with salt and a hint of refreshing sourness. The small logs mature more quickly than the rounds.
Additional notes: Quality organic milk and gentle handling ensure that the curds retain much of the sweet lactic acid so important for the heavy, moist texture and flavour of the mature cheese. The cheese also comes in a 800g cone called Rondolet.

Branxton Brie

Producer: Hunter Valley Cheese Company (NSW)
Classification: Artisan
Form: 125g & 400g thin discs, foil wrap
Milk: Cow – regional
Average fat: 34%
Rennet: Calf
Type: Traditional
Best season: Autumn
Description: A thin white-mould cheese that requires careful and gentle handling. When matured correctly, it is soft and well-flavoured, with a velvety richness.
Additional notes: The small size of this cheese can compromise the maturation because of the high proportion of rind to cheese.

Cape Wickham Double Brie

Producer: King Island Dairy (Tas)
Classification: Artisan
Form: 1kg wheel, foil wrap
Milk: Cow – island milk
Average fat: 38%
Rennet: Calf
Type: Modern
Best season: Autumn
Description: An abundant white-mould rind encases a paste that is rich, yellow and pliable. The additional cream and the distinctive island milk provide a comforting, creamy mouthfeel and slightly clotted flavour. Widely available and very approachable, this cheese can often be less than challenging because the rich, buttery texture masks more delicate flavours.
Additional notes: The size and shape of this successful cheese have become the accepted standard for Australian brie styles. Developed by Bill Kirk in 1987, it has become one of the most widely recognised white-rind cheeses made in Australia. Selected cheeses are matured for extra flavour and sold under a black label.

Caprini

Producer: Meredith Dairy (Vic)
Classification: Farmhouse
Form: 70g upright tapered cylinder, paper wrap
Milk: Goat
Average fat: 25%
Rennet: Calf
Type: Traditional
Best season: Spring & autumn
Description: When young this cheese has a thick, white, chewy rind and a dense, slightly chalky interior with a pleasant, herbal tang. It matures to a sensuous, soft, flowing texture with a mild, clean and creamy goat aftertaste.
Additional notes: A good example of a goat's milk cheese that is distinctive and interesting but not too aggressive. Ideal enjoyed mature as an individual cheese.

Cargarie

Producer: Meredith Dairy (Vic)
Classification: Farmhouse
Form: 70g upright tapered cylinder, cellophane wrap
Milk: Goat
Average fat: 25%
Rennet: Calf
Type: Traditional
Best season: Autumn
Description: Thick white-mould cheese with a dense, smooth interior texture and pleasant herbal tang when young. As it matures the texture becomes more nutty, hard and flaky with a strong goat flavour that lingers on the palate.
Additional notes: This cheese is made using a similar method to Caprini, but is wrapped

differently so that it will dry as it matures. It is ideal for grating, and delicious cut in half, drizzled with a little walnut oil, grilled and served with fresh rocket.

Charleston

Producer: Woodside Cheesewrights (SA)
Classification: Artisan
Form: 250g, 500g & 3kg wheels, waxed paper wrap
Milk: Cow – Jersey (single farm)
Average fat: 45%
Rennet: FP Chymosin
Type: Traditional
Best season: Autumn
Description: The rind of this cheese is a combination of white moulds, yeasts and *B. linens* cultures, and changes from pure white to blotchy orange as it ripens. The paste is bright marigold and grainy when young, but breaks down to the consistency of toothpaste. The flavour develops complex vegetal characteristics that balance the richness of the paste.
Additional notes: The butterfat of the Jersey milk provides a wonderful added richness to the cheese. Charleston is not made in summer. The extra-large 3kg wheels are quite rare but are well worth searching out when matured correctly.

Childers Goat Camembert

Producer: Tarago River Cheese Company (Vic)
Classification: Artisan
Form: 200g round, perforated paper wrap

Milk: Goat – local farm
Average fat: 25%
Rennet: Halal calf
Type: Traditional
Best season: Spring & autumn
Description: A dense, pure-white surface mould covers the cheese, and the interior has a fine, delicate texture that gradually softens as the cheese matures. The flavour is mild and clean, with no obvious goaty flavours. This is a cheese that will please most palates.

Clyde River Chèvre

Producer: Tasmanian Highland Cheeses (Tas)
Classification: Farmhouse
Form: 200g, waxed paper wrap
Milk: Goat
Average fat: 25%
Rennet: FP Chymosin
Type: Traditional
Best season: Cheese made in late spring
Description: Thick white-mould cheese with a pure-white, chalky curd centre. Best eaten when there is just a moderate amount of breakdown immediately under the rind. At this stage the aroma is reminiscent of the farm goats and the curd has a lemony acidity. Becomes strong and aggressive if matured too long.

Edith's Cheese

Producer: Woodside Cheesewrights (SA)
Classification: Artisan
Form: 200g squat cylinder, waxed paper wrap
Milk: Goat – local farms
Average fat: 40%
Rennet: FP Chymosin

Type: Traditional
Best season: Spring & autumn
Description: When this cheese is young, the charcoal on the rind is black and the cheese has a moist, grainy texture with a delicate, creamy, slightly acid, sweet-and-sour centre. As it ages, the rind forms a mottled grey-blue and white powdery mould, and the interior softens to a smooth, velvety texture that melts in the mouth with a long, concentrated goat flavour. With further ageing it becomes firm and eventually hard. Its characteristics also change dramatically according to the season.
Additional notes: The curd is carefully hand-ladled into tall, narrow hoops to capture as much moisture as possible. Draining and turning take place over a period of 24 hours. Once the curd is dry enough to handle, it is inoculated with white-mould spores, which are encouraged to develop for up to a week before the cheese is rolled in finely ground vine ash. This cheese can be eaten at a variety of ages and has been recognised as a benchmark.

Gippsland Brie and Camembert

Producer: Tarago River Cheese Company (Vic)
Classification: Farmhouse
Form: 200g & 1kg wheels, foil paper wrap
Milk: Cow
Average fat: 27%
Rennet: Halal calf
Type: Modern
Best season: Late autumn

Description: The young cheese has a thick, pure white-rind coating and a custard-yellow, soft texture. As it ages it becomes more buttery and slightly sticky, with a mellow, creamy flavour. The camembert rind is slightly more chewy and has a stronger influence on the taste.
Additional notes: Also sold wrapped in foil as Enterprize Dairy Brie.

Grapevine Ash Brie

Producer: Hunter Valley Cheese Company (NSW)
Classification: Artisan
Form: 125g round, foil wrap
Milk: Cow – regional
Average fat: 34%
Rennet: Calf
Type: Traditional
Best season: Spring & autumn
Description: This cheese has a covering of white mould and ash, and can be difficult to mature evenly because it is so small. When in form, it develops a flowing texture and a delicate, creamy flavour balanced with a little salt. The ash significantly slows the maturation process.

Heritage Camembert

Producer: Lactos (Tas)
Classification: Artisan
Form: 125g oval & 1kg wheel, perforated wrap
Milk: Cow – regional
Average fat: 32%
Rennet: Calf
Type: Modern
Description: The rind has a dense, even, white-mould covering with a slight mushroom

and cardboard smell. Pliable, firm, smooth, pale paste that matures to a mild and creamy flavour. A dependable and well-behaved cheese.

Jindi Brie and Camembert

Producer: Jindi Cheese (Vic)
Classification: Farmhouse
Form: 200g, 1kg & 3kg wheels, perforated wrap
Milk: Cow – Jersey
Average fat: 28%
Rennet: FP Chymosin
Type: Modern
Best season: Spring & autumn
Description: Flawless, moist, thick, white-mould rind with a predictable, mushroomy aroma and a pale golden interior. The double brie has a mild, rich and creamy flavour and soft, buttery texture. The camembert has slightly less depth.
Additional notes: Also made and sold under the Wattle Valley label.

Jindi Triple Cream

Producer: Jindi Cheese Company (Vic)
Classification: Farmhouse
Form: 1.5kg rectangular brick
Milk: Cow
Average fat: 35%
Rennet: FP Chymosin
Type: Traditional
Best season: Autumn
Description: Lush, moist white-mould coat (which shows signs of deterioration at the end of its ripening) with a yellow, slightly grainy interior. The richness of this cheese is a result of the extra cream added to the milk before cheese-making. It devel-

ops a thick, buttery texture that only partially breaks down.
Additional notes: The chalk line in the centre of the cheese is deliberate and is not a fault. The difference between the texture of the curds at the edge of the cheese and the acidity of the centre is important to produce a more balanced and palatable cheese.

Kangaroo Island Brie and Camembert

Producer: Farmhouse Cheeses of Kangaroo Island (SA)
Classification: Farmhouse
Form: 200g & 650g rounds, foil paper wrap
Milk: Cow
Average fat: 20%
Rennet: Calf
Type: Traditional
Best season: Spring & autumn
Description: This cheese has a thin, white surface mould that often colours with scattered orange blotches as the cheese ripens. The curd is a bright yellow and slowly breaks down from a firm, chalky centre to a smooth, runny texture that melts in the mouth. The sweet, creamy flavour has a hint of the ozone-rich pasture and there is an agreeable, salty bitterness reminiscent of the sea.
Additional notes: These cheeses are hand-made on a small farmhouse scale and are a good example of what can be achieved with a consistent on-farm milk supply. A hard cheese to look after, but, like many difficult cheeses, well worth a little patience.

Lady Mella Brie and Camembert

Producer: Lacrum Cheese (Tas)
Classification: Farmhouse
Form: 125g & 1kg wheel, paper wrap
Milk: Cow
Average fat: 25%
Rennet: FP Chymosin
Type: Modern
Best season: Autumn
Description: Pure white-mould rind. The interior is soft and sticky, with a pliable texture and mild, creamy flavour.

Margaret River Brie and Camembert

Producer: Margaret River Cheese Company (WA)
Classification: Artisan
Form: 250g & 1kg round, foil wrap
Milk: Cow – regional
Average fat: 22%
Rennet: FP Chymosin
Type: Traditional
Best season: Summer
Description: This cheese has a thin, white rind with a papery aroma, and the rounds are quite thin compared with many other cheeses in this category. The interior has a yellowish, chalky paste that becomes soft and creamy with a slightly bitter finish when ripe.

Phoques Cove Camembert

Producer: King Island Dairy (Tas)
Classification: Artisan
Form: 200g & 1kg wheel, foil wrap
Milk: Cow – island milk

Average fat: 27%
Rennet: Calf
Type: Modern
Best season: Autumn
Description: A thick white mould encases this moist, cream-enriched cheese. The pale yellow paste has a supple texture and mild, creamy flavour.

Saint Lukes

Producer: Tasmanian Highland Cheeses (Tas)
Classification: Farmhouse
Form: 250g cylindrical log or 50g round
Milk: Goat
Average fat: 27%
Rennet: FP Chymosin
Type: Traditional
Best season: Autumn
Description: Ashed white-mould cheese with a moist, grainy texture that breaks down to a mild, soft paste with a flowery flavour. The rapid growth rate of the exterior white mould sometimes causes the rind to separate from the cheese.
Additional notes: Farmer John Bignell has spent eight years perfecting this cheese, which is hard to find on the mainland but worth seeking out.

Seal Bay Triple Cream

Producer: King Island Dairy (Tas)
Classification: Artisan
Form: 250g & 1kg log
Milk: Cow – island milk
Average fat: 40%
Rennet: Calf
Type: Traditional
Best season: Summer & autumn

Description: A cream-enriched triple cream cheese with a rich, yellow paste covered by a fluffy shag pile of white mould that has not been suppressed by wrapping. The texture of the cheese is firm and slightly acidic, which helps to cut through the rich, buttery flavour.
Additional notes: The amazingly prolific growth of the white mould certainly makes this cheese interesting to look at.

Timboon Brie and Camembert

Producer: Timboon Farmhouse Cheese (Vic)
Classification: Farmhouse
Form: 200g & 1kg round, foil paper wrap
Milk: Cow – biodynamic
Average fat: 27%
Rennet: Microbial
Type: Traditional
Best season: Autumn
Description: This cheese has a pure-white rind and a chalky centre when young. As it matures the centre breaks down to a soft, gluey texture with a rich, buttery, flowery flavour, a sign of the quality Jersey milk used. The milk for this biodynamic cheese is not standardised and as a result is quite changeable in character throughout the year. The camembert has an added creamy length and more mushroomy flavours because of the greater ratio of rind.
Additional notes: The camembert was the first farmhouse white-rind cheese produced in Australia during the mid-1980s, and is considered a benchmark.

White Diamond

Producer: Lactos (Tas)
Classification: Artisan
Form: 1kg square, perforated paper wrap
Milk: Cow – regional
Average fat: 31%
Rennet: Calf
Type: Traditional
Best season: Autumn
Description: This cheese has a thin white rind with a slight aroma of wet paper and mushroom in the mould. The texture ripens to a smooth, silky softness with a mild, delicate flavour. Sophisticated manufacturing techniques make this a very dependable cheese, well worth maturing.

Woodburne

Producer: Meredith Dairy (Vic)
Classification: Farmhouse
Form: 200g round, cellophane wrap
Milk: Ewe
Average fat: 29%
Rennet: Calf
Type: Traditional
Best season: Spring
Description: The cheese is covered with a dense white mould that develops minor blemishes of grey at the edges as it ages. Inside, the ivory-coloured, chalky curd breaks down to a wonderfully smooth, soft, satiny texture that will sometimes flow. It has a full, rich, mild flavour with just a hint of lanolin and caramel.
Additional notes: Australia's first ewe's milk white-rind cheese – a unique regional cheese.

Gippsland Brie – Enterprize

ed

WASHED

Washed-rind

Surface-ripened washed-rind cheeses are renowned for their orange rinds and their wonderful strong smell. A mature cheese can fill every corner of a room with a stink reminiscent of the farmyard, or of socks in a sports changing room. These cheeses are something of an acquired taste, but they have many devotees among cheese enthusiasts. In a well-matured cheese it is only the rind that smells. The interior is deliciously mild and buttery, with a gentle, satisfying flavour.

Washed-rind cheeses were among the earliest surface-ripened cheeses; it is believed that they originated in the medieval monasteries. They mature in a similar way to traditional white-mould varieties, but the surface action is produced by bacteria rather than moulds. *Brevibacterium linens*, or *B. linens* for short, is the most commonly used strain of bacteria. Its presence defines these cheeses as a recognisable type, giving them their orange rinds and distinctive aroma. The bacteria on the surface of the cheese ripen the curds inside over a period of a month or longer. As with white-mould cheeses, washed-rind cheeses are shaped to provide a large surface area for the bacteria to grow on. They are often small in size, and their shapes range from a disc to a square.

After the curds are drained and salted, the exterior of the cheese is washed regularly with a brine solution, which encourages a protective skin or rind to form around the fresh cheese. The brine solution always contains a relatively high concentration of salt to control unwanted bacteria, but it can also contain some alcohol, a mixture of herbs and spices, or even orange annatto colour, depending on the cheese-maker's recipe. Regular bathing of the surface controls the growth of *B. linens* on the rind and also helps to ensure that the cheese remains moist and does not crack during maturation.

The natural yeasts and airborne flora present in the microclimate of every maturing room have a vital role in the maturation process. Each region and each dairy has its own mix of microflora, so that no two will produce identical washed-rind cheeses. Once a strain of *B. linens* has been introduced to a maturation room it thrives in the cool, damp atmosphere and develops a life of its own. It naturally migrates to the conditions that best suit it: the surface of the wet cheeses. Regular washing (often just with water after the first saline wash) prevents the cheese from becoming overpowered and sticky from the action of the *linens*. The more the cheese is washed and the more humid the room, the stronger the cheese becomes. The rind usually develops a brown-orange colour, but can vary in tone from deep red-orange to apricot, depending on the washing solution and the growth of bacteria.

Most washed-rind cheeses are made from cow's milk. Goat's milk is too volatile in flavour for this type of cheese, ewe's milk is too fatty, and buffalo milk is too delicate. The orange colours and rustic smell of washed-rind cheese are often associated with the colours and smells of autumn, because that is when the best cheeses are made.

Types

Draining time, curd handling and acidity levels vary according to the type of cheese being made. As with white-rind cheeses, the traditional techniques produce a slow-ripening cheese, while the quick, modern method produces a pre-ripened, stabilised type.

Traditional

Traditional washed-rind cheeses have a chalky centre that will slowly soften over a period of six to eight weeks. Maturation requires lots of patience and the right conditions, but when mature these cheeses have a rich, oozing, silky texture and characteristic strong, pervasive smell. If a cheese of this type does not have a good natural stink it is unlikely to have any real flavour when mature, because it is only when the rind is active that any depth of flavour can develop.

Modern

Modern washed-rind cheeses are easy to handle because the inner curd is stable and soft before maturation. As is the case with white-rind cheeses, the acid development of the curd is controlled by the use of selected thermophilic starters. Consequently surface-ripening during maturation is limited; there is only minor curd breakdown and the flavour is far milder than their traditional cousins'. These modern cheeses have a mild, inoffensive smell and consistent creamy texture, and slowly bulge as they mature. Extra cream is usually added to boost flavour and texture, and *B. linens* are often mixed with a white mould to add a little more depth of character. These mixed mould and bacteria types are recognisable by a thin, light-grey shroud over the rind.

Modern stabilised washed-rind cheeses are becoming more popular and are certainly easy to handle, but they are no substitute for a cheese made to a traditional recipe. They are best regarded as an enjoyable introduction to this type of cheese.

Ranceby

Tasting Notes

Chèvre Washed Rind

Producer: Milawa Cheese Company (Vic)
Classification: Artisan
Form: 350g wheel, foil wrap
Milk: Goat – regional
Average fat: 25%
Rennet: Calf
Type: Traditional
Best season: Autumn & spring
Description: A pale straw-coloured washed-rind cheese that is only available on a seasonal basis. Because of the volatile nature of goat's milk, it is best enjoyed young, when it has a soft, silky texture and mild, nutty flavour. As it matures it becomes strong, with nuances of billygoat.

Domaine Red Square

Producer: Lactos (Tas)
Classification: Artisan
Form: 1kg square, perforated paper wrap
Milk: Cow – regional
Average fat: 32%
Rennet: Calf
Type: Modern
Best season: Autumn
Description: A reddish-brown cheese with a thin overlay of white-mould rind. The washed rind and white mould on the exterior of this cheese produce a soft, smooth, stable texture and mild, creamy flavour with just a hint of garlic. Requires a little patience, but with care matures to a smooth, sticky texture and a creamy flavour with a touch of onion.
Additional notes: Dependable in quality, this washed-rind cheese gets a lot more interesting when it has been ripened until it develops a smelly whiff. The dairy uses ultra-filtration, which flattens out some of the seasonal variations in the milk.

Heidi Reblochon

Producer: Heidi Farm Cheese (Tas)
Classification: Farmhouse
Form: 700g disc, waxed paper wrap
Milk: Cow – Friesian
Average fat: 50%
Rennet: FP Chymosin
Type: Traditional
Best season: Late winter & spring
Description: This cheese has a thin, sticky orange-brown rind with a heady aroma of mould mingled with the smell of the dairy on a hot summer's afternoon. The interior is a moist, smooth paste that breaks down to an oozing, creamy texture. The flavour is mild but definitive, with suggestions of fresh pasture that last long on the palate.
Additional notes: Only made during the cooler months, this is a hard cheese to find but rewarding if matured carefully.

Jensen's Red

Producer: Tarago River Cheese Company (Vic)
Classification: Farmhouse
Form: 1.3kg round disc, foil wrap
Milk: Cow – Friesian
Average fat: 30%
Rennet: Halal calf
Type: Traditional
Best season: Late summer & autumn
Description: Orange terracotta rind with a buttery, mild, slightly acidic interior when young. As this cheese matures it develops a dense, supple texture and a concentrated, slightly sweet, fruity flavour reminiscent of apples.

King River Gold

Producer: Milawa Cheese Company (Vic)
Classification: Artisan
Form: 300g rectangle or round, foil wrap
Milk: Cow – co-operative
Average fat: 32%
Rennet: Calf
Type: Modern
Best season: Autumn
Description: A golden/orange rind encases a mellow, pliable, soft cheese with a sweet-sour, slightly yeasty flavour. Rarely aggressive, this cheese is at its best when soft and moist after maturation for eight weeks or more.
Additional notes: The surface-ripening bacteria thrive in the unique environment of the old butter factory at Milawa.

Lady Mella

Producer: Lacrum Cheese (Tas)
Classification: Farmhouse
Form: 250g square, perforated paper wrap
Milk: Cow
Average fat: 20%
Rennet: FP Chymosin
Type: Modern
Best season: Autumn
Description: The golden rind is speckled with a combination of white mould and bacterial

cultures, and the interior has a silky, soft, pliable texture and enjoyable, mild, creamy flavour. *Additional notes:* Made on a model farm established by pioneer cheese-maker Milan Vynalek.

Milawa Gold

Producer: Milawa Cheese Company (Vic)
Classification: Artisan
Form: 1kg wheel, foil wrap
Milk: Cow – co-operative
Average fat: 30%
Rennet: Calf
Type: Traditional
Best season: Autumn
Description: Washed to develop a deep brown-orange rind, this cheese when young has a chalky, acidic centre that can be difficult to mature. After eight weeks or more, however, it can break down to a smooth, supple texture with a strong, sweet, buttery flavour packed with wild complexity and an aroma reminiscent of wet straw in the farmyard.
Additional notes: This is one of Australia's first traditional washed-rind cheeses, originally developed by Richard Thomas in 1988. Maturation in the dairy still involves wrapping the cheese in an old sanitised plastic carrier bag to create the correct humidity-controlled conditions.

Mungabereena

Producer: Parmalat (NSW)
Classification: Artisan
Form: 200g & 1kg wheels, foil wrap

Milk: Cow – co-operative
Average fat: 27%
Rennet: FP Chymosin
Type: Modern
Best season: Spring & autumn
Description: This cheese has a bright orange rind and a soft, smooth, creamy interior texture. The addition of eucalyptus oil gives a unique Australian bush flavour.
Additional notes: Also sold as golden brie without the eucalyptus.

Pokolbin Smear Ripened

Producer: Hunter Valley Cheese Company (NSW)
Classification: Artisan
Form: 400g round, foil wrap
Milk: Cow – regional
Average fat: 34%
Rennet: Calf
Type: Traditional
Best season: Late summer & early autumn
Description: A small, round, orange cheese with a moist, slightly holey texture and mild, pleasant, sour-sweet taste that has just a hint of yeast. Although partially stable, the texture will break down to a soft, almost fluid creamy smoothness at certain periods of the year and will develop stronger, earthy flavours.
Additional notes: The Hunter Valley is famous for its wineries, and cows do not always flourish in the same climatic conditions as grapes. As a consequence this cheese is made from milk collected near Newcastle, an hour's drive south.

Ranceby

Producer: Top Paddock Cheeses (Vic)
Classification: Farmhouse
Form: 1.8kg thick disc, paper wrap
Milk: Cow
Average fat: 35%
Rennet: FP Chymosin
Type: Traditional
Best season: Early autumn
Description: Covered by a pinkish-orange washed rind, this traditional-style cheese is made with a firm, chalky, acidic centre that should mature to a rich, buttery texture after ageing. At its peak the cheese develops a powerful cowyard aroma but has a mild, tangy flavour with hints of the local eucalyptus.
Additional notes: Unpredictable, but well worth looking out for.

Stormy Washed Rind

Producer: King Island Dairy (Tas)
Classification: Artisan
Form: 250g square & 1kg round, orange waxed paper wrap
Milk: Cow – island milk
Average fat: 35%
Rennet: Calf
Type: Modern
Best season: Autumn
Description: This cheese has a thin, tangerine-coloured rind with a white mould that is designed to be edible, and an inoffensive aroma vaguely reminiscent of wet washing. The texture of the interior is rich and buttery on the tongue with a mild, sweet, clotted flavour.

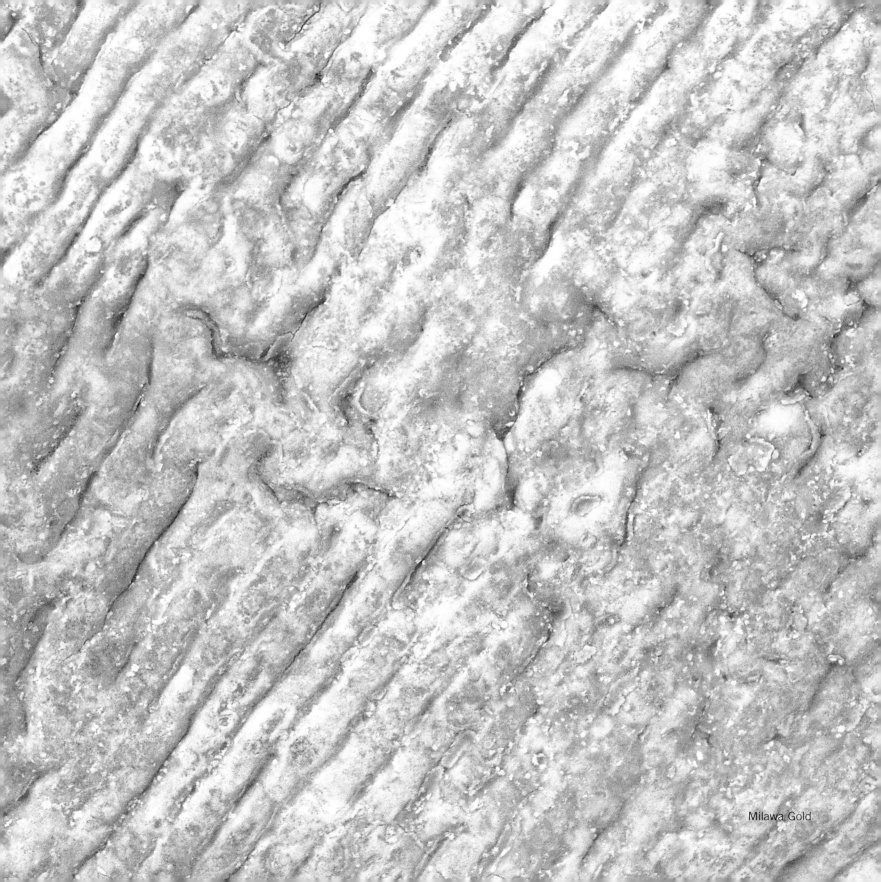

Milawa Gold

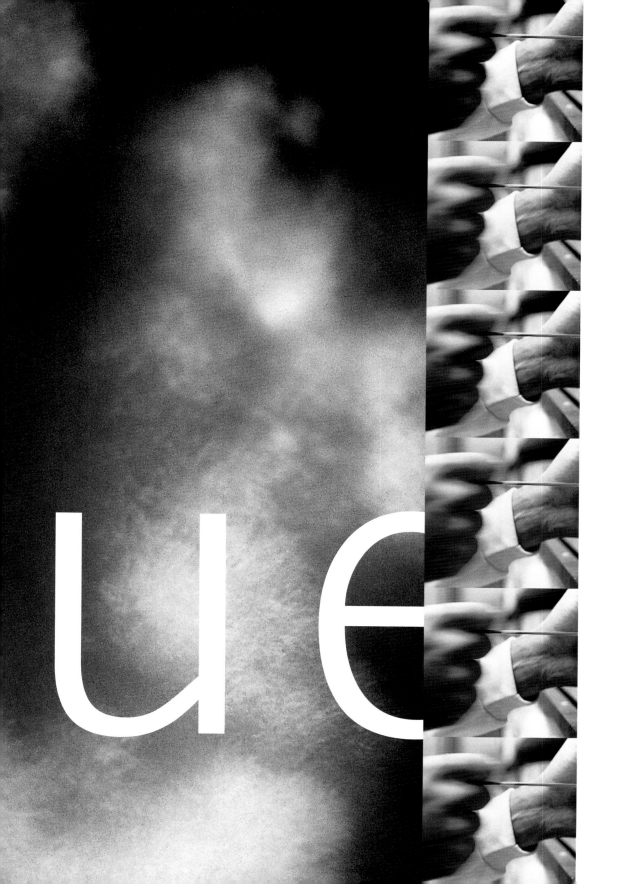

BLUE

Blue

There is a moment of truth in the making of every blue cheese. Through the long months of maturation, the secrets of the cheese remain tantalisingly locked away inside the rind, and it is only when the cheese is considered fully mature that it is cut in half to reveal its hidden treasures.

It is this internal ripening action that sets blue cheeses apart from all other categories of cheese. Whereas most cheese types ripen from the action of external moulds, blue cheese is ripened by the ventilated action of blue moulds growing from within. Particular blue-mould cultures are selected and introduced to the milk or set curds in the early stages of cheese-making. The texture of the curd and choice of mould type are very important, because they will determine the final taste profile and character of the cheese.

Blue cheeses have been made since Roman times, and were probably discovered as a result of accidental contamination by mould spores during the storage and maturation of cheeses in cool, humid caves, where moulds slowly developed under the natural rinds of poorly made dry cheeses or in cheeses that had cracked or been dropped. Among the many different types of mould present in this uncontrolled environment, only some were good to taste; others might have been downright dangerous. In time, cheese-makers learnt how to cultivate the better-tasting types of blue penicillium moulds from older cheeses or seed them on specially baked loaves of rye bread. When the bread was considered sufficiently covered in the mould, it was harvested and powdered into fine crumbs, then small quantities were mixed into the vat of milk after the curds were cut.

This old method of growing moulds was once an essential part of the craft of making blue cheese, and the distinctive strains of blue mould helped to give each cheese its regional identity. To be reliable, however, hand-grown mould cultures require highly controlled conditions, and today only a few small farm dairies in Australia use them. Most of the larger operations use dependable industrial blue cultures, which are usually imported frozen from Europe. The most common types are related to *Penicillium roqueforti*, which originated in the famous caves in France where roquefort cheese is made.

Blue-mould cultures will only flourish in specific conditions. There must be the right level of moisture and humidity inside the cheese, and a critical balance of salt concentration and acidity is required to prevent other mould types from interfering with the growth of the preferred strains of blue mould. Fortunately, most of the undesirable moulds and yeasts that might spoil a cheese rarely grow under the conditions that favour the well-flavoured moulds.

Control of moisture and texture is vital. The curds need to be loosely packed and left to drain naturally, without pressing, so that there are still tiny air spaces between the particles. This procedure ensures that the texture will not be too moist and will encourage the blue moulds to develop. If a cheese is made too moist and soft it will not hold its shape and will lack the openings and cavities required for blueing. Equally, if the cheese is made too dry there will not be enough free moisture for the blue moulds to develop, and proper ripening will be impossible.

Once the curds have been removed from the draining hoops, usually after twenty-four hours, the rinds are dry-salted and left to 'cure' in dark, temperature-controlled, humid cool rooms for four to six weeks. Inside the cheese there is little or no blueing at this stage, because the introduced mould cultures are locked inside the rind without essential oxygen. The centre of the cheese is white with a chalky and slightly bitter flavour, and is commonly known as 'green' cheese.

When the cheese-maker considers the time is just right and the cheese is sufficiently cured, it is 'spiked' with a series of fine needle-holes to let the oxygen in. The spikes were once made from wood or copper, but these days they are made of stainless steel about the thickness of a knitting needle. A series of holes is punched through the outer rind towards the centre of the cheese. The techniques and angles of these holes vary according to the cheese-maker and type of cheese; sometimes they run vertically from the top to the bottom, and sometimes they work horizontally from the sides or at an angle. In larger factories machines are used for piercing, but often in smaller farm operations each hole is individually punched by hand.

By allowing oxygen to enter the interior through the holes, the spiking reactivates the blue-mould cultures put into the milk months before. Spiking is usually carried out a number of times over a period of a few weeks until the blue veins start to form inside the lines left by the spikes. At first the veins are very light blue or green in colour, but they slowly turn a darker blue. In the more open-textured cheeses, the blue moulds also grow in small 'caves' or crevices interspersed in the curds. As the moulds develop, they liberate ammonia and other aromatics, which provide the essential secondary flavour and character of all good blue cheese.

The maturity of the cheese is normally judged by the distribution of the blue veins. A well-made cheese should have veins that progressively spread out from the centre towards the rind. Unlike most other traditional cheeses, almost all blue cheeses are cut in half before they leave the makers, so that the cheese-maker can be reassured that the heart of the cheese has matured evenly.

CLUB BLUE

The introduction of 'club blue cheese' is an unfortunate development that can be traced back to the old habit of putting inferior cheese in pots, often with port. Originally this was done to use up odd bits from cheeses that had not matured properly, or in more recent times the trimmings left over from cutting. Minced or chopped mature blue cheese, sometimes mixed with cheddar, is pressed and re-formed to be sold in interesting shapes, often hidden under a wax coat and pretty label. It is a clever cosmetic move that prevents wastage and allows producers to use up poor-grade or imperfect cheese, but the result can never match the flavours of a good blue cheese.

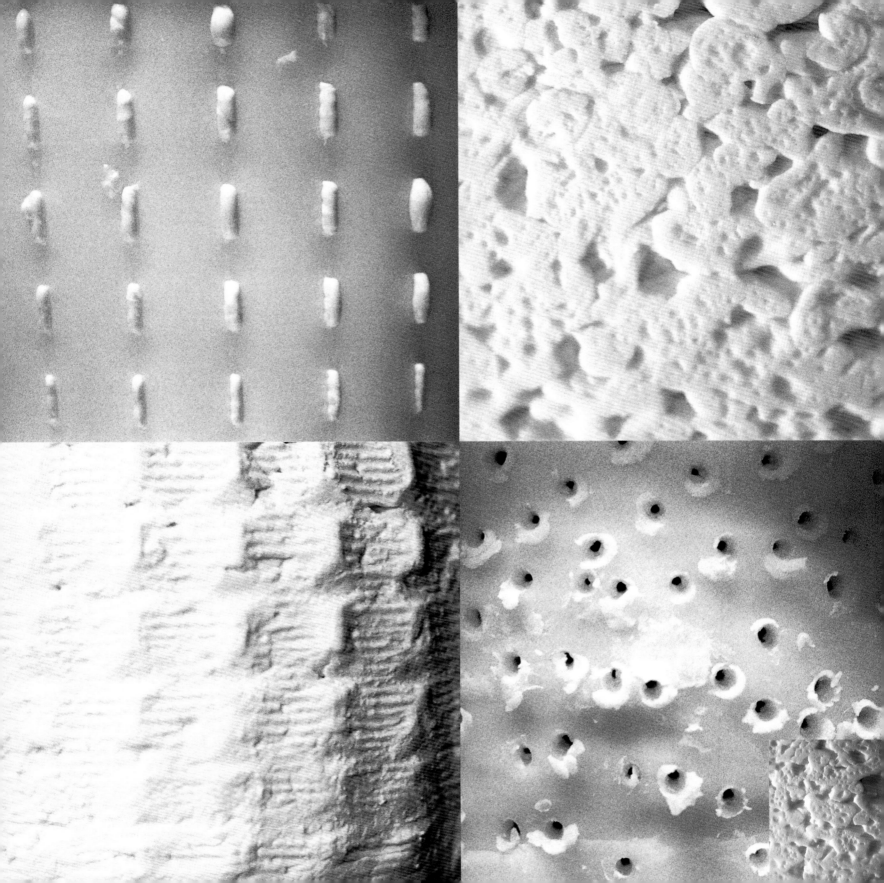

Types

In 1980 there was just one Australian blue cheese, but this changed rapidly after Gippsland Blue, Australia's first farmhouse blue, was launched at Hillcrest Farm in Gippsland, Victoria in 1981. Today there are more than twenty varieties of Australian blue cheeses to choose from, although many of these new cheeses are seasonal and are made in limited quantities by small, specialist farmhouse or artisan cheese-makers.

Most Australian blue cheeses are made from cow's milk, but three dairies also make blue cheese from ewe's and goat's milk. The character of ewe's milk blue cheeses tends to vary considerably according to the season and pasture conditions, while the volatility of goat's milk makes it particularly difficult to produce good blue cheese. Goat's milk blue is at its best when made with spring milk and eaten young to avoid a strong goaty flavour.

Collectively blue cheeses offer a wide variety of tastes and textures, with flavours ranging from very mild to strong and textures from soft to hard. Three different rind types help to identify the sub-groups and their respective characteristics.

Natural rind

These cheeses are identified by their natural, crusty rind, which is usually grey in colour with the occasional orange or yeasty blotch. Usually the flavour of these cheeses is closely associated with the rind activity, which requires carefully controlled conditions. The interior is rich and condensed because the cheese has been breathing and moisture has been allowed to evaporate. The result is a creamy, buttery texture and distinct blue-mould flavour with a syrupy sweetness.

Scraped rind

Identified by their lack of a developed rind, these blue cheeses are usually sold in wax or tight foil wrapping. This covering helps to prevent a natural rind from forming during maturation, and any external moulds that do grow are regularly scraped off. Control of any rind growth gives the cheese-maker a great advantage: control over shelf life. The shelf life of cheese maturing without a rind is easily extended by reducing the temperature. As a result, these types of blue are common, particularly among large industrial producers. Scraped rind cheeses have a crumbly, acid texture and are often quite sharp and salty with a strong fruity bite when mature, particularly if waxed.

White-rind/blue-mould

The mildest of all, these blue cheeses are a crossover type, because they incorporate a surface white rind. The inner blue mould is encouraged to grow quickly in warm rooms before the white rind begins to cover the holes. Once the external white mould has grown, it limits the oxygen available for further blue mould growth inside the cheese and halts blue maturation. Consequently these blue cheeses tend to have a characteristic mild flavour, which is often enhanced with added cream. Soft and mild, this type of blue cheese should be considered a novice's blue.

Strzelecki Goat Blue

Tasting Notes

Admiralty Blue

Producer: King Island Dairy (Tas)
Classification: Artisan
Form: 6kg cut into discs,
cellophane wrap
Milk: Cow – island milk
Average fat: 35%
Rennet: Calf
Rind: Natural
Best season: Autumn to winter
Description: A distinctive grey,
crusty rind with a rich, warm,
creamy, yellow interior coarsely
veined with blue-green mould.
Slightly dry and acid in texture
when cut too young, but
develops a creamy blue flavour
with a spicy tang.

Bass Strait Blue

Producer: King Island Dairies
(Tas)
Classification: Artisan
Form: 2.5kg wheel (whole
or halves), foil wrap
Milk: Cow – island milk
Average fat: 35%
Rennet: Calf
Rind: Natural
Best season: Autumn & winter
Description: Soft, moist and
slightly acidic, this cheese
has a rich, fudgy mouthfeel
and mild, blue, tangy flavour
with a delicately honeyed
aftertaste.

Blue Orchid

Producer: Tarago River Cheese
Company (Vic)
Classification: Farmhouse
Form: 4kg wheel, sold cut into
quarters
Milk: Cow
Average fat: 30%

Rennet: Halal calf
Rind: Blue wax
Best season: Summer to winter
Description: When young this
cheese can be bitter and acid,
but as it matures it develops
a rich and succulent texture
with a hint of caramel, which
balances the robust flavours
of the heavy blue mould.
The texture is high in moisture,
and the cheese has a tendency
to weep slightly.
Additional notes: The name
for this cheese is taken from
the sun-veined blue orchid,
which grows in the surrounding
alpine region. The texture is
silky because of the addition
of retentate, the separated
protein solids derived from
ultra-filtration of milk.
The retentate adds structure
to the milk and gives the
cheese a less fragile texture.

Domaine Deep Blue

Producer: Lactos (Tas)
Classification: Artisan
Form: 1kg wheel sold in
quarters, foil wrap
Milk: Cow – regional
Average fat: 35%
Rennet: Calf
Rind: Scraped
Description: Well-developed
blue veining produces a slightly
crumbly, creamy cheese with
a gentle, sweet, acid finish.
The strength of the roqueforti
mould used is balanced by
the creaminess of the texture.
Additional notes: Made
using ultra-filtered milk,
which ensures a consistent,
appealing texture.

Enterprize Foundation Blue

Producer: Tarago River Cheese
Company (Vic)
Classification: Farmhouse
Form: 3.2kg wheel sold in
quarters, foil wrap
Milk: Cow
Average fat: 35%
Rennet: Halal calf
Rind: Natural
Description: Made using
enriched milk, this cheese
has a natural rind, soft, moist,
creamy texture and distinctive
blue-mould flavour arising
from the use of unique mould
cultures grown on bread.
Additional notes: Named
in honour of the schooner
Enterprize, which brought the
first settlers and their cows to
the site of Melbourne in 1835.

Gippsland Blue

Producer: Tarago River Cheese
Company (Vic)
Classification: Farmhouse
Form: 5.5kg wheel sold in
halves or quarters, foil wrap
Milk: Cow
Average fat: 26%
Rennet: Halal calf
Rind: Natural
Best season: Late spring
& early winter
Description: The natural, grey,
crusty rind is flecked with
orange and white moulds,
and the interior ripens to a soft,
sticky, creamy texture punctuated
with grey and steely-blue veins.
Rich in flavour with hints of
pasture, and ammonia as it
ages. Best when bought from
the whole wheel.

Additional notes: Australia's first farmhouse blue cheese was developed by Laurie Jensen, Richard Thomas and farmers Rob and Lyn Johnson. The combination of yeasts and mould cultures used in this cheese has produced one of Australia's finest benchmark specialist blue cheeses.

Heritage True Blue

Producer: Lactos (Tas)
Classification: Artisan
Form: 125g oval & 1kg wheel, perforated paper wrap
Milk: Cow – regional
Average fat: 43%
Rennet: Calf
Rind: White mould
Description: A modern cheese that combines the surface-ripening ability of white mould with internal blue mould veining. The result is a pleasant cheese, delicate and creamy – a good cheese for beginners who want to learn about blue cheese but are not prepared for the complex, fully developed flavour of a traditional blue.
Additional notes: There is a theory in the cheese-making industry that you tempt fate by making blue-mould and white-mould cheeses in the same factory. Cheeses such as this show that under controlled situations it is possible.

Jumbunna Blue

Producer: Top Paddock Cheese (Vic)
Classification: Farmhouse
Form: 1.5kg cylindrical truckle, foil wrap

Milk: Cow
Average fat: 35%
Rennet: FP Chymosin
Rind: Natural
Best season: Winter to spring
Description: Moist, coarse and crumbly, this cheese has natural turquoise-blue veins scattered through the large, creamy curds. It is best eaten when quite young and balanced in acidity. Can be powerful and aggressively hot when mature.
Additional notes: This cheese is made using a unique method in which blue mould is treated as a surface-ripening agent on the exterior of the coarse conglomerate of curds. The cheese is not punctured to allow oxygen to enter, but instead the mould grows in the numerous large air pockets formed when the firm, dry curds are hooped.

Lighthouse Blue Brie

Producer: King Island Dairy (Tas)
Classification: Artisan
Form: 1.5kg paper-wrapped rounds
Milk: Cow – island milk
Average fat: 35%
Rennet: Calf
Rind: White mould
Best season: Spring & summer
Description: White-mould surface rind with a mild, creamy interior.
Additional notes: Named after the lighthouse that was built last century to warn ships of the treacherous waters around King Island.

Meredith Blue

Producer: Meredith Dairy (Vic)
Classification: Farmhouse
Form: 500g & 1kg rounds, paper wrap
Milk: Ewe
Average fat: 29%
Rennet: Calf
Rind: Natural
Best season: Autumn & late winter
Description: The natural, grey, dusty rind covers an ivory-coloured interior that is flecked with blue-green mould, depending on season and maturity. The cheese is most popular when soft and satiny with sweet, herbaceous hints of fresh grass and herbs.
Additional notes: This is Australia's first farmhouse blue cheese made from pure ewe's milk, and was developed by Richard Thomas and Julie Cameron. While it is quite variable depending on the season, at its best it is a delicious benchmark cheese.

Milawa Blue

Producer: Milawa Cheese Company (Vic)
Classification: Artisan
Form: 6kg wheel sold in halves or quarters, foil wrap
Milk: Cow – co-operative
Average fat: 28%
Rennet: Calf
Rind: Natural
Best season: Autumn & winter
Description: This cheese has a grey natural rind mottled with orange and blue moulds, and a slightly chalky acid interior that varies with the

season. When matured evenly, it becomes soft and tacky with a rich, buttery texture balanced by a gentle blue-mould flavour.

Mt Buffalo Blue

Producer: Milawa Cheese Company (Vic)
Classification: Artisan
Form: 5kg wheel sold in quarters, foil wrap
Milk: Goat – regional
Average fat: 32%
Rennet: Calf
Rind: Natural
Best season: Spring
Description: A crusty grey-rind cheese with a semi-soft texture. The combination of the ammonia-producing blue mould spores and volatile goat's milk can make this a powerful blue that commands respect when mature.
Additional notes: Best tried last on a cheese board.

Roaring Forties

Producer: King Island Dairies (Tas)
Classification: Artisan
Form: 1.2kg round, blue wax coat
Milk: Cow, island milk
Average fat: 35%
Rennet: Calf
Rind: Wax
Best season: Spring & summer
Description: This cheese has a semi-hard texture with some acidity and a rich mouthfeel with a salty, fruity tang and just a hint of hazelnuts.
Additional notes: Waxing blue cheese alters the flavour by

Lighthouse Blue Brie

Timbozola

restricting airflow to internal blue moulds. This cheese starts life using similar production methods to Bass Strait Blue, but the wax coat alters the maturation characteristics.

Roc

Producer: Milawa Cheese Company (Vic)
Classification: Artisan
Form: 4kg wheel sold in quarters with foil wrap
Milk: Ewe – regional
Average fat: 38%
Rennet: Calf
Rind: Natural
Best season: Late spring
Description: A grey natural rind encloses an ivory-white interior marbled with irregular blue veins. Matures to a semi-soft, creamy texture.

Royal Victorian Blue

Producer: Tarago River Cheese Company (Vic)
Classification: Farmhouse
Form: 3.5kg wheel sold in quarters with foil wrap
Milk: Cow
Average fat: 27%
Rennet: Halal calf
Rind: White wax
Best season: Winter & late spring
Description: A visually striking cheese with a unique combination of white and orange annato-coloured curds interspersed with tributaries of blue veins. The maturation under wax maintains moisture, and the interior is soft and easily crumbles. Flavour is deep and powerful when mature, with

an acid, steely finish.
Additional notes: Waxed blue cheeses often weep droplets of syrupy moisture, which can be messy. Wrap the cut cheese in absorbent paper towel to contain the problem.

St Joseph's Blue

Producer: Timboon Farmhouse Cheese (Vic)
Classification: Farmhouse
Form: 500g round, foil wrap
Milk: Cow – biodynamic
Average fat: 43%
Rennet: Microbial
Rind: Natural
Description: The washed-rind treatment of this cheese provides an added dimension to the mild, creamy flavour of the golden interior, which is ribbed with pale blue moulds. The rind is then treated with geotrichum, which helps to prevent the cheese from becoming sticky.
Additional notes: A close cousin of Timbozola (see below).

Shadows of Blue

Producer: Tarago River Cheese Company (Vic)
Classification: Farmhouse
Form: 3.5kg wheel sold in halves with foil wrap
Milk: Cow
Average fat: 35%
Rennet: Halal calf
Rind: Yellow wax
Best season: Summer to winter
Description: Made using whole milk with added cream, this cheese has a soft, creamy texture and distinctive, mild, blue-mould flavour.
Additional notes: The blue

moulds used for this cheese are quite unique and are carefully cultured on bread at the dairy.

Strzelecki Goat Blue

Producer: Tarago River Cheese Company (Vic)
Classification: Artisan
Form: 2kg wheel, paper wrap
Milk: Goat – local farm
Average fat: 25%
Rennet: Halal calf
Rind: Natural
Best season: Spring
Description: A rough grey rind mottled with orange yeasts and moulds. The young cheese has a white, chalky centre that breaks down to a soft, sensuous, melting texture with just a mild hint of blue.
Additional notes: Only the finest quality milk is used for this unusual cheese because of the volatile nature of goat's milk. The window of opportunity when the cheese is mature is short, two weeks at best, and the cheese quickly deteriorates to develop strong ammoniac flavours if kept too long.

Timbozola

Producer: Timboon Farmhouse Cheese (Vic)
Classification: Farmhouse
Form: 500g round, foil wrap
Milk: Cow – biodynamic
Average fat: 42%
Rennet: Microbial
Rind: White mould
Description: The white mould envelops a soft, golden buttery interior ribbed with pale blue mould. Mild and creamy in flavour.

Unity Blue

Producer: Queensco–Unity Foods (Qld)
Classification: Industrial
Form: 2.5kg, foil wrap
Milk: Cow
Average fat: 33%
Rennet: FP Chymosin
Rind: Scraped
Description: From the Darling Downs, this typical scraped blue has a slightly salty, sharp, pronounced acid flavour and varied creamy texture. Also sold under other brand names.
Additional notes: Australia's only blue cheese until 1980.

semi

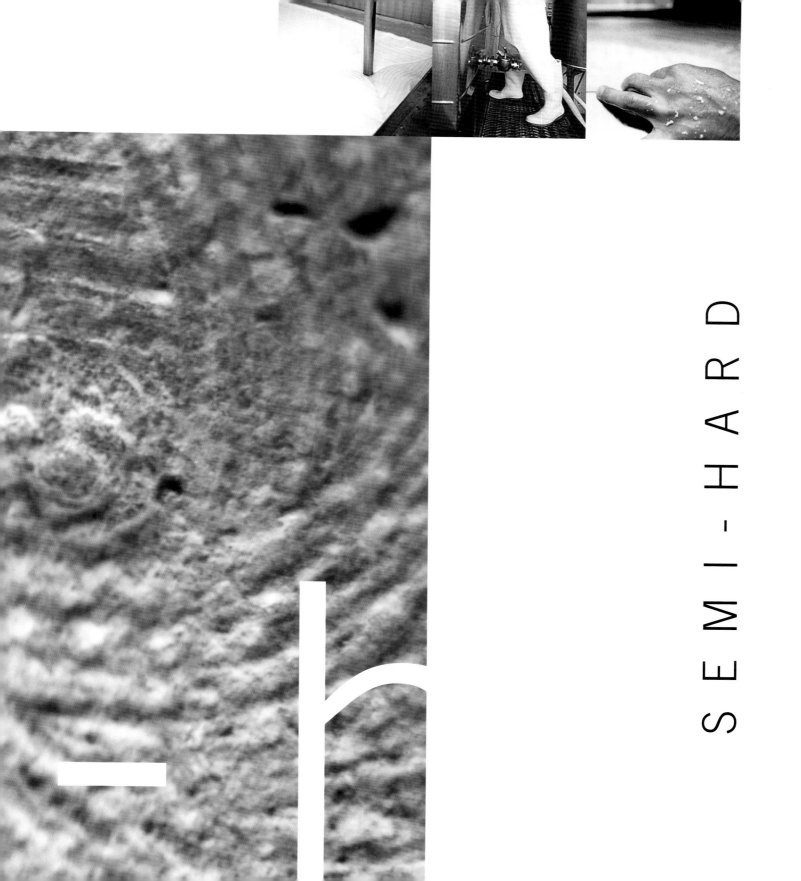

SEMI-HARD

Semi-hard

If you offered me a desert island with just one kind of food, a farmhouse cheddar would be my unhesitating choice: its mouth-watering texture and flavour could never bore, but only change for the better through the months of eating.

Patrick Rance, *The Great British Cheese Book*

A great deal of the cheese Australia produces and exports falls into this category, which includes varieties as diverse as cheddar, edam, havarti and mozzarella. Many of these cheeses are mass-produced by large industrial co-operatives, but in recent years small cheese-makers have also shown a growing interest in adapting traditional techniques to make specialist semi-hard cheeses.

Semi-hard cheeses differ from the less mature cheeses in two main ways. To begin with, the cheese-making process involves scalding the curds so that they shrink and expel moisture. Secondly, the curds are then pressed to release further free moisture. The result is a concentrated cheese curd with relatively low moisture content that will mature for an extended period of time. Depending on the size and the maturation conditions, the flavour and texture of these cheeses will improve for six months, a year or even longer.

Semi-hard cheeses can be divided into three broad groups:

- cheddar types;
- washed-curd types; and
- stretched-curd types.

Cheddar Types

Cheddar is among the world's most popular cheeses and represents more than 60 per cent of all cheese eaten in Australia, but what cheddar actually means is not entirely clear.

Cheddar

The name 'cheddar' originated several centuries ago in the west country of England, but the method was not standardised commercially until 1856, when the procedure was recorded by Joseph Harding.

'Cheddaring' refers to the way the curds are handled during the cheese-making process. After scalding, the whey is drained from the vat and the rubbery, warm curd is cut into large blocks. These blocks are then stacked and re-stacked in small towers to squash the individual curd particles and force out the whey over a period of two hours or more. This stacking is known as cheddaring. As the curds drain, the lactic acid becomes evenly distributed through the curd, controlling bacterial growth and texture and reducing spoilage. The curd is then milled into walnut-sized pieces and salted.

In traditional cheese-making the pieces are then put into large hoops lined with cheesecloth to be pressed for twenty-four hours. Finally, the young pressed cheese is dressed with more cheesecloth, smeared with lard and left to mature for six to twelve months in cellars at around 12°C. The traditional cloth wrapping not only provides a natural protection for the cheese but also allows the rind to breathe, releasing moisture and stale air and letting fresh air in.

Maturation is carefully monitored, and every few weeks the cheeses are hand-turned to ensure that they ripen evenly. Great care has to be taken not to crack or bruise the outside of the cheese, as this allows mould to enter. The cloth surrounding the cheese is also brushed frequently, sometimes with a mild brine solution, to minimise the presence of cheese mites, or 'jumpers', as they are known.

Cheddars are traditionally matured in large wheels – around 25 kg – to ensure that they achieve the right balance of moisture loss, rounded flavour and rich texture. Small cheeses, sometimes known as 'truckles', often dry out before they have developed a real flavour. Originally these were made from leftover curds, and were designed to be eaten young.

This traditional method was used in farmhouses and small dairies to make the first Australian cheddar cheese types, but with the growth of the export industry from the 1880s, Australian and New Zealand manufacturers rapidly modernised the making of cheddar. Australia has the distinction of having developed rindless tinned cheddar, and during the 1950s and 1960s cheese-making was revolutionised by another Australian invention: the first fully mechanised cheese manufacturing system, known as the Bell-Siro cheese-maker. Operating around the clock, the system produced up to 100 tonnes of cheese per day. This system has since been superseded by even larger, fully enclosed systems, and Australia is still one of the world's most efficient mass producers of industrial cheddar. Most of this cheese is sold at bargain prices and ends up as an ingredient used in secondary manufacture overseas. For example, in some European countries it is not unusual to mix young Australian cheddar with local cooked varieties to make processed cheeses, which are then re-exported around the world.

Almost all the cheddar-type cheese manufactured in Australia is now made by these huge, cost-efficient industrial plants and matured in vast coolrooms with convenient pallet racking and minimum handling. It is produced in technically perfect 20-kg vacuum-packed blocks, which are easy to process, mature, cut and wrap, with price and 'export quality' the main considerations. The standardised cheddar pushed out from these modern factories is special only in its outstanding lack of individual character or anything other than a brand name to differentiate it from other industrial cheeses. Traditional cheddar is far more interesting, simply because it tastes different from day to day, farm to farm and season to season.

At present there are few Australian producers making cheddar in the traditional way. In our rush for efficiency we have sadly lost most of the time-honoured techniques, and for the most part the buying public no longer knows the difference between traditional cheddar and the industrial version. The good news, however, is that there is now a new interest in reviving this forgotten art. The challenge for small cheese-makers in the future is to rescue what we can of this heritage and again produce unique Australian cheddars that are a pleasure to eat.

Stirred-curd (Colby) cheese
Stirred-curd or Colby cheese is often referred to as 'cheddar' and is similar in appearance, but it is made somewhat differently. Instead of being 'cheddared' in stacks, the curd is toughened by being stirred in the vat of warm whey before draining. It is then pressed and matured in a similar manner to cheddar. The resulting cheese looks like cheddar and has a similar flavour, but it is moister and sweeter, with an open texture and a shorter shelf life.

This method is said to have been invented during the late nineteenth century in Wisconsin, USA, although there is speculation that it is much older, and might even pre-date cheddaring. The technique soon came into wide use because it was relatively simple to mechanise for mass production. The oldest specialist cheese in Australia, Pyengana, which dates back to 1901, is hand-made using a variation of the stirred-curd technique and is still matured under cloth.

Club cheddar
This term refers to matured cheese that has been re-worked through a milling process. After maturing in vacuum bags, selected cheeses are blended and minced into small pieces. The milling alters the texture and airs the cheese, allowing moisture and gas to escape. The flavour of the resulting club cheese is manipulated by adding ingredients such as herbs, garlic or sun-dried tomato, then the mixture is pressed into shape. The texture of these cheeses is often grainy or crumbly, and they are presented in foil, or with a seductive coating of wax.

NATURAL RINDS AND WAX COATS

A natural rind is an indication of a handmade cheese. In semi-hard cheeses the rind may be cloth-bound or scalded, washed or oiled, but it plays a vital part in the maturation process because it allows the cheese to breathe.

The increased market interest in specialist cheese has brought a rash of boutique cheeses with colourful wax coats and rustic labels. These cheeses are not what they seem. It is difficult to ripen a cheese under wax over a long period, because the wax prevents the cheese from breathing, and any free moisture is trapped between the cheese and the wax coat. This will form a mould unless a chemical inhibitor is used. Most waxed cheeses are matured in sterile vacuum packs and are only taken out of the bag and waxed at the last minute before leaving the factory. The brightly coloured wax might look attractive, but the cheese inside often has a suffocated 'baggy' taint and a cloying texture that sticks to your teeth.

Washed-curd Types

The hallmark of a washed-curd cheese is its smooth, soft texture, which is achieved by diluting the whey with hot water in the vat after the curd has been cut. This is commonly known as washing the curd. The hot water reduces the production of acid, and when the cheese is hooped the curd particles 'knit' together into a solid mass, forming a close-textured cheese with a mild, bland flavour.

Washed-curd cheeses come in a host of varieties, depending on differences in temperature, rind treatment and maturation.

Trappist cheeses

These cheeses are named after the Trappist order of monks, who developed washing as a simple but effective method of controlling the natural maturation of soft cheese. The most famous traditional Trappist cheese is Port Salut, which was developed in 1815 in northern France by Trappist monks returning from exile after the Napoleonic wars.

Trappist cheeses are often given extra flavour and character by being coated with *Brevibacterium linens*, sometimes with a range of herbs and spices for extra flavouring. *B. linens* is the same bacterium used in surface-ripened washed-rind cheeses, but in Trappist cheeses the coat is encouraged to dry gradually, without cracking or splitting, to form a semi-permeable rind. The result should be a cheese that will store for three or four months, with a mild aromatic flavour and dependable semi-soft texture.

Eye cheeses

Many eye cheeses (so called because of the 'eyes' that form inside the cheese) are produced on a large industrial scale, and the milk is standardised before hot water is added to the vat. Edam and gouda are among the best-known eye cheeses.

Washing the curd removes some of the lactose and reduces – but does not eliminate – acidity. The result is a cheese that is mildly acidic but not sour. The eyes vary in number and size depending on the maturation temperature and the propionic starter used; the higher the temperature, the more eyes develop. Because these cheeses are often produced on a large scale and are quite moist, they are rarely matured for more than six to nine months. They are generally wrapped in wax or plastic to prevent moisture loss, but it is well worth trying a mature eye cheese with a natural rind if you are lucky enough to come across one.

Mature Stretched-curd Types

Mature stretched-curd cheeses are made on similar principles to many washed-curd types. Hot whey and water are used to scald the curds in order to firm them, reduce moisture and prevent further acid development. The crucial difference is that the water added at the end of the process is heated to 90–95°C. This makes the curds melt and consolidate into a thick, fibrous, pliable mass at the bottom of the vat. The warm curd mass is kneaded by hand or machine until it is smooth and shiny, then is cut into small pieces and pulled into long threads.

Mature stretched-curd cheese was traditionally eaten in many parts of central and eastern Europe, and was widely made from ewe's milk in remote mountain regions, where it was sometimes smoked, and often plaited or moulded into interesting shapes. By far the most familiar stretched-curd cheeses today are those that originated in Italy, such as provolone, provole, pancette, caciocavallo and scarmorza.

By comparison with fresh stretched-curd cheeses (see p.72) these harder stretched cheese types are worked more intensively to expel more moisture. They are made in a wide variety of shapes, from giant truncated cones to pear-shaped bells that are brined and thinly waxed before being left to age for several months. Shape and maturation influence the flavour, though this is rarely challenging. Young cheeses are mild and aromatic with a buttery sweetness, but aged cheeses become more piquant and sharp. After about a year the cheeses become quite firm and oily, and are best used in cooking. The most common shape made in Australia is the small waxed sausage tied and hung with a cord. These are best eaten within a few months.

Industrial pizza cheese
Pizza cheese is a mild, low-fat industrial version of matured stretched-curd cheese, often made as a by-product in large cream or butter factories. The cow's milk curds are machine-stretched and folded until they have a low moisture content, which enables them to be matured in vacuum-wrapped blocks. They are then sliced or shredded for the supermarket or bulk pizza trade. The result is a tasteless, rubbery cheese with no real flavour. Its only redeeming feature is its texture – and how it melts. If an industrial pizza cheese burns easily, it is a sign that it has been made with too much added skim milk powder.

Vacuum packing, automation, waxing and mixed club cheeses are the reality of modern cheese-making. It would be hard to argue against all forms of progress in the mass production of cheese, but in many cases modern methods flatten out the peaks of flavour and quality for the sake of avoiding the troughs. It is particularly misleading to slap 'rustic' labels on industrial semi-hard cheeses and dress them up with a wax coat. Why not support the minority of cheese-makers who are prepared to make the effort to produce genuine specialist cheeses with a unique flavour and changeable character?

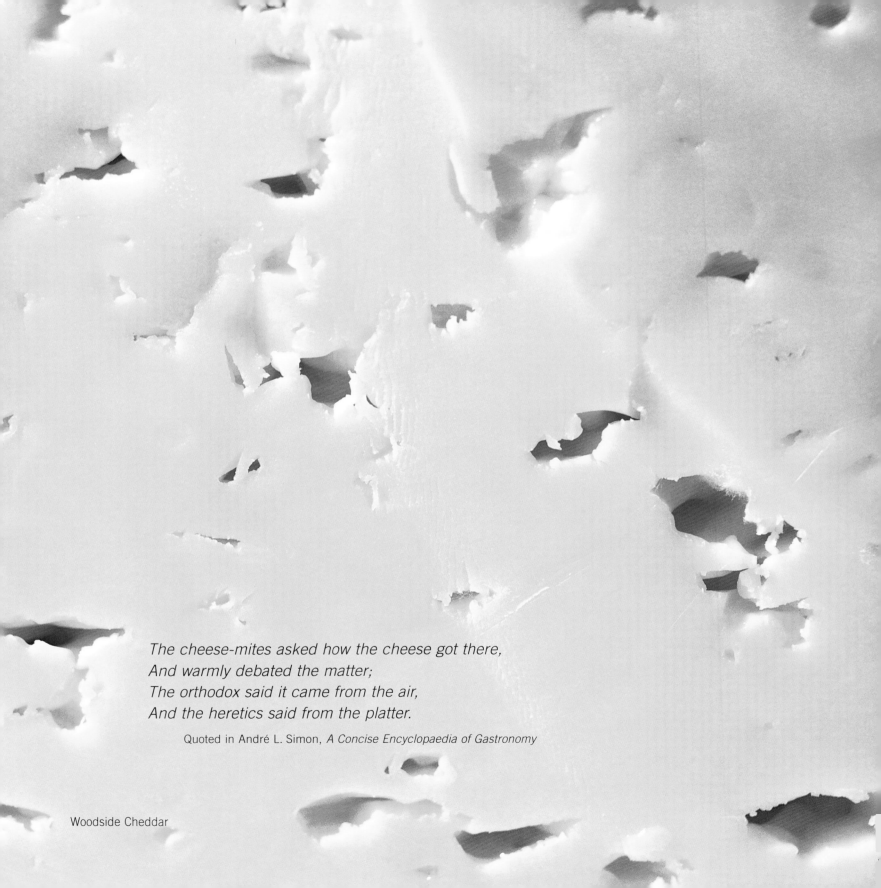

The cheese-mites asked how the cheese got there,
And warmly debated the matter;
The orthodox said it came from the air,
And the heretics said from the platter.

Quoted in André L. Simon, *A Concise Encyclopaedia of Gastronomy*

Woodside Cheddar

Tasting Notes

Ashgrove Mature Cheddar

Producer: Ashgrove Farms (Tas)
Classification: Farmhouse
Form: 20kg blocks & 5kg wheels; vacuum-packed random weights
Milk: Cow – Friesian
Average fat: 33%
Rennet: FP Chymosin
Type: Cheddar
Best season: Cheeses made in early summer
Description: Made using a traditional cheddar method and matured for a minimum of twelve months, this cheese has a firm, slightly open texture and distinct fruity tang, with just a suggestion of rich pastures. This is as good as farmhouse cheddar gets after maturation under vacuum pack.
Additional notes: Also sold as vintage when matured for 8–10 months.

Bass River Red

Producer: Top Paddock Cheese (Vic)
Classification: Farmhouse
Form: 2kg waxed truckle & 5kg cloth-wrapped round
Milk: Cow
Average fat: 45%
Rennet: FP Chymosin
Type: Cheddar
Best season: Best when made with late spring milk (matured 4–6 months)
Description: This orange-red cheese was inspired by the English Red Leicester and has a firm, slightly crumbly texture and rich, mellow flavour with just a suggestion of bitterness from annatto. Rounds matured in traditional cloth have a more open texture and a more complex, rounded earthy tang.

Brolga Cloth Bound

Producer: Purrumbete Buffalo Cheese (Vic)
Classification: Artisan
Form: 1kg round, cloth-bound
Milk: Buffalo – local farm
Average fat: 34%
Rennet: FP Chymosin
Type: Washed-curd
Best season: Cheese made in spring and summer (matured for 9–12 months)
Description: Similar to Dancing Brolga (see p. 132) but the fresh pressed cheese is wrapped in cheesecloth and naturally matured in humid cellar rooms. As it matures it becomes rich and fudgy in texture, with a sweet nuttiness reminiscent of fresh shelled almonds.

Buetten

Producer: Timboon Farmhouse Cheese (Vic)
Classification: Farmhouse
Form: 2kg brick, yellow wax coat
Milk: Cow – biodynamic
Average fat: 32%
Rennet: Microbial
Type: Washed-curd
Best season: Cheese made in late spring/early summer
Description: Washed-curd cheese based on a traditional German recipe that originally used wooden vats. The cheese has a soft, smooth, pliable texture and mild, buttery flavour that matures with age. Matured for 3–6 months.

Additional notes: Also smoked over red-gum chips and sold in rectangular form with purple wax.

Buffalino Melt

Producer: Purrumbete Buffalo Cheese (Vic)
Classification: Artisan
Form: 1kg & 3kg pre-cut vacuum-packed blocks
Milk: Buffalo – local farm
Average fat: 37%
Rennet: FP Chymosin
Type: Stretched-curd
Description: Semi-hard buffalo mozzarella with a semi-pliable texture and unique, slightly sweet, lactic flavour. Ideal standby for cooking, when it melts to a thick, creamy, stringy consistency.

Chevrotin

Producer: Faudel Goat Cheese Company (Vic)
Classification: Farmhouse
Form: 1.5kg round, natural cloth rind or waxed, and 150g flat cylinders, plain or waxed
Milk: Goat
Average fat: 25%
Rennet: FP Chymosin
Type: Washed-curd
Best season: Cheese made in spring & summer (matured for 3–6 months)
Description: A firm, smooth cheese with a fine texture and clean, mild but distinctive flavour.

Creamy Lancashire

Producer: Ashgrove Farm (Tas)
Classification: Farmhouse
Form: 20kg block & 5kg wheel; cuts vacuum-packed
Milk: Cow – Friesian
Average fat: 33%
Rennet: FP Chymosin
Type: Cheddar
Best season: Cheese made from late spring & summer milk
Description: Handmade to a traditional English recipe, this territorial creamy cheese is at the young stage of tasty Lancashire. It is pale gold in colour, and the texture is moist and distinctly crumbly with a mild, slightly acid flavour.
Additional notes: Ideal for toasting and melting. Also sold smoked and with added indigenous bush pepper berries.

Dancing Brolga

Producer: Purrumbete Buffalo Cheese (Vic)
Classification: Artisan
Form: 1kg red waxed round
Milk: Buffalo – local farm
Average fat: 34%
Rennet: FP Chymosin
Type: Washed-curd
Best season: Cheese made in spring and summer (matured for 6–8 months)
Description: Ivory-white in colour, this semi-hard cheese is quite unique, because buffalo milk is more commonly used for mozzarella and fresh cheese. The cheese is moist and has a compact, silky texture and mild, creamy taste with an extraordinary sweetness balanced by a slight citrus tang.

Additional notes: Named after the water birds that inhabit the Western District.

Farmhouse Havarti

Producer: Top Paddock Cheeses (Vic)
Classification: Farmhouse
Form: 700g waxed truckle
Milk: Cow
Average fat: 35%
Rennet: FP Chymosin
Type: Washed-curd
Description: Smooth-textured washed-curd cheese with a mild, creamy flavour. Sold plain or flavoured with herb & garlic, olive & tomato or smoked with pecan nuts (with different coloured waxes).

Finniss

Producer: Helen & Derek Fenton (SA)
Classification: Farmhouse
Form: 1.2kg round
Milk: Cow – Jersey
Average fat: 30%
Rennet: FP Chymosin
Best season: Spring to autumn
Description: Made from the milk of just one cow, this deep marigold-coloured cheese has a variegated rind covered with beeswax, a moist texture and creamy, clotted flavour. It can be eaten after a few months, when it is still slightly acidic, but ages to become sweet and nutty with a complex flavour of grass and herbage and a delicate, honeyed aroma. Depending on the time of year the cheeses are made and therefore the temperature and humidity of the stone cellar in which they mature, they vary

from fresh to semi-hard through to a parmesan-style cheese.
Additional notes: This is a difficult cheese to find outside South Australia, but if you come across it, buy it.

Goat Mature

Producer: Tarago River Cheese Company (Vic)
Classification: Artisan
Form: 2kg round, plastic-coated
Milk: Goat – one farm
Average fat: 32%
Rennet: Halal calf
Type: Washed-curd
Best season: Cheeses made from early autumn milk (matured for 4–6 months)
Description: This scalded washed-curd cheese has a firm, smooth, fudgy texture and lingering creamy goat taste with a mixture of earthy and slightly fruity flavours.

Heidi Raclette

Producer: Heidi Farm Cheese (Tas)
Classification: Farmhouse
Form: 6.5–7kg wheel & 15kg squares
Milk: Cow – Friesian
Average fat: 28%
Rennet: FP Chymosin
Type: Washed-curd
Best season: Cheese made in autumn/winter
Description: Moist, washed and smeared-rind cheese with a pliable texture. The cheese has a pungent aroma that is delightful to some and repugnant to others. The rich, milky flavour and doughy texture are best appreciated when the

cheese is melted or cooked.
Additional notes: The best cheeses are fully matured for five months. Raclette is derived from *racler*, which means to scrape. Traditionally, this mountain cheese was eaten with boiled waxy potatoes and pickles.

Hillcrest Mature

Producer: Tarago River Cheese Company (Vic)
Classification: Farmhouse
Form: 5kg round barrel, natural grey rind
Milk: Cow
Average fat: 32%
Rennet: Halal calf
Type: Washed-curd
Best season: Cheeses made from late spring milk (matured for 6–12 months)
Description: This cheese is matured in underground cellars, where the rind becomes flecked with orange and white moulds. The interior has a dense, smooth texture with small holes. The flavour is sweet and fruity, with a hint of mushroom when young. The more mature cheeses develop a nutty texture and a delightful medley of complex flavours with overtones of mould and milky sweetness.

Jannei Mature

Producer: Jannei Goat Dairy (NSW)
Classification: Farmhouse
Form: 1–1.5kg red waxed round
Milk: Goat
Average fat: 32%
Rennet: FP Chymosin
Type: Cheddar

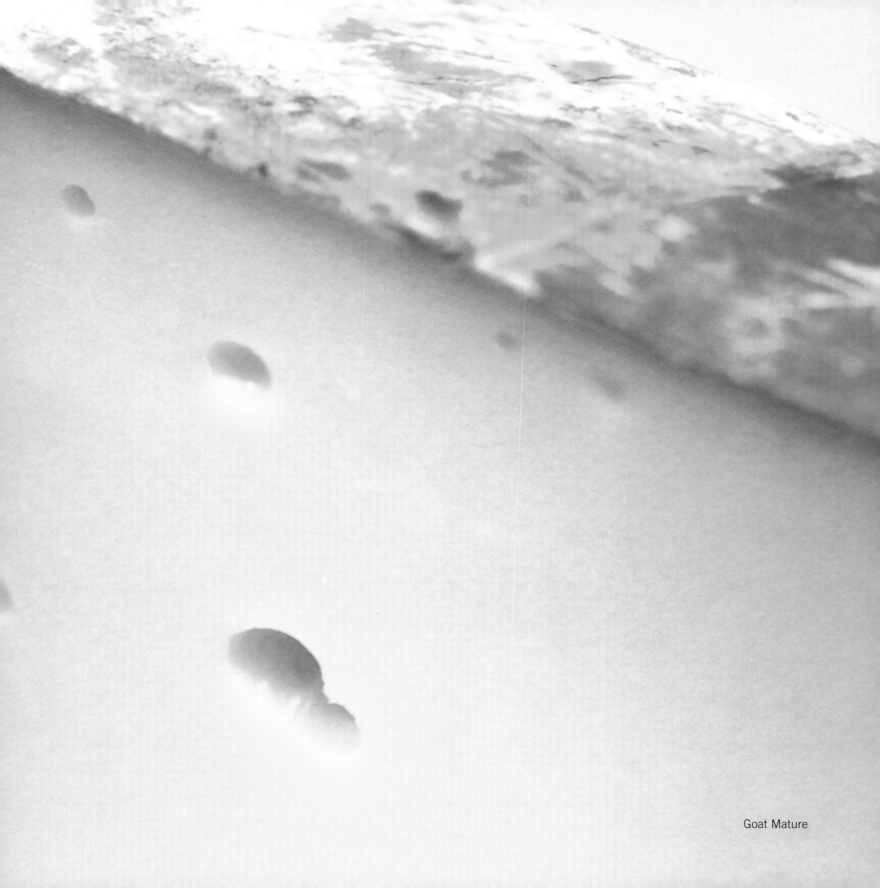

Goat Mature

Pyengana Cheddar

Best season: Cheese made in spring (matured for 3–6 months)
Description: A firm, chalky cheese with a fine texture and slightly sharp, goaty taste.

Maffra Longhold Cheddar

Producer: Crescent Creek Cheese Makers (Vic)
Classification: Farmhouse
Form: 14kg wheels, cloth-bound and waxed; pre-cut pieces vacuum-packed
Milk: Cow – Friesian
Average fat: 50%
Rennet: Calf
Type: Cheddar
Best season: Cheeses made with late spring milk (matured for 9–12 months)
Description: Handmade traditional cheddared cheese washed in large vats. Open, crumbly yet moist texture with a well-developed, tangy flavour. Best when matured for 18 months.
Additional notes: This cheddar can be hard to find as production is limited.

Malling Red Whey Cheddar

Producer: Kenilworth (Qld)
Classification: Industrial
Form: 2.4kg & 4.8kg wheels, wax coated
Milk: Cow
Average fat: 33%
Rennet: FP Chymosin
Type: Stirred-curd
Description: Crumbly straw-coloured curds with a rich, creamy tang and slight sweetness. This cheese is made using traditional stirred-curd Colby techniques, and utilises a unique local whey starter developed by the company founder, Papa Peter Hansen. Cheese is cloth-wrapped before maturation in the bag and later waxing.
Additional notes: Also available as extra mature vintage, matured for up two years.

Meadow Cheese

Producer: Elgaar Farm Cheese (Tas)
Classification: Farmhouse
Form: 5 & 10kg wheels
Milk: Cow
Average fat: 32%
Rennet: FP Chymosin
Type: Washed-curd
Best season: Cheeses made with late spring or autumn milk (matured for 3–4 months)
Description: These distinctive cheeses have a smooth rind pockmarked with small holes and mould, and a pale yellow interior with variable aromas of green grass or fresh hay according to season. A mild and savoury cheese with a subtle tang.
Additional notes: Hard to find on the mainland, but worth seeking.

Mersey Valley Vintage Club

Producer: Lactos (Tas)
Classification: Industrial
Form: 2kg block, vacuum-packed with foil wrap
Milk: Cow
Average fat: 33%
Rennet: Calf
Type: Club cheddar
Description: This club cheese is made from a mixture of selected cheddars and some-times mature gouda. It is moist and crumbly in texture, with an acidic and slightly fruity flavour.
Additional notes: Australia's most successful club cheddar. Also made with peppercorns and sun-dried tomatoes.

Nineteenth Century Cheddar

Producer: Bega (NSW)
Classification: Industrial
Form: 4.5kg brown waxed wheels
Milk: Cow
Average fat: 35%
Rennet: FP Chymosin
Type: Cheddar
Description: Made in a modern automated dairy using an adaptation of traditional cheddar methods. The rounds are wrapped in cloth but matured under vacuum before later being unwrapped and waxed. The mature cheese is moist, rich and dense with a delicate, creamy/buttery aftertaste and primrose yellow colour.
Additional notes: The Bega Co-operative Creamery Company was established in 1899 and takes milk from 135 farms. This cheese is sold under a number of other brand names.

Osheiepok

Producer: Mountain Shepherd Cheese (Vic)
Classification: Artisan
Form: 250g & 500g rounds or ovals, vacuum-packed
Milk: Cow – co-operative
Average fat: 21%
Rennet: Kosher chymosin
Type: Stretched-curd
Description: Small round or oval-shaped smoked cheeses with a pattern embossed on the skin. Texture is similar to many stretched-curd cheeses, with slight resilience and bounciness. Koliba (meaning shepherd's hut) is the unsmoked version; the name comes from the Slavic region of the former Yugoslavia.

Pyengana Cheddar

Producer: Healey's Pyengana Cheese (Tas)
Classification: Farmhouse
Form: 1.2, 2.5, 4.5, 7 and 18.5kg wheels, natural cloth-bound
Milk: Cows – Friesian
Average fat: 32%
Rennet: Calf
Type: Stirred-curd
Best season: Cheeses made with spring or autumn milk
Description: These cheeses are made using a traditional stirred-curd technique. The honey-coloured curds are pressed and bound in cheesecloth and naturally matured on wood in humidified rooms, where the exterior of the cheese develops a grey, dusty rind. Maturation time varies depending on size. The cheeses are released at 6–9 months or one year, when they have developed a fine, open texture and a rich, complex flavour. The best are matured for up to 18 months, when they become drier and more granular with a tangy flavour reminiscent of honey and green grass.
Additional notes: Pyengana dates back to 1901, and is

Australia's oldest traditional specialist cheese still made on the farm. The cheeses are made entirely by hand, and the dairy still uses a wood-fired boiler to heat the water and an original Victorian bed press to press the cheeses. Each cheese is tagged with its date of manufacture.

Raclette

Producer: Parmalat (NSW)
Classification: Artisan
Form: 5kg wheel
Milk: Cow – co-operative
Average fat: 28%
Rennet: FP Chymosin
Type: Washed-curd
Description: Has a bright terracotta-coloured rind with a smooth, semi-soft, silky texture and a big, pongy aroma that intensifies with heat.

Romney Fresca

Producer: Mount Emu Creek Dairy (Vic)
Classification: Artisan
Form: 1kg rounds, black wax
Milk: Ewe – local farms
Average fat: 30%
Rennet: FP Chymosin
Type: Washed-curd
Best season: Cheeses made from spring milk (matured for 3 months)
Description: Ivory-coloured cheese with a semi-soft, springy texture, tiny holes and a mild, sweet, milky flavour.
Additional notes: Named after the local breed of Romney sheep that graze along the banks of Mount Emu Creek. Also flavoured with lavender and sold in a purple wax coat.

Romney Mature

Producer: Mount Emu Creek Dairy (Vic)
Classification: Artisan
Form: 1.5kg rounds, natural cloth rind
Milk: Ewe – local farms
Average fat: 30%
Rennet: FP Chymosin
Type: Washed-curd
Best season: Cheeses made from late winter or spring milk (matured 9–12 months)
Description: An ivory-coloured cheese surrounded by a rough, grey-brown cloth wrap. When mature it has a dense, flaky texture and sweet, nutty, butterscotch flavour with a hint of mould.
Additional notes: Made by the same method as Fresca (see previous entry) but matured naturally under cloth. Avoid mature cheeses that have brown discolouration or have a strong smell of lanolin.

St Claire

Producer: Lactos (Tas)
Classification: Artisan
Form: 4kg & 10kg yellow waxed wheel
Milk: Cow – regional
Average fat: 28%
Rennet: Calf
Type: Scalded eye
Description: A predictable cheese with an elastic, mild, creamy texture and slightly sweet aftertaste. Australia's most successful gouda style.

Surprise Bay Cheddar

Producer: King Island Dairy (Tas)
Classification: Artisan
Form: 5kg red waxed round
Milk: Cow – island milk
Average fat: 30%
Rennet: Calf
Type: Stirred-curd
Description: The crumbly, golden curds have a moist sweetness achieved by gentle cooking and stirring. When mature the cheese has a creamy, caramel flavour balanced with acidity. Also sold as a black waxed vintage cheese with a serious bite.
Additional notes: A unique cheese first developed in 1987 by Bill Kirk, who came up with this successful cheese-making technique while experimenting with variations on Romano methods.

Tilba Cheese

Producer: Tilba Cheese Company (NSW)
Classification: Industrial
Form: 2kg rounds, pre-cut vacuum-packed
Milk: Cow
Average fat: 30%
Rennet: FP Chymosin
Type: Club cheddar
Description: One of the most successful club cheeses. Made in the historical village of Tilba, New South Wales, from a mixture of selected cheddar blended with savoury or sweet flavourings and marketed under a variety of exotic names.

Top Paddock Washed Rind

Producer: Top Paddock Cheeses (Vic)
Classification: Farmhouse
Form: 600g round, paper wrap
Milk: Cow
Average fat: 35%
Rennet: FP Chymosin
Type: Washed-curd
Best season: Late autumn
Description: Soft washed-curd cheese based on traditional monastic methods. The terracotta orange rind is mottled with blotches of blue and has a yeasty, herbaceous aroma. The texture of the interior is semi-soft and springy, with a pale, buttery colour and tiny holes. Once mature it develops a mild, rounded, creamy flavour with a background of grass and pasture and a hint of eucalyptus.
Additional notes: This cheese changes to a soft, sensuous texture during late autumn as the late lactation milk and feed conditions alter the composition of the milk.

Top Paddock Wine Washed

Producer: Top Paddock Cheeses (Vic)
Classification: Farmhouse
Form: 1.6kg round, paper wrap
Milk: Cow
Average fat: 35%
Rennet: FP Chymosin
Type: Washed-curd
Best season: Autumn
Description: Soft washed-curd cheese with a grey-brown, leathery rind mottled with blue mould. The rind is washed in pinot noir, which gives this unusual cheese a winey aroma

reminiscent of the inside of old oak barrels. The texture is smooth and supple with a pleasant hint of sweet, grapey fruitiness.

Additional notes: Close relative of the washed-rind except larger and with a different wash. The curd is washed and scalded to remove excess whey, creating a low-acid, stable cheese.

Watsonia Cheddar

Producer: Watsonia Cheese Company (WA)
Classification: Industrial
Form: 500g canary-yellow waxed rounds
Milk: Cow
Average fat: 33%
Rennet: FP Chymosin
Type: Club cheddar
Description: A club cheddar made with selected cheddar from Mount Barker and other regions. Crumbly with a slightly fruity aftertaste.

Woodside Cheddar

Producer: Woodside Cheesewrights (SA)
Classification: Artisan
Form: 25kg wheels, natural rind, cheesecloth-bound
Milk: Cow – local farm
Average fat: 30%
Rennet: FP Chymosin
Type: Cheddar
Best season: Cheeses made with late spring or autumn milk (matured 12–18 months)
Description: Pale yellow in colour, with variable aromas of green grass or fresh hay according to season. When mature the cheese has an open yet dewy texture and a rich, savoury tang that is well balanced with acidity.

Additional notes: Handmade using Friesian milk in small batches and pressed in an antique cheese press, this is one of Australia's few cheddars still made using the traditional cheddaring technique and correct temperature maturation in cloth. If you are lucky enough to find a cheddar aged for 24 months or more, it will have developed a much more powerful, earthy tang and rough open texture with small knots of blue mould in the body.

ha

Hard

The most concentrated, driest and richest forms of cheese are the hard-cooked cheeses. These dense cheeses are the lowest in moisture content and the longest-keeping of all specialist cheese types, sometimes being matured for two or three years or more.

Hard-cooked cheese originated in the cold mountain regions of northern Europe, where they were traditionally only made during the warm summer months. Cows in these alpine regions produced plenty of rich milk during spring and summer, but the supply dried up in winter. It was therefore important to make cheeses of a kind that could be stored for many months.

The size and shape of any cheese have important implications for maturation, and these alpine cheeses are among the largest and most concentrated of all. Large wheels can be kept for extended periods because their size allows long, slow, controlled maturation. It takes a lot of milk to produce just one cheese – about 350 litres for the average 30-kg wheel. To produce such large cheeses with small herds in remote locations, farmers traditionally set up co-operative arrangements to pool their raw milk at a local village dairy, known in France as a *fruitièr*.

Many of these cheese types are no longer only made during the summer and copies of varying sizes have been made around the world, but the original large cheeses still have the most flavour. In Australia we do not have a tradition of making cheese in the Alps, but the rich early summer milk from animals fed on green paddocks has proved ideal for making hard-cooked cheese.

In the traditional method of making hard-cooked cheeses, the cut curds are heated in the liquid whey so that they release their surplus moisture. The cooking temperature can be as high as 60°C, and the process may last for more than three hours. The curds are then cut finely so that the maximum amount of moisture is expelled. Cooking the curd also starts to caramelise the remaining lactose, leaving the cheese with a characteristic sweetness.

After cooking, the warm curds are removed from the whey, often in a single action. A bulging cheesecloth sack full of dripping curds is hauled up and gently laid into a large circular hoop, then pressed in a hydraulic press. This pressing forces more moisture from the cheese, further concentrating the texture and flavour.

The whole pressed cheeses are bathed in brine to encourage rind development, then placed in dark, warm maturing cellars for six months or more. The maturation temperature and rind treatment determine how the cheese will mature.

Hard-cooked cheeses fall into two sub-groups: granular and smooth. The major differences between the two are the way in which the curds are cut and cooked, and the starters and cultures used in fermentation.

Granular

The granular texture of hard cheeses is produced by cutting the curd finely, almost to the size of a rice grain, then cooking and scalding it at a high temperature. As a result the texture is dense but dry and quite brittle. After hooping into large wheels, the cheeses are generally oiled to form a rind and matured in warm cellars for at least a year. They are often made with low-fat cow's milk to prevent them from seeping fatty liquids as they mature. The different varieties are associated with the regions of Italy where they originated: cow's milk cheeses such as grana padano and parmigiano reggiano are made in the colder northern regions, and ewe's milk cheeses such as pecorino romano and pecorino sardo come from the warmer south.

A good granular cheese should be slightly grainy but melt in the mouth with a concentrated flavour, slight caramel sweetness and lingering salty tang.

There are many passable Australian granular cheeses, but virtually all are made and matured under plastic in block form, and lack the subtle nuances and mature character of the originals. Worse still, some industrial producers have an infuriating habit of calling cheeses 'pecorino' (meaning sheep) when in fact they are made entirely from cow's milk. Some of the best Australian granular cheeses are made from ewe's milk on a small scale.

Smooth

Smooth hard-cooked cheese types have a more elastic and pliable texture than the granular cheeses, often developing eyeholes. The main difference lies in the treatment of the curd particles, which are not scalded for as long or cut as small, and in the controlled development of acidity as the cheese ripens. These cheeses have a smooth, nutty texture and retain more moisture than granular types. The eyeholes in smooth curd cheeses are produced by the action of what are known as 'propionic starters', which are added to the milk. When the cheese is matured in warm cellars the heat activates micro-organisms in the starter, producing bubbles of carbon dioxide that become trapped in the body of the cheese.

The size of the holes depends on the cheese size, rind treatment and temperature of maturation. Cheeses such as emmental have walnut-sized, shiny eyeholes and a supple, slightly oily texture with a sweet, fruity flavour. Most of these cheeses have a semi-sealed oiled or plasticised rind and are matured at 20–24°C for six to eight weeks. As a general rule, the larger the holes, the sweeter the cheese.

The other major type of smooth curd cheese has only small, scattered eyeholes the size of a pea. These cheeses are firmer and more fatty with developed acidity, which results in a stronger, more aromatic cheese; gruyère is one of the best-known cheeses of this kind. These cheeses are matured at a lower temperature (16–18°C) and often have a washed rind that can breathe and release some of the gas. They also have horizontal fissures, which are used as a guide to the cheese's maturity. When small white specks of lactate appear in the fissures, the cheese is considered ready to sell.

Australian Hard-cooked Cheeses

There are relatively few hard-cooked specialist cheeses made in Australia, although the number is growing every year. Hard cheeses have made a slow start partly because Australia's climate is warmer than Europe's and the seasonal demand for this type of cheese is limited. The long maturation time and relatively high cost have also deterred smaller cheese-makers, and there is strong competition from similar industrial European cheeses, which generally travel well. It is much more profitable for local cheese-makers to make fresh cheese than to tie their milk up in maturation rooms for long periods without much extra reward.

On the other hand, as consumers develop a greater interest in and knowledge of specialist cheese, they are learning to appreciate the difference and are prepared to pay for it. Any encouragement is welcome.

Heidi Barrel

Tasting Notes

Graviera

Producer: Hellenic Farm (Vic)
Classification: Artisan
Form: 4kg waxed rounds, pre-cut wedges
Milk: Ewe – mixed source
Average fat: 24%
Rennet: FP Chymosin
Best season: Cheeses made with winter & spring milk (matured for 3–6 months)
Description: A close, dense, granular cheese that is soft when young but as it ages develops a semi-hard, pliable texture and slightly sweet, nutty character. Avoid cheeses with too much bite.

Heidi Barrel

Producer: Heidi Farm Cheese (Tas)
Classification: Farmhouse
Form: 1.5kg, paper wrap
Milk: Cow
Average fat: 35%
Rennet: FP Chymosin
Best season: Cheeses made with spring and early summer milk (matured for 2–12 months)
Description: This small 'truckle' cheese has a washed rind and matures more quickly than its larger cousins. It has a closed, smooth, soft texture with tiny holes and a mild flavour.

Heidi Emmental

Producer: Heidi Farm Cheese (Tas)
Classification: Farmhouse
Form: 50–55kg oiled wheels
Milk: Cow
Average fat: 35%
Rennet: FP Chymosin
Best season: Cheeses made in late spring (matured for 6–18 months)
Description: This cheese has a dry, leathery rind and a pale, elastic paste that is full of imperfect round eyes of varying sizes. Delicate, sweet and fruity with a savoury finish.
Additional notes: Cheeses that have been aged are especially worth seeking.

Heidi Gruyère

Producer: Heidi Farm Cheese (Tas)
Classification: Farmhouse
Form: 30kg wheel, waxed paper wrap
Milk: Cow – Friesian
Average fat: 48%
Rennet: FP Chymosin
Best season: Cheeses made in late spring
Description: These large wheels have a brown, orange-crusted rind that has a strong aroma from washing and maturation in the cellar. When young the texture is moist and smooth, gradually becoming drier and denser with age. At 9 months the flavour is well-rounded, slightly sweet and nutty, with suggestions of scalded cream, green pastures and honey. By 18 months the texture has become more concentrated and flaky and the flavour is deep, with hints of creamy, caramel sweetness balanced with salt.
Additional notes: A benchmark recognised as one of the finest Australian farmhouse cheeses.

Kardella

Producer: Top Paddock Cheeses (Vic)
Classification: Farmhouse
Form: 2–3kg, natural rind
Milk: Cow
Average fat: 35%
Rennet: FP Chymosin
Best season: Cheeses made from spring & autumn milk (matured for 6–9 months)
Description: The natural rusty-coloured rind is smeared with a mixture of white wine and herbs over a 3-month period. The texture is dense and compact, with a strong, earthy flavour and slightly sweet aftertaste.

Loch

Producer: Top Paddock Cheeses (Vic)
Classification: Farmhouse
Form: 5kg wheel
Milk: Cow
Average fat: 40%
Rennet: FP Chymosin
Best season: Cheeses made in spring (matured for 6–9 months)
Description: This cheese has a rough, mottled, natural rind and a smooth, firm, golden-yellow interior with a sweet flavour reminiscent of cashew nuts.

Merino Gold

Producer: Hellenic Cheese Farm (Vic)
Classification: Artisan
Form: 4kg wheel, vacuum-packed
Milk: Ewe – mixed source
Average fat: 25%
Rennet: FP Chymosin

Best season: Winter to late spring
Description: Close, dense, granular cheese aged with dried capsicum paste, wine and salt until it develops a crumbly texture and pleasant, sweet, nutty character.

Mount Elephant

Producer: Mount Emu Creek Dairy (Vic)
Classification: Artisan
Form: 2.5kg wheels
Milk: Ewe – local farm
Average fat: 30%
Rennet: FP Chymosin
Best season: Cheeses made from late winter/spring milk (matured for 12–18 months)
Description: The grey, mottled rind encases a hard, dense, granular interior with an antique ivory colour and slightly oily texture. Initial tasting reveals strong nutty flavours (brazil nuts) and a slight lanolin taste, but the sweetness of the ewe's milk lingers long after the primary flavours.
Additional notes: Described by cheese-maker Robert Manifold as a stylised pecorino, this hard ewe's milk cheese is made only with the milk from his farm. Also sold matured for one month – a milder version.

Petite Fleur

Producer: Timboon Farmhouse Cheese (Vic)
Classification: Farmhouse
Form: 1kg upright drum, foil wrap
Milk: Cow – biodynamic
Average fat: 28%
Rennet: Microbial

Best season: Cheeses made in late spring (matured for 3–9 months)
Description: The light-brown washed rind can be a bit smelly and sticky. Soft and moist in texture, this cheese will develop a strong, nutty flavour with hints of yeast and vegemite.

Swissfield Emmental

Producer: Parmalat (NSW)
Classification: Artisan
Form: 5kg wheels and pre-cut pieces vacuum-packed
Milk: Cow – co-operative
Average fat: 28%
Rennet: FP Chymosin
Description: This cheese has a golden plastic-coated rind and a semi-soft, elastic body with small eyeholes. Mild, with a distinctive, fruity flavour.
Additional notes: The best cheeses have olive-sized holes evenly dispersed.

Swissfield Gruyère

Producer: Parmalat (NSW)
Classification: Artisan
Form: 5kg wheels and pre-cut pieces vacuum-packed
Milk: Cow – co-operative
Average fat: 28%
Rennet: FP Chymosin
Description: A full-bodied, smooth-textured cheese with tiny eyes and possibly a few fine cracks. Mellow, with a gentle, fruity, slightly nutty taste.

Mount Elephant

ben

Ch

BENCHMARKS

Piccante gorgonzola

European Classics

How often do we come across cheeses whose flavours and textures are a source of unqualified delight? We don't forget such rare experiences, and naturally seek to renew them. At the same time, when we recognise a particularly enjoyable flavour or texture, we unconsciously use it as the benchmark against which we measure others.

Australians have a good deal to learn from many of the benchmark cheeses, particularly the European classics. Only when we have experienced the pleasure of these cheeses can we speak with any authority about the quality of the local product. I sometimes fear that the Australian specialist cheese industry is in danger of succumbing to a complacent, naïve nationalism. Far too often I hear people say that Australia has the best cheese in the world, an ignorant statement made only by those who have never bothered to look at what the rest of the world has to offer. We certainly have some wonderful cheese, and good milk with unique potential, but we must continue to learn what makes good milk into great cheese. This is not the time for arrogance. If specialist Australian cheese-making is to keep improving, we must take the time to study the classic masterpieces made for hundreds, even thousands, of years.

The more delicate of these cheeses have not always been seen in Australia at their best. They are difficult to ship because of quarantine restrictions, the long sea voyage, and the expense and temperature control problems associated with the 24-hour air trip. To provide cheeses in top condition, it is necessary to treat them with great care and understand their individual requirements. Too often wholesalers and retailers pay insufficient attention to providing the right conditions, and as a result many cheeses are sold well over the hill. But in the right skilled hands there are a number of excellent examples of these benchmark cheeses, which are well worth seeking out. To experience their flavour and texture is a reward in itself, and provides an interesting contrast to the local specialist cheeses.

Fresh

Fresh cheeses are rarely imported to Australia, although gas flushing (see p. 61) has seen the introduction of modern classics such as Boursin. The classic benchmark cheeses available in this category are made from goat's milk.

Goat's Milk Cheeses

Some of the earliest cheeses recorded in France were made from goat's milk and were introduced by the Saracens, people of Arab descent who moved north into France from Spain. When these invaders were finally expelled during the eighth century, they left behind an enduring legacy of making goat's milk cheese. These cheeses are made in various shapes and sizes, and are often distinguished by their association with the name of a specific village or region. More than 70 per cent of all goat's milk cheeses in France, including many of the benchmark goat's milk cheeses, are made in the region south-west of the Loire River.

The classification of regional milk and the use of traditional techniques are strictly enforced. Coagulation is mainly lactic, with only a small amount of rennet added, and takes up to twenty-four hours. The curds are scooped by hand, ladled into hoops and drained for a further twenty-four hours. A geotrichum and glaucum mould is introduced to the surface of the cheese, producing a wrinkled look. In some cases (sainte-maure, for example) cheeses are coated with a mix of salt and powdered charcoal (*sel noir*).

These traditional cheeses are moist and sweet when young but as they age they develop a natural covering of grey and blue mould that draws out the moisture from the curds. After they have undergone *affinage* (maturation) for three weeks, they have a much drier texture and stronger, more deeply concentrated flavour. These cheeses are usually mature on arrival in Australia. Texture tends to vary according to season. They are at their best when made between early spring and autumn. Some of the best examples are made by Soignon.

Chabichou du Poitou
Small, round, upright cylinders with a cream-coloured, wrinkled rind that gradually becomes covered in blue-grey moulds. The cheese is rich and slightly salty, with a concentrated, creamy goat flavour.

Pouligny-saint-pierre
A pointed pyramid-shaped cheese (nicknamed the 'Eiffel Tower') with a thin, wrinkled, ivory-coloured rind that develops an array of grey and reddish moulds as it ages. Concentrated and moist, the cheese has a sweetness that hints of hay. It is considered one of the best goat's milk cheeses for maturation.

Sainte-maure de Touraine
Small log-shaped cheeses coated with ash that gradually develop blue and grey moulds across the surface. The cheese is fine and close-textured, with a contrasting lemony tang that becomes stronger with age.

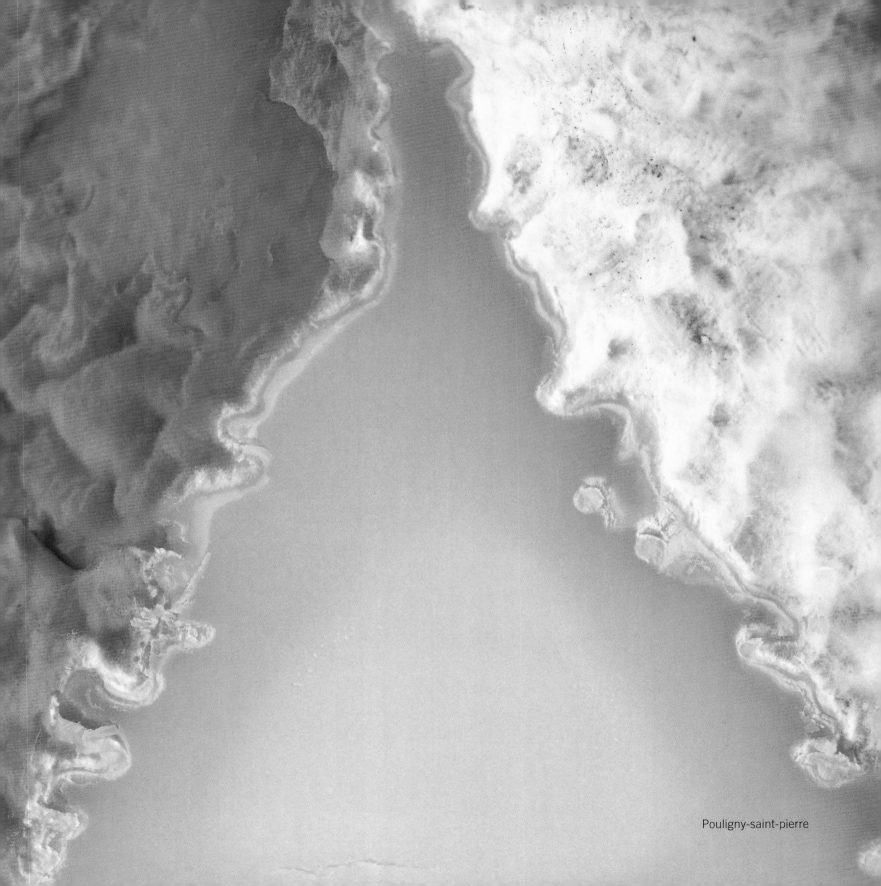

Pouligny-saint-pierre

Normandy Camembert

White

Brie de Meaux

Brie cheese is one of the world's most widely copied and misrepresented cheeses. It originated from the plains north and south of the village of Meaux, close to the Seine and Marne rivers south-east of Paris. The 'brie' or 'brye' of Ile-de-France was famous for many centuries, and was accorded the title of Prince of Cheeses (later elevated to King) at the Congress of Vienna after the defeat of Napoleon in 1815.

Brie de Meaux is made in large, round, flattish discs weighing about 2 kg. This shape exposes a large area for surface-ripening of the centre, which is chalky and acid when young. Matured under the right conditions, an authentic brie will develop a moist, white, peeling, flaky crust speckled with a touch of orange and red moulds and a rich centre that is clotted and gluey, oozing with a seductive sensory expectancy.

To carry the name, Brie de Meaux must be made from raw milk, and in Australia we are only able to buy a pasteurised version called Fromage de Meaux, matured by Affineurs Rouzaire. Brie des Coulommiers is another classic cheese available from the region.

Camembert

Any surface-ripened white-mould cheese that vaguely resembles this marvellous cheese can use the name 'camembert', but the genuine article is only made in Normandy from raw milk, and is identified by the mark *Véritable Camembert de Normandie* (VCN), instituted by government decree in 1983. Camembert owes some of its fame to one Monsieur Ridel, who in 1880 invented a small poplar-wood box that made it possible to transport the cheese outside the region for the first time.

The authentic cheese must be made to a particular size (11 cm in diameter, with a weight of 250 gm). The centre is chalky when young but always slightly moist, and the crust is white with some red flecking. As it ripens, a good camembert develops a rich, distinctive flavour and an aroma that is often referred to as '*les pieds de dieu*' (literally 'the feet of God'); more prosaically, it is reminiscent of cooked cauliflower.

Most 'camemberts' available in Australia do not even resemble this magnificent cheese, although some have their own distinctive flavours and qualities. The French brands to look out for are those made by Isigny St Mere.

Washed

Taleggio

The technique of making this ancient soft cheese originated during the eleventh century in the Valsassina valley in Lombardy. The mountains of this lush valley are capped with snow for much of the year, and their sides are honeycombed with granite caves and natural fissures. As the snow melts, the cold run-off and the flow of wet air into the caves produce a unique microclimate ideal for maturing cheese. This is where the best local cheese-makers still mature their cheeses.

Taleggio was once referred to as 'stracchino' cheese, because it was made from the milk produced in autumn when the cows were tired (*stracche*) after descending from the high alpine pastures. It has been known as taleggio since the early twentieth century, when the cheese-makers of Val Taleggio coined the name to distinguish their cheese from other cheeses in the region.

Taleggio is a soft, square cheese, unusually deep for a surface-ripened cheese, and the salted, washed rind plays a crucial part in its flavour and quality. The rind should be thin, lightly flecked with pinkish-brown and dusted with white mould. It should not be cracked, and must be sturdy enough to contain the bulging, buttery texture of the mature cheese. The white, chalky centre turns a smooth ivory as the cheese matures over two months or more. If well cared for, taleggio should mature until it begins to show signs of oozing at the edge.

When fully mature, it has a complex, subtle texture that dissolves on the tongue, and a slightly salty and yeasty creaminess that is hard to resist.

Many industrial manufacturers produce taleggio, sometimes waxing or vacuum-packing their cheeses rather than taking the trouble to mature them in the caves. The resulting cheeses are pale imitations of the original, and do a sad injustice to this great cheese. Two of the best brands available on the Australian market are Mauri and Cademartori.

Pont l'évêque

Pont l'évêque is a distinctive square orange-russet cheese dating back to the twelfth-century monasteries, where it was used as a substitute for meat on fast days and was known as 'white meat'. It is a close cousin of livarot, which is a round cheese. Both originate from particular localities in the Pays d'Auge of Normandy, which was made famous by camembert. These washed-curd cheeses were originally made with the rich raw milk of the local Normandes breed cows, but today there are versions made from pasteurised milk. They are usually sold in poplar-wood boxes.

Traditional cheeses ripen to a rust colour, and the rind often has a granular texture from its coating of dry salt. The texture is soft and melt-in-the-mouth, sometimes with a meaty flavour. These cheeses are hard to find in Australia; the brand to look out for is made by Graindorge.

Taleggio

Blue

Gorgonzola

Gorgonzola is one of the oldest named cheeses in the world, dating back to 879 AD, and comes from a designated region of Lombardy just south of the Italian Alps. The town of Gorgonzola was established as a rest point for cattle on their way back from the summer alpine pastures. There are many theories about how the cheese evolved, but there is little doubt that the late-season milk from these cattle would have been made into *stracchino* cheese, as was the case with taleggio.

Traditional gorgonzola relied on an unusual method in which the curd from two separate milkings was combined. The adoption of this method, which gives gorgonzola its open texture, may have been influenced by the fact that the volume of milk from a single autumn milking was not sufficient to produce a full vat for making cheese. The evening curd was cut and rested overnight, then mixed with warm, drained curd from the next morning's milking, along with spores of the blue mould *Penicillium gorgonzola*. Because of differences of temperature and acidity, the two curds did not blend together smoothly, and this left small cracks and fissures along which the blue mould could grow. After being trussed in pine slats and incubated in warm rooms for several weeks, the cheeses were pierced and transferred to cooler, humid maturation rooms.

There are more than eighty producers of gorgonzola. A few still mature their cheeses in mountain caves, but most use a huge underground facility built at Novara.

There are two distinct types of gorgonzola, and confusing them can often lead to disappointment.

Piccante (piquant) gorgonzola is made by the traditional method in large 12-kg wheels, and is firm and slightly chalky in texture. It takes at least three or four months to mature and should be well blued from the centre. Its strong, spicy blue-mould flavour contrasts with its dense texture. Always try to buy gorgonzola from a shop that is cutting from a whole wheel. The best brand to look for here is made by the Mauri company.

Dolce (sweet) gorgonzola is a modern, faster-maturing version developed for those who found the original too strong. Milk for this cheese is collected from the defined region and still carries the 'g' sign of gorgonzola, but the cheese is made from only one vat of milk. It should be soft, luscious and slightly sweet, but it lacks some of the complexity of mature piccante. Sweet gorgonzola also has a shorter shelf life, particularly when pre-cut. When shipped to Australia it tends to lose flavour and is often sold with butterfat leaking from the foil, well past its sweet youth.

Roquefort

No respectable list of benchmark cheeses could fail to mention roquefort, which has been around since at least the time of the Holy Roman Empire and is widely recognised as the king of French blue cheeses. Roquefort is made in the dramatic rocky mountains of the Rouergue region in the Causses, just south-east of the geographical centre of France, using milk from the region's million-strong flock of Lacaune breed ewes. Most of the milk is collected in small *bidons* (churns) rather than tankers to avoid breaking up the delicate fat globules, and only seven companies still make the cheese. The making season runs from December to July. Quality is strictly supervised, and all roquefort is made from raw milk.

Roquefort cheeses must be matured for at least three months in the deep limestone caves of Cambalou, next to the town of Roquefort-sur-Soulzon. The natural air currents in these vaulted caves maintain a damp, cool environment ideal for the growth of *Penicillium roqueforti*. This famous mould was traditionally grown using baked rye bread as a host. Some companies still use this method, introducing the sifted crumbs into the fresh milk.

Roquefort has a scraped foil-wrapped rind, and when mature it has a distinctive aroma and an ivory colour with well-interspersed greeny-blue mould. Crumbly and slightly fatty in texture, it should have a strong yet subtle flavour that is both sweet and slightly sharp, balanced by the blue mould and a lingering saltiness.

Because roquefort is only made for seven months of the year, its maturation is often stalled by low-temperature storage and vacuum packing, which do nothing to improve the cheese. The best advice is to find a reliable retailer and avoid cheeses with too much 'weeping' whey.

Australia banned the importation of roquefort in 1995 because, being made only from raw milk, it did not conform to national food laws. International trade pressure will eventually overturn this ridiculous ruling, and perhaps will be the catalyst for local producers to gain the right to make raw-milk cheeses in Australia.

Stilton

This king of English cheeses is made by just seven dairies situated in the Midland counties of Nottinghamshire, Derbyshire and Leicestershire. Stilton has had a form of legal protection since 1910, when makers formed themselves into an association to regulate the cheese-making process. The origins of stilton probably date back to the Norman invasion of England in 1066, and in shape and flavour it resembles fourme d'Ambert, which is made in the Auvergne in France. Stilton was not widely recognised in England until the 1790s, when the village of Stilton became an important coach terminus on the newly built Great North Road. Travellers stopping there soon came to appreciate the unique character of the blue-vein cheese being sold at the local taverns, and demand quickly outstripped the seasonal farm supply.

Stilton is made in 8-kg cylinders, and its quality varies according to its age and the size of the factory. Stilton sold in Australia is mostly shipped young from the larger producers, waxed or vacuum-packed (even frozen), making it easier for those who know no better to keep the cheese for long periods. The methods of production in these large concerns are often rushed, and packaging without air alters the essential flavour and character that make this cheese so special. Good, mature stilton should have a natural crusty rind, be well marbled with blue veins stretching from the centre of the cheese to the outer rind, and have a soft melt-in-the-mouth smoothness that leaves a lingering, spicy, syrupy flavour. The best-tasting cheeses are those from smaller dairies such as Cropwell Bishop or Colston Basset.

Semi-hard

English farmhouse cheddar

There is no legal protection of the name 'cheddar', which is indiscriminately applied to thousands of tonnes of undistinguished industrial cheese made all over the world. The origin of real cheddar, however, is indisputably the fertile countryside of Devon, Dorset and Somerset in south-west England, and the traditional cheddaring method probably dates back to Roman times. The cheese only drew its name from the Somerset village of Cheddar by association with the caves and gorge there, which have attracted tourists for centuries. In fact, no cheese of note is made in Cheddar and possibly never has been, but the tag was applied to the cheeses from the surrounding region.

The unique English farmhouse cheddar almost became extinct during the twentieth century as a result of two world wars and disastrous government controls. In recent times, however, real cheddars have enjoyed a renaissance in demand thanks to the valiant efforts of committed cheese lovers, notably the cheese writer Patrick Rance and Randolph Hodgson of Neal's Yard Dairy in London. Even so, there are only six cheese-makers who still make traditional cloth-bound cheddar, and only three who are true to the tradition of using raw milk. The problem now is that there is not enough traditional cheddar to go around, and cheeses are sometimes sold too young, before their flavour has had a chance to develop.

Some of the most important qualities that make English farmhouse cheddar different are the milk quality, careful methods of hand production, classic 25-kg size, calico and lard binding and maturation temperature. While every cheese made on the farm is by definition different, the traditional methods produce exceptional cheeses – firm, open yet moist in texture, with an ageing, earthy aroma that just bursts with richness, and a kaleidoscope of evocative flavours.

The best cheddars available in Australia are mature cheeses of eighteen months or more made by Quickes Farm (the only traditional maker left in Devon) and Chewton (Somerset).

Hard

Parmigiano reggiano

Parmigiano reggiano is recognised as one of the finest cheeses made in the world and its quality is very dependable. It is a hard-cooked cheese made to exacting standards, which were first set down by the Consorzio del Formaggio Parmigiano Reggiano in 1934. Production is based in five authorised provinces. One of the most extraordinary features of this cheese is that a large volume is made by more than 500 small producers, with the average dairy making eight wheels a day.

The methods of manufacture and maturation are strictly regulated. Cheese can only be made using fresh, unpasteurised, partially skimmed milk from cows who have been fed freshly cut grass in summer or hay in winter. All milk has to be 'poured' – not pumped – into the vats, and the curds must be cooked in copper-lined kettles before draining into large hoops overnight. The young rounds weigh from 30 to 40 kg, and their outer rim is stencilled with the words 'Parmigiano Reggiano' in tiny dots to guarantee authenticity. The rounds are then floated in a brine bath for up to three weeks to seal the rind.

Maturation takes at least fourteen months. Often cheeses from the smaller dairies are matured in huge centrally controlled warehouses or *cascina*, each batch being classified according to maker and season.

An oval space is left on each cheese to identify the manufacturer and receive the grader's stamp of approval. There are five different grades sold. All are acceptable, but price is usually a reflection of quality. The flavour should be sweet and delicate, slightly nutty, but never strong. Cheeses aged for two years are called *vecchio*; those aged for three years are called *stravecchio*. The premium cheese is made in autumn with late-lactation milk. A well-aged cheese will always have tiny sweet crystals. Parmigiano reggiano is best bought broken from a whole wheel; pre-cut wedges do not have the same texture and aroma.

Grana padano

Grana means 'grainy', and this type of cheese has been made in the Po valley of northern Italy since Roman times. The name was established by regulation in 1954 to prevent confusion with parmesan, which can be made anywhere. Often considered the poor relation to parmigiano reggiano, grana padano is made from milk collected from twenty-seven provinces. All cheese maturation is controlled and graded, but production quality is far less dependable than for parmigiano reggiano. There are some very good grana padano cheeses, but in Australia it is common to find young, low-grade cheeses being sold on price rather than quality. Avoid cheeses that are semi-soft, have eyeholes, or are discoloured, dry or cracked.

It is important to differentiate between parmesan, parmigiano and grana. Only cheese made by traditional methods can be called parmigiano reggiano or grana padano. The name 'parmesan' is widely misused to represent these great cheeses.

Gruyère

This famous cooked mountain cheese is a close cousin of emmental and is often associated with Switzerland, but the name is best regarded as a technical term applied to the cheese-making method and shape, which have survived for centuries in the European Alps. Gruyère is named after the pine forests that lie just below the snow line. In the days of the Holy Roman Empire, these forests were managed by a special corps of *officiers gruyers*. Wood from the forests was bartered for mountain cheeses, which in turn were cooked in large copper vats, using the wood as fuel.

Cows mainly grazed the high alpine meadows in summer after the snows had melted. Herds were small, and their milk was pooled for making into large cheeses that would keep well until the end of the season. Gruyère is a potent example of what can be achieved by good co-operative milk under close control. By law, it must still be made from raw milk, and the traditional method produces large, flat, crusty wheels of 35 kg or more. Importation into Australia is allowed because the cooking process is regarded as equivalent to pasteurisation.

Gruyère is made in both France and Switzerland. French comté gruyère is made by more than 300 small village dairies (*fruitières*), then matured in the region by affineurs for nine months or more. Surprisingly, there is far more comté gruyère than Swiss gruyère. The making of comté gruyère is strictly regulated. Each cheese is labelled with the maker's name and the month of manufacture.

The best cheeses are still made with the milk collected during the summer, when cows are grazed on the high alpine pastures. The best comté gruyère to look for in Australia has a green cowbell stamped on the rind.

In Switzerland cheese is made and and marketed on a regional co-operative basis, strictly controlled by a national council, and the quality is always dependable. Gruyère comes from the canton of Fribourg and is matured for at least six months before sale. A well-aged gruyère is wonderfully complex – sweet, buttery, nutty and full of alpine flavours. The Swiss gruyères are slightly less salty and full-flavoured than the French equivalents.

Be warned: gruyère is increasingly being sold in oblong plastic-wrapped blocks, which are easy to ship and store in bulk. These are usually exported young, and lack the unique depth of a piece cut from the wheel. Always buy from the wheel if you want cheese worth remembering.

Naming the Classic Cheeses

For many centuries the cheeses of Europe have been recognised by names relating to a cheese type, region and technique of production. In the postwar period the naming of these cheeses in Italy and France has increasingly been subject to a stringent system of accreditation.

Denominazione di Origine Controllata (DOC)

The Denominazione di Origine Controllata (DOC) system was developed by the Italian Ministry of Agriculture and Forest Regulation in 1954 to protect the trade names of Italian cheeses and prevent copies from being passed off as the real thing. DOC status is not a specific mark of quality but a guarantee of origin. To qualify, cheeses must be made exclusively from milk produced in a particular region according to specified methods. The logo, which varies according to the cheese, is either punched into the rind or marked on the wrapping.

A review of names is conducted every five years. At last count there were twenty-six DOC cheese types, but it is anticipated there will eventually be more than thirty.

The DOC cheeses most familiar in Australia are:

Washed-rind	*Taleggio*
Blue	*Gorgonzola*
Semi-hard	*Asiago*
	Fontina
	Montasio
	Provolone
Hard	*Grana padano*
	Parmigiano reggiano
	Pecorino romano

Some of the common DOC logos are:

Appellation d'Origine Contrôlée (AOC)

The regional names of certain traditional French wines have been protected by the Appellation d'Origine Contrôlée (AOC) system since 1919. Since then the system has been greatly expanded. The first cheese included was roquefort (in 1955) and the use of names is now regulated by a branch of the French Ministry of Agriculture.

Before they are entitled to use the AOC symbol, cheeses must meet a strict set of criteria relating to the breed of animal, region of production, feed quality, making season, methods of production and maturation. Like the Italian DOC, the AOC symbol is a guarantee of origin but not of quality, which may vary between different producers. Many of the traditional AOC cheeses are made with raw milk, others with pasteurised milk. There are thirty-four cheeses registered at present, and more are expected to apply for classification in coming years. Production of AOC cheese is becoming important to the French economy and has gradually increased, with annual production reaching more than 160,000 tonnes in the mid-1990s.

AOC cheeses available in Australia:

Fresh	*Chabichou du Poitou*
	Pouligny-saint-pierre
	Sainte-maure de Touraine
White-rind	*Chaource*
Washed-rind	*Livarot*
	Munster
	Pont l'évêque
	Saint-nectaire
Blue	*Bleu d'Auvergne*
	Fourme d'Ambert
Semi-hard	*Cantal*
Hard	*Beaufort*
	Comté
	Ossau-iraty

AOC cheeses are identified by a single logo:

Naming Australian Cheeses

The great cheeses of Europe generally draw their names from the regions in which they have been made. In its short history, the Australian cheese industry has not produced the same intimate association between specialist cheeses and their regions of origin. Instead, Australian producers have tended to copy the names and styles of traditional European cheeses.

The practice of using European names is unlikely to be allowed to continue indefinitely. There are moves to prevent overseas producers from using European regional cheese names. The number of traditional cheeses for which European producers are now claiming international naming rights grows every year. Similar restrictions already apply to the naming of many wines.

Some Australian producers regard this trend as a threat, but it is better seen as a challenge, an opportunity to develop a new image for Australian specialist cheeses and to name them accordingly. Copying is hardly innovative, often misleading, and masks the distinctive qualities of local specialist cheeses. Using European names invites people to judge the cheese against the 'true' cheese, but a copy can rarely claim to be better than the original.

If Australian cheese producers are determined to replicate a European cheese, they should at least stay within the parameters of the cheese's manufacture. A brie, for example, is not just any size or shape of white-mould cheese, pecorino is not made from cow's milk, and real mozzarella is not a plastic-wrapped ball with a texture like rubber and a shelf life to match.

It is important for the future of Australian specialist cheese that international consumers learn to recognise these cheeses in their own right. For this reason, it is highly desirable that more cheese-makers identify their cheeses by unique, creative names rather than cashing in on European names that may well be banned in the future.

Kervella Affine

Australian Benchmarks

Australia provides a wide range of environments for dairy farming, and each region offers its own distinctive combination of soils, climate and pasture types, which lend themselves to producing particular kinds of cheeses. Understanding the characteristics of these regions and the cheeses each makes best is an important part of learning to appreciate the unique qualities and potential of Australia's specialist cheeses.

South Australia

South Australia produces some of the finest wines in Australia, but it is also Australia's driest State. Hot, dry summers and mild winters are good for growing grapes, but only small areas are suitable for dairy farming. As a consequence dairying has been restricted to the mild southern coastal fringe, the only part of the State that receives enough reliable rainfall to support green pasture growth and milk production. Milk quality and output have become more consistent with the development of irrigation and the availability of supplementary feed. South Australia first exported cheese in the 1840s, and the influence of the colony's strong German community has been evident in the making of cheese, wine and other foodstuffs since the nineteenth century. Today the State produces 5 per cent of Australian cow's milk output, and is home to some distinctive but hard-to-find specialist cheeses.

Finniss

In 1986 Derek Fenton sold his Adelaide restaurant and moved to a bare hilltop overlooking Finniss near Strathalbyn to pursue his dream of living in harmony with the environment. As part of this self-sufficient lifestyle the family bought a pair of cows and began making butter. Then, during the early summer when there was an excess of milk, Derek decided to teach himself how to make cheese.

Today he has perfected an original regional cheese that is made in small batches with the organic whole milk of just one Jersey cow. The small semi-hard rounds weigh just over a kilo, and each is carefully pressed, 'baptised' with a light coating of local beeswax and given an individual name. They are then matured for several months in a maturing cave lined with field-stone and insulated with local seaweed. Here the cheeses develop a variegated rind, deep yellow colour and rich buttery texture with a thick condensed-milk flavour.

Kangaroo Island Cheese

The view of Kangaroo Island from the sea has changed little in the 180 years since sealers first began to farm this exposed, windy island off the South Australian coast. Thanks to its isolation from the mainland, Kangaroo Island has an abundance of unique flora and protected fauna.

Mos and Liz Howard are third-generation farmers on the island, and are proud owners of its only dairy herd. The seaside climate is moderate enough to produce a good supply of milk all year, and the pastures, rich in many varieties of unusual herbage, are kept green with regular irrigation. All the milk produced on the farm is used by the small dairy, which makes surface-ripened white-rind cheeses as well as a distinctive double cream. The operation is very much a family affair, with several generations involved. Mos is committed to producing 'a traditional cheese with some real character' and is always seeking ways and ideas to make an even better cheese.

The small but practical dairy has special maturation rooms built to grow the white mould on the outside of the cheese. Open the door to these dark rooms and you can immediately tell how ripe the cheeses are. When they are ready to pack, the room will be full of the characteristic aroma of fermented apples.

The cheeses are then wrapped in silver foil with a smiling cow logo. The white-rind cheeses have a chalky and slightly bitter flavour when young, but as they mature over a month or more the centre gradually breaks down to a smooth soft, oozing texture and sticky, slightly fudge-like flavour. They are not easy cheeses to look after, but they will reward a little patience.

Woodside Cheesewrights

Situated in the picturesque green hills north of Adelaide is the village of Woodside, site of this small artisan dairy. In 1994 Paula Jenkins, a winemaker, and her friend Simon Burr decided to diversify into cheese-making after spending almost a year in Europe studying many small farmhouse operations. On their return they converted a disused Farmers' Union factory in the village and named it Woodside Cheesewrights. Their objective was 'to prove quality does matter and you can make a business work by specialising in flavour rather than volume'. Since then the dairy has established a notable reputation for excellent cheese, winning a number of prestigious national awards with its range, which includes both cow's and goat's milk cheeses.

The Jersey cow's milk used for the white-rind cheese comes exclusively from the nearby farm run by Molly and Syd Lewis. Jerseys produce the richest cow's milk of all, with a golden colour and large fat globules. Paula has found the milk ideal for the soft double-cream surface-ripened cheese she calls Charleston. The cheese, which is made in several sizes, has a chalky centre that gradually softens as it matures over three to four weeks. Ripening is encouraged by the growth of a distinctive lightly mottled outer coat containing a combination of natural cultures. When mature the rind looks and smells very different from the pure white velvet coverings found in more industrial cheese. It plays a vital role in ripening the rich golden curds to a deep, distinctive flavour and a bulging, creamy softness as the cheese matures.

Woodside Cheesewrights are also one of the few producers in Australia now making traditional cloth-wrapped cheddar. They use Friesian milk from two local farms, standardised to avoid too much fat tainting the cheeses as they mature. Production volume is small, only two 25-kg bandaged wheels per day, and each wheel is pressed on a heavy, old upright press that was found in a shed in Glastonbury, England, and carefully restored. The wheels are encouraged to develop a dusty, grey surface mould, which helps to give the cheese's rich flavour a slightly earthy tang when it is aged for a year or more.

The dairy also makes a range of goat's milk cheeses from organic goat's milk collected from four farms, all of which are certified disease-free. All soft cheeses are made using a gentle 24-hour method to acidify the milk with minimum amounts of rennet, and the set curds are gently ladled from the small vats by hand. This monotonous, slow process ensures that moisture and flavour are retained in the delicate curds. The Woodside goat's cheeses include a light, fluffy, fresh curd, a seasonal white-rind cheese called Capricorn, and a mature charcoal-covered cheese known as Edith's cheese, which was developed from a French farmhouse recipe in Bourg en Bresse and has won many awards.

Tasmania

One of the most pleasurable memories from the autumns of my childhood is that of eating a fresh windfall apple cut into quarters with a small piece of good farm cheddar perched on top. This perfect combination, with the sweet yet acid flavour of the apple balancing the complex,

slightly salty tang of the cheddar, was engraved on my tastebuds forever. Growing apples and making cow's milk cheese require similar climatic conditions, so it is no coincidence that Tasmania, long recognised as Australia's premier apple-growing region, has now gained a reputation for its exceptional specialist cheeses.

Tasmania is well known for its clean air, rich soils, cool temperate climate, year-round green paddocks and charming, gentle countryside. This island State is home to only 2.6 per cent of Australia's population, but produces more than 5 per cent of the national output of cow's milk. Milk production exceeds local requirements, and producers are cut off from the liquid milk market in the mainland cities. These circumstances have encouraged the development of a Tasmanian cheese industry based on 'exports' to the mainland.

Dairy farming is concentrated on the island's wet northern coast, and extends north-west to King Island in Bass Strait. Northern Tasmania is a region of green, undulating hills and tall, unkempt hawthorn hedges, a haunting reminder of the early European settlers' hopes of re-creating an English landscape in the antipodes. Conditions are ideal for dairy farming, with remarkably clean air, rich volcanic and peat soils and good, dependable rainfall evenly spread throughout the year.

Two of Australia's largest and best-known cheese-makers, Lactos and King Island, are based in north-western Tasmania, along with a number of small producers, including Lacrum and Ashgrove Farm. The north-east is home to Heidi and Pyengana, two of Tasmania's most significant small specialist cheese producers.

North-eastern Tasmania

Heidi Farmhouse Cheese

Heidi Farm dairy was established by Frank Marchand in 1984. It overlooks the lush green meadows beneath Rolley's Hill near the village of Exton, and makes some of the most respected hard-cooked cheeses available in Australia, mainly using milk from the farm's herd of 300 Friesian cows. The best-known is Heidi gruyère, which has won many awards. This is one of Australia's largest cheeses, weighing in at 25 to 30kg (eclipsed only by the emmental at more than 35kg). It takes a lot of milk to produce just one gruyère, about 350 litres per 30-kg cheese.

After hooping and pressing, these huge round wheels are lifted to and from the brining tank with a hydraulic block, then slowly matured on old seasoned hardwood shelving in a warm, humid maturation room. Visitors entering the room are warned to brace themselves for the smell of ammonia, which is strong enough to check the breath and sting the eyes. The gruyère wheels are regularly hand-turned with the aid of a special wooden wedge and rubbed with a brine solution to encourage a thick orange-brown rind to form.

The gruyère is deliberately made with a dense texture, and has fewer holes than the sweeter European types. It is generally matured for seven to eight months, although some wheels are kept for sixteen months or longer. This cheese just keeps getting better with age, but it is much in demand and the longer-matured cheeses can be hard to find. Every batch is graded for quality by removing a plug from the cheese with a special corer. When the small fissure cracks begin to calcify, it is a sign the cheese has developed a sweet, nutty flavour and a moist, elastic texture and is ready to be sold. Look for cheeses with tiny, sweet teardrops in the small eyes. These are known as 'angel's tears', and are a sign of perfect cheese maturation.

The dairy, now owned by Lactos, works closely with the seasons. It makes about forty tonnes of gruyère a year, usually over a nine-month period from late winter until autumn. Cheese is not made here in winter, because the milk is considered too poor and conditions too cold. Early summer, when the Tasmanian pasture is green and covered with wildflowers, is the time when the best cheeses are made.

Other cheeses made only in certain seasons include an excellent raclette, large farm emmental, Exton farm barrel and a washed-rind style based on reblochon.

Pyengana Cheese

Pyengana cheese is made in far north-eastern Tasmania using an original method that has been passed down from generation to generation. Apart from having to pasteurise the milk, farmer and cheese-maker Jon Healey still follows the method established by his great-grandfather at the turn of the century. This tradition helps to establish Pyengana as one of Australia's oldest specialist cheeses. The name 'Pyengana' is an Aboriginal term meaning 'meeting place of rivers'.

Fresh milk is selected from the farm's herd of 180 Friesians, which graze in the lush valley of the George River. Cows are milked throughout the year. The herd is split into winter and summer milkers, enabling Jon to produce fresh bottled milk to sell to nearby towns.

The milk is never standardised, so it varies according to the season. 'Nothing added, nothing taken away' is Pyengana's motto.

Cheese is also made throughout the year, but the peak period is during spring and autumn, when the volume of milk and complex balance of flavours are at their best. The cheese is all made in a small 1400-litre vat heated by a wood-fired boiler. After adding starter and traditional calf rennet, Jon uses a special technique of stirring the cut curd gently in the warm whey to ensure an even acid development and fine, crumbly texture. After draining and hand-tearing, the salted curds are hooped in cloth bags and the larger cheeses are pressed overnight using a nineteenth-century mechanical bed press. They are then transferred to the humid maturing room behind the shop, which has a framed window for customers to look through.

The cheeses are made in five sizes – barrels ranging from 1.2 kilos to 7 kilos, and 18.5 kilo wheels. Jon sells the smaller cheeses at one or two months of age, when they are still moist in texture and have a mild, milky flavour. The larger cheeses take longer to mature, particularly the big wheels, which often do not develop full flavour until a year or more. The result is usually an open-textured cheese with an aroma reminiscent of honey and summer grass and a well-developed, rounded flavour.

North-western Tasmania

Lactos

Lactos, based in Burnie, is now part of the French-owned Bongrain group, one of Europe's largest producers of specialist cheese. The company was originally founded in 1955 by Czech-born Milan Vynalek, a pioneer who challenged local traditions by introducing new cheeses such as St Claire, a type of gouda, and Mersey Valley, a mixed club cheese, at a time when most Australian producers confined themselves to making tasty cheddar. Bongrain took over the operation in 1981, drawn to the area by its natural environmental advantages and high-quality local milk.

The Lactos facilities for making specialist cheese are among the most advanced in Australia, and have benefited from the transfer of sophisticated European technology. Under its Domaine Heritage brand, Lactos has expanded its range of consistent quality cheeses, including blue-mould and white-rind types. These are widely available in Australian stores and supermarkets, and have also been successfully exported to Asia, with the stabilised long-life white-rind cheeses finding a niche market in Japan. It is harder to find the company's more specialised cheeses, particularly Red Square and White Diamond. Both are unusual square cheeses that ripen over time from the outer rind towards the centre.

King Island Dairy

Guarding the western entrance to Bass Strait, King Island is exposed to the Roaring Forties and surrounded by deep ocean waters. The island was originally famous for the number of tragic shipwrecks that occurred along its isolated coast, and the straw mattresses that washed up from some of the wrecks are said to have been responsible

Gippsland Blue

for introducing the unusual and varied grasses on which the island's cattle now graze, giving their milk its distinctive flavour.

The King Island Dairy was founded in 1902 as a co-operative, but it was not until 1986 that Bill and Robin Kirk, who had started to develop specialist cheese on the mainland at Interlandi near Warragul some years before, recognised the unique opportunities that the island's milk offered for making specialist cheeses. Although the Kirk family moved on, the influence of their original work assured the initial success of the King Island brand of cheese, which today is produced in large quantities and is widely available in stores and supermarkets throughout the country.

The milk of King Island is collected daily from a number of dairy farms scattered cross the island. The dairy has named most of its cheeses after local places and nautical features such as Lighthouse Blue, Surprise Bay Cheddar and Bass Strait Blue. The unique flavours of King Island milk are most obvious in the double cream, which changes in thickness over the season but always has a luscious, sweet roundness from the rich milk, with overtones of seaside pastures.

Victoria

Gippsland

In 1840, after traversing the Snowy Mountains, the Polish-born explorer and scientist Paul Edmund de Strzelecki travelled south to eastern Victoria, which he called 'Gippsland' in honour of George Gipps, the governor of New South Wales. He encountered an almost impenetrable terrain of extensive coastal swamps backing on to steep ranges clothed with forbidding forests of mountain ash. The going was so rough that Strzelecki was forced to abandon many of his geological specimens and set his horses loose.

This first encounter set the pattern of Gippsland's history for the next sixty years. While most of Victoria grew and prospered, Gippsland was left behind. Settlers barely eked out a living, sometimes making temporary homes in the stumps of huge trees. They ringbarked and burnt the forests, only to discover that the soils were thin and leached. Gradually the forests and swamps gave way to farmland, but it was not until the 1920s, when the government set out to encourage soldier settlers to take up dairying, that the region's potential for dairy farming began to be realised.

Today there is little left of Gippsland's noble forests, and its well-watered hills and valleys are home to large, efficient dairy factories as well as to a significant number of specialist cheese-makers. The temperate climate and usually reliable rainfall provide excellent conditions for pasture growth. Winters are cold and wet, but in spring the bright yellow wattles and flowering blackwoods herald the start of the growing season, when the pastures are thick and lush.

The finest cheeses are made during this spring and early summer flush. In spite of its unpromising start, Gippsland is now one of Australia's prime dairy regions, producing almost 20 per cent of the country's cow's milk.

Faudel Goat's Milk Cheese

The biggest challenge for south Gippsland goat farmers is the adverse effect of the short, cold, wet winter days on these lean, sensitive animals. Rod Faudell of Faudel Dairy near Korumburra has become the first goat farmer in Gippsland to produce a consistent milk supply all year round. His mixed herd has been bred over fifteen years specifically to cope with the climate, and produces a rich milk high in solids, ideal for cheese production. Rod studied how temperate European countries achieved consistently good-quality milk, and decided to house his goats in sheds through winter as protection from the elements, giving them access to the paddocks during summer. Goats are social animals, and they seldom wander far in the paddocks except on warm days, preferring the company and warmth inside. They are fed a specially controlled diet balanced with minerals and sweet-smelling wilted silage cut from Rod's farm paddocks.

With help from his family, Rod makes the cheese by hand every day in a tiny dairy close to the milking shed. The milk is batch pasteurised at 63°C for thirty minutes because Rod believes that 'the lower the temperature the softer and fluffier the cheese'. The curds are drained naturally, not minced as in many other operations, for making into a fresh creamy fromage de chèvre or delicate fromage frais. During the summer flush Rod makes a hard cheese called South Gippsland Chèvre, which is matured in a black wax for three months before sale.

Jindi Cheese

Jindi Cheese is hidden away along the evocatively named Old Telegraph Road, a winding, unmade bush track near Neerim South. This farmhouse operation uses the rich milk from the Jersey herd of farmer George Ronalds, and was originally established in 1985 with help from Laurie Jensen of Tarago River (see next entry). The dairy specialises in surface-ripened white-rind cheeses, including triple cream. The 3-kg Jindi double brie has won a number of prestigious prizes.

Tarago River Cheese Company

The Tarago River Cheese Company is set high on a hill overlooking the gleaming Tarago dam and distant blue hills near the town of Neerim South in north-west Gippsland. Initially established in 1983 by Laurie Jensen, Richard Thomas and farmer Rob Johnson, this farm was responsible for introducing farmhouse cheese-making to Australia. Today the operation is on a much grander scale, although most of the milk is still sourced from the farm's 400 Friesian cows.

Originally adapted from a sweet gorgonzola recipe, Gippsland Blue has developed a unique regional identity of its own. Today it is an Australian benchmark, soft and creamy with a distinct mould flavour and grey natural rind. The cheeses are matured in underground cellars, a rare facility in specialist cheese-making anywhere, and unique in Australia. It is fascinating to enter this dimly lit area, with its unforgettable smell of ammonia, and feel the still dampness among the rows of entombed cheeses waiting for their moment of release.

Other blue cheeses are matured in large, humid rooms upstairs. Because these are all made with waxed or scraped rinds, they require different humidity and temperature conditions. Some use rich Jersey cream from other local farms. Next door is a facility for making white-rind and fresh cheese varieties, kept strictly separate from the blue cheese rooms to avoid contamination by blue-mould spores. Here 'double' brie and camembert styles are made from local farm Jersey milk, and fresh, sweet goat's cheese with milk collected from nearby Wild Dog Valley.

From the tearoom at Tarago River, looking out through the picture windows across the blue reservoir to the distant hills, you can often see trucks piled high with logs from the Gippsland forests. A hundred and fifty years on, the clearing continues.

Top Paddock Dairy
The Top Paddock Dairy perches on the side of a picture-book green hill just across the road from Rod Faudell's farm. The farm has a herd of red cows bred specially for cheese-making from a mixture of Jerseys, Illawarra Shorthorns and Swedish Reds. These cows' milk is especially good for semi-hard traditional cheeses because it has smaller fat globules than the more common Friesian milk.

The cows are milked throughout the year and rotated through the farm paddocks to ensure a well-balanced diet of fresh green pasture. They receive supplementary crushed barley at milking time, and in a dry summer they are occasionally fed silage or turnip tops. All the milk used for cheese-making comes from a combination of evening and morning milk, selected according to the types of cheeses to be made and batch pasteurised by gentle heating to 62°C for thirty minutes. Fred Leppin, who established the dairy in 1990, believes this slow method of pasteurisation is preferable because 'it

preserves more of the essential character and individual farm flavour to the milk, which is important for our cheese'. This is what farmhouse cheeses are all about.

The dairy was originally designed to make only cloth-bound cheeses, but since then Top Paddock has gained something of a name for innovation, and the range has diversified to include semi-hard washed-curd, washed-rind, fresh and blue cheeses. The best-known are Top Paddock Washed Rind and a fresh cow's milk cheese called Whitelaw.

The Western District

When Major Thomas Mitchell first surveyed the open grasslands west of Port Phillip in 1836, he dubbed the region 'Australia Felix', the 'fortunate south land'. This is Victoria's Western District, where wide plains with an endless horizon are broken by spectacular deep lakes and strangely shaped hills, including some of Australia's youngest volcanoes.

The defining feature of the Western District is a recent basalt flow stretching from the west of Port Phillip Bay to Mount Gambier in South Australia. When Europeans first saw it, much of this plain was covered with lush native grasses, ideal for grazing sheep and cattle. Among the first white settlers were the Henty family, who landed near Portland from Tasmania in 1834 and proudly dispatched Victoria's first cheese and butter exports back to Launceston two years later.

Rainfall slowly decreases as you move inland, and the open grasslands and dry conditions of the interior are best suited to grazing sheep. Sections of the Princes Highway between Geelong and Warrnambool follow the dividing line, with cow country to the south and sheep country to the north. Today the Western District produces 18 per cent of Australia's cow's milk and has some of the largest and most efficient cheese factories in the country, as well as a number of small specialist cheese-makers using a variety of milk types.

Meredith Dairy

On the eastern edge of the Western District is the village of Meredith and the Cameron family farm. Originally opened up as dairy farms for soldier settlers after the First World War, Meredith does not enjoy the rich volcanic soils found further to the west, and its open grasslands were found to be ideal for extensive sheep farming.

The Meredith Dairy is one of Australia's leading producers of ewe's milk. Sandy Cameron, who trained as a vet, has crossed East Frieslands with his parents' wool-producing sheep to create a prime flock of milking ewes. Ewes' lactation period is only three months, but Sandy has managed to secure a consistent milk supply by careful husbandry and the use of irrigation during summer.

The cheeses made here were originally developed with help from partner Richard Thomas and are unique in flavour and technique. Sandy's wife Julie makes all the cheeses, keeping a keen eye on their quality and noting how every cheese develops. All milk comes from the farm, so these are true farmhouse cheeses, and their character changes with the seasons despite the year-round supply of milk.

Meredith Blue and Woodburne are just two of the range. Meredith Blue is a natural crusty-rinded 1.5-kg cheese matured for six to eight weeks. It is most consistent in autumn and late winter, when it has a semi-firm texture and well-distributed blue veining. From early spring,

as the grasses grow and animals lactate, it starts to hold more moisture; the flavour then becomes milder and the texture very soft, almost creamy. Woodburne, named after a local village, is a surface-ripened white-rind cheese. In spring it has a deliciously soft and silky texture and a luscious, creamy centre. With summer, as the sheep shift to irrigated pasture, the cheese becomes firmer with a more fudgy texture and mild, creamy flavour. There is no single 'right' time for either of these cheeses. Their charm lies in the fact that their seasonal changes appeal to different tastes, which is part of what makes them so interesting.

Meredith is well known for a pure ewe's milk yoghurt and a delicious, delicate fromage frais. The fresh cheeses are not vacuum-packed, and are best eaten within a few days to enjoy them at their sweetest, lemony best.

The farm is also home to more than 300 dairy goats, whose milk is collected daily for cheese-making. This part of the business has grown dramatically in recent years. Julie makes a natural, sweet, fresh goat's curd cheese, a marinated feta infused in oil, garlic and fresh herbs, and a small white-rind egg-cup-sized cheese known as Caprini.

Mt Emu Creek Dairy

From the highlands near Ballarat, Mt Emu Creek winds down into the Western District proper towards Camperdown, where the flat grasslands are grazed by flocks of Romney sheep. Each day a small tanker visits several of the local farms to collect ewe's milk for the owner of Mt Emu Creek Dairy, Robert Manifold, whose forebears built the historic Purrumbete homestead and helped to pioneer the development of dairying in this part of the Western District.

The Romneys were originally bred for their wool, but are now being crossed with East Frieslands to increase milk yields. The milking is done with a unique portable milking machine so that the ewes do not have to trek to a central dairy. According to Robert, this saves their feet. The cheese is then made at a Camperdown dairy, with the busy period running from September to December. All the cheese here is made from pure ewe's milk, with no cow's milk solids to boost the yield.

Ewe's milk whey ricotta, brined feta and marinated feta are some of the more traditional types made. Under the guidance of cheesemaker John Staaks, Mt Emu Creek also produces a range of natural-rind mature cheeses. The best-known of these is Romney Mature, a washed-curd cheese made to a Spanish monk's recipe in small 1.5-kg rounds and matured for six months. Inside the mouldy cloth exterior is a delicious cheese with the characteristic translucent ivory colour of ewe's milk and a nutty, flaky texture with a sweet, lingering flavour.

There is also a hard-cooked cheese named Mt Elephant after the foreboding black-humped hill that is visible for miles across the grasslands of the district.

Purrumbete Buffalo Cheese

Roger Haldane is a man with a vision, and it seems apt that his property, Purrumbete, was the first to introduce Shorthorn dairy cattle to Victoria in the 1840s. Based just outside Camperdown, the property is graced by a magnificent restored bluestone house overlooking the fresh, deep waters of Lake Purrumbete. Beneath the house is the cave where the pioneering Manifold brothers sheltered after forging an overland path across the aptly named 'stony rises' to the east. The meadows that surround the homestead were once criss-crossed by more than 160 kilometres of specially commissioned dry-stone walls to keep out the rabbits. Many of these walls remain as a testament to the vast wealth generated by the region, giving the landscape a sense of long, continuous occupation more commonly associated with ancient parts of Ireland or northern England.

Purrumbete is now home to Australia's first milking buffalo herd. These huge animals are extraordinary to meet for the first time, with their coarse, hairy coats, piercing black prehistoric eyes and inquisitive, searching nostrils. They move with a wonderful measured pace, suggesting an unhurried, calm character. Buffalo are suspicious of strangers, but can be also friendly and obedient. They will come across a paddock to Roger's whistle and roll over for a tummy-stroke.

Each animal yields an average of just eight litres of sweet, creamy milk per day for eleven months of the year. The volume may be low, but the milk is rich in solids and calcium, and it takes only 4.5 litres to make a kilogram of cheese.

Buffalo like warm conditions and are sensitive to the cold. Earlier attempts to develop milking buffalo in Gippsland failed because the buffalo could not adapt to the cold winters. The climate in the west is less chilly, and Roger has provided huge open sheds to keep the herd warm during winter. The richest milk is produced during the warmer months, when a variety of summer-flowering pastures and herbage grow beside the lake and the buffalo are in full lactation.

The fresh milk is transformed into a range of exciting products, of which the fresh mozzarella is the prize. Hand-stretched, pure porcelain in colour and encased in a thin skin, this delicate but firm cheese oozes with delicious, creamy whey. Other products include a sweet semi-hard cheese named Dancing Brolga after the colourful local water birds, and a natural set yoghurt with a thick head, extraordinarily creamy texture and long, perfumed finish.

Timboon Biodynamic Cheese

Timboon Farmhouse Cheese is a registered biodynamic farm, utilising a combination of organic and celestial techniques developed by Steiner in the 1930s. Enter the farm gate by the dairy shop and you can see and feel the difference in pasture immediately. Herman Schultz is committed to farming by natural methods so that the cheese reflects 'the quality of the animals, the grass, the sunshine and the rich mineral soil of the region'. In 1984, tired of seeing his premium milk vanish into the mixing vats at the local co-operative, he decided to develop a specialist camembert, and so became Australia's first true farmhouse producer making white-rind cheese on the farm with milk from the farm. This original cheese is still made by hand according to traditional techniques. Like all traditional white-rind cheeses it requires a little understanding, care and patience to ripen the chalky centre to perfection.

Today Herman's daughter Audrey oversees the operation, which has grown considerably, and the cheeses have become quite widely available around Australia. The range now includes a fresh curd herb torte, a popular marinated feta, a semi-hard natural-rind cheese known as Petite Fleur and a blue/white-mould creamy cheese known as Timbozola.

Western Australia

Western Australia's ancient, hungry soils and varied flora offer unique conditions for dairying. The southern coastal strip from Bunbury to Albany is cow country, accounting for just 4 per cent of Australia's cow's milk production. This was one of the last dairying regions in Australia to be developed. The local market in the settlements around the Swan River remained tiny until the gold rushes of the 1890s, and even then the growth of agriculture and dairying was slow. Clearing the region's forests of giant jarrah and karri trees was a time-consuming and costly task, and the soils suffered from a deficiency of phosphate. It was not until the 1920s that the numbers of dairy cows increased, thanks to new mechanical clearing techniques, the widespread use of fertilisers, better knowledge of pasture management and a range of government initiatives, including the establishment of state-owned dairy farms running Ayrshire cows.

The native wildflowers that bloom in the southern parts of Western Australia in late winter and early spring are part of a vibrant burst of seasonal growth that gives a distinctive character to the region's specialist cheeses. Geographical isolation and strict quarantine controls have protected Western Australia from many of the introduced pests that have overrun the eastern States.

The region has a reliable Mediterranean climate with heavy winter rains and dry summers. During the mild winters pastures are lush and varied, and conditions for animals kept outdoors are better than almost anywhere in Australia, but the change of season brings a dramatic transformation. By early October, the meadows of the south-west are covered with yellow flowers and lush herbage. The spring flowering occurs at least a month earlier than in other States, producing an early flush of high-quality milk. Then, as the inevitable hot, dry summer sets in, the supply of green feed falls away sharply. To keep their herds in good condition, farmers have to time the calving carefully and provide pasture irrigation and supplementary feed.

The seasonal extremes of climate are not the only challenge facing Western Australia's cheese-makers. The State's population is still relatively small, just over 1.75 million, so specialist cheese-makers have been obliged to seek markets interstate and in Asia. Distance, however, remains an obstacle. It is more than 3000 kilometres of hard travelling from Perth to the markets of the eastern States by land or sea, and fresh specialist cheeses produced in the West have to be exceptionally good to command a sufficient premium to cover the cost of air freight.

Kervella Cheese
Since establishing her goat farm in 1985, Gabrielle Kervella has become something of an Australian legend. At its seasonal best, her fromage de chèvre is widely recognised as a benchmark of the best Australia has to offer.

Her carefully planned 200-acre property is tucked away at Gidgegannup in the hills north of Perth, overlooking the beautiful, winding Avon River and surrounding hills. Gabrielle is passionately opposed to the use of sprays and nitrogenous fertilisers on these fragile soils, and runs her farm on a strictly organic basis.

Meet Gabrielle's happy, well-kept goats and it is immediately obvious why their cheese has become so well respected. The flock of 120 is registered disease-free, and each milker has her own name handwritten on her collar. On one of my visits, a goat named Erica was particularly attentive, and followed me around like a charming and inquisitive child.

The hills provide a warm, sheltered environment with pastures that are green in winter and sparse and dry in summer. These are ideal conditions for goats, which are happiest browsing on a varied diet rather than just grazing green pasture. The moderate winters make it unnecessary to construct elaborate sheds, and light corrugated-iron shelters are enough to provide the shade required in summer.

The flock has been carefully bred for the local conditions. Anglo-Nubian goats, which originated in the Middle East and can handle the hot summers, have been bred with Swiss Saanens, which are well known for their long lactation and high-volume milk production.

The goats are kept in small flocks in individual paddocks, where their consumption of grass and other feed is closely controlled. As well as nibbling the tops of the grasses, the goats are given supplementary feeding with organic hay, barley, lupins and minerals. The milk quality is excellent and provides an ideal basis for making good cheese. Gabrielle's breeding program has ensured a year-round supply of milk, but in winter milk production is only half that of spring and summer.

The year's richest cheeses are made in autumn, when the milk volume drops and solid content rises. The more complex, lively cheeses are made after lactation in spring, when the seasonal wildflowers carpet the valley.

Gabrielle and her daughter Maite make fresh goat cheeses in a variety of shapes and sizes, a semi-mature 'affine' cheese with an ash and white-mould coat, and a hooped cutting cheese known as Halo. The ashed pyramids are usually eaten fresh, but if they are left to mature in humid conditions a variety of bluish blooms will appear on the rind, and after a few weeks the cheese will develop a nutty, flaky texture and long, sweet flavour that lingers at the back of the palate.

Margaret River Cheese Company
The Margaret River Cheese Company, which specialises in white-rind cheeses, is situated in the heart of the famous Margaret River wine-growing area and is part of the Fonti Farm group. The fresh milk for this small operation is taken from several surrounding farms, which graze Friesian cows on the region's gentle, undulating meadows.

From May to September these pastures are 'so green it makes the eyes hurt', as one local put it, and this is when the cows give their richest milk. Cheese made at this time of the year has a light marigold colour. Then, as the meadows dry off, the cows are fed a combination of grain and silage and produce milk of a pale ivory colour, much like that of many winter European cheeses. The flavour and character of the cheeses become much more predictable in summer.

The white-rind cheeses are surface-ripened according to a traditional recipe, and it usually takes about forty days of maturation to soften the chalk line in the centre of the cheese. Terry Scott, the production manager, is convinced that the unique character of Margaret River cheese lies in the recipe and skill employed in the making these cheeses and the growth of white moulds in the humid climate of the maturing room. Cheese is made three times a week from a single batch of milk inoculated with *Penicillium candidum*, which is left to grow naturally from the curds rather than being sprayed on the surface later. This method leaves a sparse, thin rind with a slight crust.

Other Regions

If it isn't pasture that draws a cheese-maker to a certain spot, then it's likely to be a winery. Cheese and wine are natural companions, and there are many similarities in their basic making principles. The climatic conditions conducive to growing vines, however, are not ideal for the production of cow's milk. Small boutique cheese-makers who have established themselves in wine-making regions often have to buy milk from other areas to craft into their own regional cheeses.

Hunter Valley Cheese Company
North and west of the city of Newcastle lies the Hunter Valley, Australia's oldest wine region, where the first vineyard was established in 1825 by John Busby. The climate is difficult and often fickle for growing vines, but this drawback is far outweighed by the benefits of having more than four million people within a few hours' drive. The Hunter region is popular with tourists eager to sniff, taste and buy the local wines. The first specialist cheese factory to cater for these visitors was the Hunter Valley Cheese Company, established next to the McGuigan winery by David Brown of the Milawa Cheese Company (see the following entry).

The factory has a small shop and café where visitors are encouraged to taste the handmade cheeses. There is also a novel viewing window into the maturation room. The dairy obtains cow's and goat's milk from neighbouring regions and cheeses from Milawa, and cheese-maker Peter Curtis makes a range of surface-ripened cheeses, including white-mould and washed-rind types, which vary in character according to the quality of milk and the season.

One of the more unusual offerings is the Grapevine Ash cheese, a surface-ripened cow's milk cheese developed from an old French recipe. The fresh curd disc is smothered in powdered black grapevine ash, then inoculated with white-mould cultures. Other cheeses to look for are Branxton Brie and Pokolbin Gold.

Milawa Cheese Company

The Milawa Cheese Company is housed in an old red-brick butter factory just a short distance from the famous Brown Brothers winery in the village of Milawa in north-eastern Victoria. This was the first of the small boutique dairies to open close to a winery and was initially established in 1988 by Richard Thomas and David and Anne Brown, although Richard left several years later.

Milawa cheeses are made from cow's milk collected from the region further north. They were the first company to produce surface-ripened washed-rind cheese in Australia. The airborne moulds and flora present in the maturing rooms of the old factory have been encouraged to develop on the rinds of the young cheeses by regular washing in local well water. This regional combination has resulted in perhaps Australia's wildest and most pungent washed-rind cheese, Milawa Gold (not to be confused with its milder and more delicate cousin, King River Gold).

This cheese is at its best in late autumn, when walnuts ripen in the groves beneath the nearby alpine slopes. It has a powerful smell but a surprisingly mild, slightly fermented fruity flavour, and is worth maturing.

The dairy also makes a range of other cheeses, including some from other milk types. These include a blue cheese and goat's milk cheeses (fresh and ashed), all of which are sold from the dairy shop adjoining the factory.

Yarra Valley Dairy

Just one hour's drive to the east of Melbourne lies the Yarra Valley. Once known as Billanook after the many billabongs found along the rich river flats, the region has a long history of wine-growing, and in recent years has again developed an enviable reputation as a cool-climate wine region.

The Yarra Valley Dairy is on part of an old dairy property once known as Hubertswood, and was established by farmers Mary and Leo Mooney, initially with help from Richard Thomas. The boutique cheese room and café were carefully designed inside the wooden shell of the farm's 100-year-old milking shed. The goat's milk used in cheese-making is collected from the nearby Yarra Glen hills, but cow's milk comes from the farm's own dairy herd of 200 Friesians. To reduce handling and provide cheese as fresh as possible, the milking facility is right next door to the making room. The tasting room café enjoys splendid views across the farm's lush paddocks to the distant blue hills.

The cheese types made vary with the season. The benchmark is the 'Persian Feta', a soft, marinated cow's milk cheese preserved in oil, fresh herbs and local pink garlic. Fresh goat's milk cheeses and clotted cream are made during the warmer months.

CHOOSING

Choosing

The season of the year is very important to the quality and consequently the taste of great cheeses.

Pierre Androuët

One of the great advantages of good cheeses is that you do not need to be a millionaire to enjoy them. The ability to taste is a common birthright of rich and poor alike, and a little good cheese goes a long way in providing pleasure to the senses. We develop 'good taste' through experience and experimentation. We remember foods we have tasted in the past, and these memories are organised and catalogued by various parts of the brain. You will never know what the flavour of a cheese is unless you have tried it, and if you want to repeat the experience you may need to think consciously about it too.

Because specialist cheese-making in Australia is so new, most Australians have only quite recently begun to develop a taste for specialist cheeses and do not necessarily know what to expect, particularly when it comes to some of the more complex types. Some cheese-makers, misreading this as a permanent state of affairs, have opted for reliable, safe, bland styles of cheese. This not only underestimates Australian consumers, who are rapidly developing a more sophisticated palate, but also misses the whole point of specialist cheese as a gastronomic experience.

The pleasure of eating a cheese at its absolute peak is a memorable experience. There are no certainties about specialist cheeses, only predictable tendencies. Taste and texture changes are part of what make these cheeses so fascinating. We all have different palates and perceive cheeses differently, but stopping to think about taste and unravel the complex sensory experiences it involves can help us work out what we like and why we like it.

The Elements of Taste

Taking a Sniff

Flavour begins with smell. Our basic survival instinct makes us automatically – even unconsciously – smell food before we place it in our mouths. With cheese, a quick sniff before tasting gives a very good indication of what to expect and acts as an early warning of any potential problems.

Taste and the Tongue

The first task for the tongue and lips is to tell us the temperature of the food we are eating – another survival instinct – but the tongue's main function is to register taste. There are four important 'zones' in the tongue. It is sensitive to sweetness at the tip, saltiness and then sourness around the sides, and bitterness towards the back.

All the tastes of cheese are registered in these zones to different degrees. The taste of fresh and mild cheeses is a combination of sweetness and acidity, which are detected at the front of the tongue. Maturation produces greater strength and complexity of taste; surface-ripened and hard cheeses bring the whole of the tongue into play.

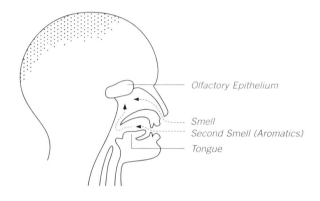

Olfactory Epithelium

Smell
Second Smell (Aromatics)
Tongue

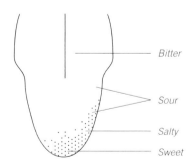

Bitter

Sour

Salty
Sweet

Texture

The mouth and tongue also detect subtle differences in texture, which is generally referred to as 'mouthfeel'. Texture will always tell you something about the character of the cheese. Textures range from soft and succulent through to hard and crumbly.

Some of the words used to describe textures in cheese-speak are clotted, chalky, creamy, crumbly, dry, fatty, flaky, moussey, oily and thin.

The Second Smell

The sense of smell again comes into play when we chew on a piece of cheese. The chewing action releases aromatics that pass up the back of the nasal passage to the specialised olfactory epithelium at the top of the back of the nose, sometimes referred to as the retronasal region. The olfactory nerves then carry the information to the brain. Most of us do not consciously register this sensation as important, but it is one of the things that makes the difference between a good cheese and a great one.

This secondary smell makes the real difference to our perception of the overall structure of a cheese and its length and complexity of flavour. Like a good wine, a good cheese should have a 'long' taste, which comes from the vapours lingering in the back of the nasal passage. Often it is not until a cheese is actually swallowed that the full secondary flavours are released. 'Smelling as you taste' is quite obvious in smelly washed-rind and blue cheeses, which often have a slight ammonia tang, but it is subtly present even in mild, fresh cheese, particularly goat's milk cheese.

Most cheese types can be identified by the aromas found in this secondary smell released after chewing:

- *fresh* – aromatic, lactic, refreshing pasture flavours, particularly in goat's milk cheese
- *white* – rotting brassica, moulds and ammonia
- *washed* – distinct cowyard and yeasty tastes
- *blue* – strong, robust moulds and ammonia
- *semi-hard* – earthy mushrooms and truffles
- *hard* – condensed and lactic

There are many ways to describe the smell and flavour of a cheese, but there is no substitute for tasting it yourself. Here are a few useful cheese descriptions

- *dairy aromas* – buttery, cheesy, condensed-milk, creamy, lactic, processed, rindy, sour, toasted
- *aromatics* – ammonia, animal, artificial, blue, burnt, caramel, cardboard, chemical, cowyard, earthy, eggy, fat, fermented, floral, fresh, fruity, grassy, goaty, hay, herbal, malty, meaty, metallic, mouldy, mushroom, nutty, oily, oxidised, perfumed, plastic, pungent, rancid, smoked, sharp, soapy, spicy, vegemite, watery, waxy, winy, woody, yeasty.

Selecting Cheeses

A good cheesemonger that I can trust is enough.

Pierre Androuët

If you want to buy really good cheese you must first find a good shop to turn your expectations into reality. This might be a local dairy, a wholesaler who also sells direct to the public or a retail shop that stocks a wide range of farmhouse cheeses. Look for a shop with a thoughtful and knowledgeable display, particularly of whole cheeses with natural rinds. A good cheese display should be fresh, colourful and imaginative, making full use of the fascinating range of shapes, colours and sizes in which cheeses are made. The very best shops to find are those that buy in young cheeses and carefully mature them in a purpose-built cellar until they develop their true potential. There is not much point in making wonderful cheese if it fails to get to the customer in perfect condition.

Avoid places that buy cheese in blocks or pre-cut wedges and resell them without any thought for condition or maturation. A large range of refrigerated waxed cheeses or rows of plastic-wrapped rectangles are a sure sign of a selection that is unlikely to provide any real flavour satisfaction.

Once you have found a shop you trust, let your senses and intuition guide you to making your own personal selection of cheese. You should try before you buy, and the retailer should be happy to let you do so. A good cheese shop will have a wide, balanced range of cheese types to choose from. While a large range can be confusing, it can also be exciting to explore. Making a choice on the basis of your own personal judgement is part of what makes buying and eating cheese so enjoyable.

It is important to be flexible and open to suggestions. Don't arrive with a preconceived idea about what brand or type of cheese you want; seasonal variations and maturation conditions may leave you disappointed. Be adventurous: cheeses vary from week to week, and what is good in one season might be scarce and not so good in another. In winter, for example, you can expect few traditional white-rind or fresh cheeses, but a good array of hard and semi-hard types. If the cheese you have set your heart on is not up to scratch, don't compromise; substitute another cheese or do without.

Once you have developed a relationship of trust with the people on the other side of the counter, ask them to recommend a cheese that is at its best. Selling good cheese requires vigilance, experience and enthusiasm. Retailers should know what is good because they will have tasted the cheese, and they may also be able to tell you more about the cheese, such as how and where it is made. The price you pay may be a bit higher, but this reflects the time spent on selection and maturation. This extra service is important, because it is what makes customers come back and buy more.

Never hurry a visit to a good cheese shop; you need time to taste and think. The most important rule is to think carefully about when you intend to eat the cheese and to buy just enough, as close as possible to the day you want to eat it. It can spoil a meal to offer great slabs of cheese that have been bought days before and are well past their prime, or a few miserable slivers that would not grace a mousetrap. Unless you have just the right storage conditions, don't buy more than just enough to last you a week. It requires special care to keep good cheese at home for a long period.

Fresh

Buying fresh cheese means putting your eyes and nose to work. Smell and appearance are the most important guides to assessing quality. These cheeses should have a light, delicate, floral perfume reminiscent of baby's talcum powder, with a light, moist, tender texture. A high moisture content is crucial for the texture and flavour, but also makes them extremely fragile, as the all-important whey can easily evaporate or turn rancid if not stored and handled properly.

Vacuum-packed fresh cheeses never have the same flavour and texture as a true fresh cheese, because the vacuum draws out the precious sweet whey from the curd. Avoid fresh cheeses with a soured, rancid or musty aroma and a dull or tacky surface.

Some of the best fresh cheeses are made during the spring and autumn, when the grass is greenest. Ewe's milk cheeses are the first to appear; when you see spring lamb in butchers' windows, you can be assured that fresh ewe's milk cheeses are appearing in dairies too. Goats are next on the scene with the first batch of good-quality cheese in spring, but they produce their richest cheeses from autumn milk. Cow's milk fresh cheeses are at their best in late spring, but are generally available year-round.

White

Surface-ripened white-rind cheese is generally considered at its best or '*à point*' when it is soft to touch and slightly gooey in texture, with a light, glossy sheen.

With white-rind cheese, it is easier to say what to avoid than what to look for. Bad cheeses can be identified by dry, hard edges and cracked rinds, which are usually caused by poor storage conditions and lack of humidity, a common fault in Australia because of the dry heat. Excessive warmth or lack of air can cause sweating, which produces a cheese with a poor mould cover and an ammoniac smell. These symptoms can also mean that the cheese is at the end of its shelf life. When cheeses are excessively liquid and run out of their rinds, it is a sign of seasonal changes or poor manufacturing technique. Large white cheeses made in autumn often suffer from this problem, which is sometimes referred to as 'slip-coat'. Late spring and autumn are the best making seasons.

Washed

The look of the rind and internal texture are good guides to choosing washed-rind cheeses, but always taste the cheese if possible, as the smell and appearance can be misleading. A washed-rind cheese in good condition should have an evenly coloured rind, a semi-soft to soft centre, and a strong but not ammoniac smell. Avoid cheeses with chalky centres and rinds that are cracked, sticky or slimy. All of these indicate that the cheese has not been matured in an ideal way.

Cheeses made in autumn are considered the most exciting. Their orange-gold coats provide a warm reminder of autumn on cold winter days.

Blue

Check the colour and distribution of the blue veins in the centre of the cheese before buying. An even distribution of mould is a sign of balanced maturation, but try the cheese too.

The most dependable season for making good blue cheese is during the spring and early summer when the grass is still green. These spring cheeses usually ripen from November through to January.

Blue cheeses made from cow's milk during the summer months can be hard and dry in texture with a stronger blue flavour and uncontrolled mould growth. This seasonal change relates not only to milk quality but also to the difficulties of providing adequate maturation facilities in the hot Australian summer, particularly for smaller producers.

Semi-hard

Always look for cuts from whole wheels with a natural rind. Check that the cheese hasn't suffered from poor wrapping and isn't dry or cracked. Remember that the best semi-hard cheeses are made with the richest spring and early summer milk. When buying these cheeses it is worth trying to establish the manufacture date, which is sometimes stamped on the cheese in a code that corresponds to the day of the year it was manufactured.

Hard

All smooth hard-cooked cheeses tend to be slightly waxy in texture and quite sweet and nutty in flavour. With 'eye' cheeses, the guide to a good mature cheese is an evenly balanced distribution of eyes through the cheese. The best cheeses are considered at the perfect peak of maturity when they have tiny teardrops in the eyeholes ('angel's tears').

Granular hard-cooked cheeses should not develop any internal eyes. Most granular cheese is close-grained in texture and becomes harder and more concentrated with age. These cheese types should have an even texture and colour and should be moist, not dry or cracked.

The best Australian hard cheeses are made with spring and early summer milk and take at least six months to mature, so they make ideal buying in winter. Mature cheeses of eighteen months or more can be quite exceptional if you are lucky enough to find them.

Wrapping and Storing

Cheese is a living product, and once cut the open surfaces need to be wrapped to prevent drying. Wrapping in any form of plastic film should be avoided, especially for long periods. Plastic does not allow the cheese to breathe and will asphyxiate any living organisms. It will also cause sweating when the cheese is brought to a higher temperature for serving.

If you buy a cheese correctly wrapped, it is best to continue to use the original packaging. Alternatively, use waxed cheese paper – a good cheese retailer will always have some. Waxed paper prevents the cheese from drying out and at the same time allows the cheese and the associated living organisms to breathe, and it is ideal for bringing cheese to serving temperature.

Cheese can be practically stored in the vegetable compartment of the fridge, which is usually warmer and moister than other areas. Make sure the cheese is not touching any vegetables. Perhaps keep it in a separate box, but don't seal the lid. Never freeze cheese.

Fresh

Fresh cheese is not dependent on moulds and can be kept cool in a container with a loose-fitting lid. Alternatively, place it on a plate or in a bowl and cover it loosely with plastic wrap. Do not wrap it too tightly, as this will trap gases and draw off moisture. Fresh curd can be kept for up to a week in this way. Simply spoon off any whey that forms.

Fresh cheeses benefit from being stored at around 2–4°C; if they become too warm they lose moisture and condition.

White and Washed

The bacteria and moulds in surface-ripened cheeses need cool, damp, humid conditions to flourish. The best way to store these types of cheese is to keep them wrapped – preferably in the original wrapper – in the vegetable compartment of the fridge or in a similarly cool, damp place.

The type of wrapping used for these cheese types can have a major influence on their eventual flavour characteristics. The wax-coated paper often used to wrap traditional cheeses allows the cheese to breathe slowly and creates a slightly moist microclimate. These cheeses often have mottled rinds and a slightly yeasty smell.

Plain foil or paper-backed butter wrap, which is commonly used in Australia, tends to make the cheese sweat a little and develop a slight ammonia smell as it matures. Modern perforated white plastic wrap, which is used by large industrial dairies, allows the rind to breathe and in white rinds encourages a pristine white downy coat and mild mushroom smell.

Blue

Avoid storing blue cheeses with other cheeses that are susceptible to mould or flavour contamination. Blue cheeses can be stored at a lower temperature than many surface-ripened types, but make sure you give the cheese plenty of time to breathe and warm to serving temperature. Blue cheese is often sold in foil, but this is best replaced with waxed paper. The foil stops the crust from growing, and when the metal is weakened by the acidity in the cheese, it fragments into little pieces that are hard to remove.

Semi-hard and Hard

The exposed cut surfaces of these cheeses quickly oxidise and lose their subtle sweetness, so it is essential to keep the surface wrapped. Hard, granular cheeses and smooth-curd types are traditionally stored in damped calico cloth or waxed paper. If you have no alternative, apply a film of plastic wrap firmly across the smooth cut surface of the cheese and press it down gently with a slightly damp cloth. Ensure the rind is not covered and still has breathing space, as this controls texture and flavour development.

Maturing

Age is not important unless you're a cheese.

Helen Hayes

If you want to buy cheese for maturation, you will need to take special measures. There is an optimal age for every cheese, and this can vary from a few days to several years, so it is difficult to make sweeping statements about how to mature cheese. The one general principle is that it requires patience and care and a means of achieving the right humidity and temperature conditions.

All cheeses with rinds depend on the action of moulds to mature, and are therefore best kept in cool, damp conditions where the moulds can continue to develop. Trying to achieve the ideal temperature and humidity is a real challenge in Australian summers, but it is possible in winter in some cooler areas.

To start with, it is best to buy a whole cheese, as small cuts of cheese do not store well and rarely mature. Maturation is relatively easy for small, whole surface-ripened cheeses, which are often suitably packaged and do not take up a lot of room. But most hard cheeses are made in large wheels for a reason – because they mature more slowly and develop better flavours. It is rarely satisfying to mature small replicas of traditional hard cheese such as cheddar truckles because the cheese will dry out long before it develops any real flavour dimensions.

Temperature

It is important to create just the right conditions to mature a cheese. Avoid shocking it into submission by frequent temperature changes. If cheese is kept too cold, it rarely recovers; the active organisms stop working and maturation is interrupted, often leaving a bland, boring cheese. On the other hand, if it is kept too warm or overwrapped it will sweat, developing a tacky rind, soggy base, soft, rubbery texture and strange smell.

As a general rule you are better off erring on the warmer side, but if you want to slow the ripening process you can store cheese in a cooler place, wrapping it well.

The ideal temperature for maturing most types of cheese is 10–14°C, which is quite a lot warmer than normal refrigeration temperature. Blue cheeses prefer the cooler end of this range, around 10–12°C.

Humidity

Humidity is just as important as temperature. The essential character of any cheese is determined by its moisture level, and can be destroyed if it is stored under the wrong conditions.

The ideal storage humidity for most natural cheeses is 80–85 per cent, but these conditions are not available in most houses or even in refrigerators, which are much too dry. Refrigeration draws moisture from the air – and from your cheese, if you are not careful about wrapping.

There are all sorts of constructive ways of creating the right kind of microclimate. A simple, practical method is to store your cheese in a polystyrene box with a hole the size of a 20-cent piece in the top. This can be kept in or out of the fridge, depending on the weather. A linen cloth kept damp and placed over the wrapped cheese will maintain essential humidity and prevent airflow from drying the cheese out, while the hole will allow cool air to circulate.

All cheeses should be loosely wrapped and turned or brushed regularly. It is also important to keep a close and careful eye on the cheese and get to know it by touch, smell and appearance. You will learn to recognise how it is maturing. When you think it is ripe, have a taste. If it is ready, eat and enjoy.

g

EATING

The Cheese Board

There is much to recommend the French custom of bringing the cheese board to the table after the main course. A good cheese board should be a feast for the eyes as well as the palate, and signals the time when the hosts can relax, enjoy the fruits of someone else's labour and join the conversation around the table. A well-thought-out cheese board also provides an interval between the savoury main course and the dessert, and the sweetness of the dessert helps with the digestion of the cheese.

How much cheese to serve on a cheese board depends on your guests' appetites, how good the cheese is, what else you have planned for the meal and of course how many people there will be. Always buy enough cheese to offer a generous serve. As a general guide, aim at 50 g per person when cheese is an important part of a light meal, or about 25 g when it is part of a larger meal.

Selection

A good selection might include anything from one to five cheeses. Do not buy on numbers to impress. One really great cheese is far better than several mediocre ones, and different flavours can confuse the palate.

There are many different principles that can be used to assemble an interesting cheese board that will appeal to a range of different palates.

Types

You can combine the different types of cheeses to produce a pleasant contrast of textures, colours and flavours. You might choose four or five, including a soft fresh cheese, a traditional white-rind, a washed orange rind, a well-rounded blue, and a semi-hard or interesting mature hard cheese.

Single types

A selection of cheese of just one type can work well – for example, several blue cheeses or a selection of mature goat's milk cheese. This approach is particularly appropriate for strong cheeses such as blues, which tend to monopolise a table. It also makes a lot of sense if the type of cheese selected is in peak season, and has the added advantage of matching well with just one style of wine.

Region

A selection of cheeses from a particular region, either similar types or a range of varieties, will often match well with a regional wine selection.

Shapes and colours

Different shapes and colours can add interest to your cheese board. Rather than having all shapes the same, it is more visually appealing to offer a mixture of pyramids, logs, cylinders, rounds and pieces cut off whole wheels.

Milk types

A selection of cheeses made from different milk types can produce attractive flavour contrasts. In spring, you might try fresh cheeses from ewe's, cow's, goat's and buffalo milk with seasonal fruits; in autumn, try three surface-ripened cheeses.

Serving Temperature

After removing cheese from storage it is important to look after it carefully and serve it at a temperature that will best reveal its true flavour and texture. Many cheese books advise serving cheese at room temperature. This is all very well in a cool European climate, but is clearly ridiculous when the mercury climbs into the thirties in Australia. On a hot day or in a hot kitchen, it can be difficult to leave cheese out before serving because it will soon sweat, spoil or ooze away. In these conditions it is best to remove cheese from the refrigerator only an hour or so before serving, leaving it wrapped in its waxed paper, and cover it with a damp cloth so that it will not dry out. In winter, remove cheeses from the refrigerator at least four to six hours before serving or, if you are serving a large wedge of one particular cheese, allow up to twelve hours for it to come to room temperature.

Fresh soft cheeses are usually best served much cooler than other types to avoid losing the flavour of the whey and to emphasise the fresh character of the cheese.

Presentation

So much work goes into making a cheese that the least it deserves is special treatment when it is displayed at the table.

Real cheeses look best on natural materials. Straw trays, wooden or marble boards, straw mats, waxed paper, seasonal leaves, wicker trays and ceramic tiles are just a few options. Whatever you do, keep it simple and allow air to circulate between the selected cheeses. Don't devalue your careful selection by cramping it.

If your selection includes one cheese that has a particularly strong character – blue cheese or mature ash-covered goat cheese, for example – present it on a separate tray to avoid its flavour contaminating milder cheeses. For the same reason, always provide individual knives for cutting each cheese.

Always offer both a knife and a fork for the cheese course; not everyone wants to eat the rind of a natural cheese.

Cutting

When buying cut cheese you expect to get a fair share of the centre of the cheese and a share of the outside rind too. On a cheese board, similar rules apply. Always cut cheese with the next person in mind. For example, a triangular wedge should be cut from tip to outer rind. If you cut across the tip, the people who follow you will get more than a fair share of the rind.

When tasting cheeses, it is best to begin with the mildest, progress to stronger, mature types and finish with blue cheeses. Otherwise the lingering flavours of the stronger cheeses will interfere with your appreciation of the milder types.

How to cut different styles of cheese

Fresh, White and Washed

 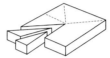

Blue and Semi-hard

Hard

Accompaniments

Good cheese has a beauty of its own, and does not need to be dressed up. The best combination is usually the simplest, and you can't beat the simplicity of good bread and wine. Some other alternatives include:

Butter
Unsalted butter can temper flavours in some stronger varieties, particularly of blue cheese.

Dried fruits
Dried figs and muscatels on the vine look and taste delicious with most cheese types.

Fresh fruit
Apples, pears and figs in season can be perfect partners for the right cheese types. They tend to work best with semi-hard and cooked types, where they are refreshing on the palate and do not overpower the flavour.

Apricots, peaches, nectarines and berries are best in late spring and early summer, and are a natural seasonal match for fresh cheeses. Fruits such as strawberries or raspberries can lift young, fresh, acidic cheeses, but are inappropriate with rinded cheeses and are best served as dessert.

Fresh herbs
Roughly chopped garlic with fresh herbs or rocket can be stirred through fresh cheese to make a cool summer dish.

Honey
A drizzling of honey can enhance the flavour of fresh goat's cheese or blue cheese.

Nuts
Fresh seasonal nuts in shells have a lovely sweetness that balances well with stronger cheeses. Walnuts are particularly good with blue cheese, hazelnuts with cheddar.

Preserves
The use of vinegar-based pickles is an English custom that works well with hard cheddar cheeses. Sweet mustard fruits balance well with mature, salty cheeses. In Spain and Italy, fruit pastes are used to accompany hard ewe's milk cheeses.

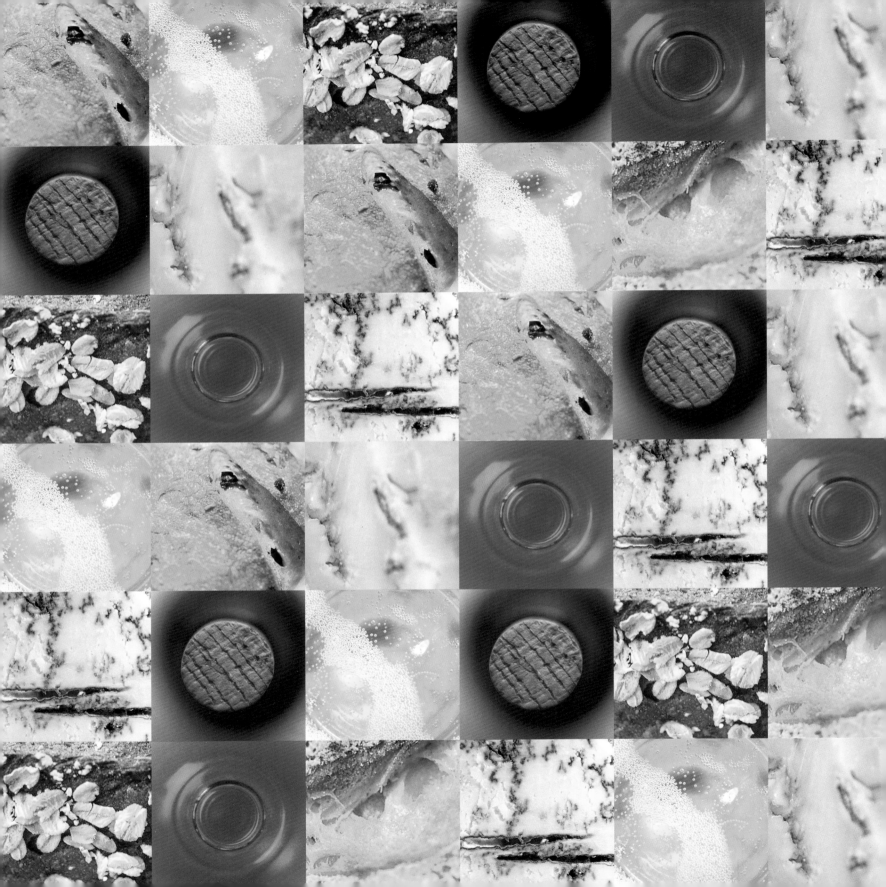

Bread, Cheese and Wine

Bread

Cheese and bread make a classic food combination that has delighted the rich and sustained the poor since ancient times. Both these traditional foods are created using natural fermentation techniques, and the quality of both depends on the quality of the raw ingredients and the skills of the maker.

In modern times, dry biscuits have tended to replace bread as an accompaniment to cheese. Certainly plain biscuits are convenient, but their crunchy texture often interferes with the full appreciation of the cheese. Biscuits can never match the subtle taste and texture combination of bread and cheese.

Bread balances the flavours of many cheeses and enhances their sensual texture. It can also make the difference between appreciating a good cheese or dismissing it as too strong. Just as cheeses made using traditional techniques have more character than mass-produced items, so bread is at its best when traditional methods are employed, using natural starters without improving agents.

There are no hard-and-fast rules on combining bread and cheese, but the general rule is to try to match the strength and texture of the bread to the strength of the cheese. Soft, fresh cheeses and white-rind types are best eaten with light, crusty breads. Washed-rind cheeses will balance well with fruit bread. Blue cheeses can be quite delicious with stronger sourdoughs and rye bread in any form. Semi-hard cheeses combine well with strong wholemeal or walnut breads. Fruit bread complements the strengths and masks the weaknesses of hard-cooked cheeses.

Wine

Bread and cheese also have an affinity with another fermented food – wine. The combination of the three is sometimes referred to as the 'holy trinity'. Like cheese, wine is a fermented food used since ancient times to preserve the seasonal surplus for later consumption. There is an old saying that you can't make a silk purse from a sow's ear, and this applies especially to cheese and wine. The character and flavour of the final product is primarily dependent on the quality of the basic ingredient used.

A key influence on quality is the character of the region, or *terroir* as the French call it. In making wine, the quality of the harvest and the particular grape varieties used are determined by regional climate and geography. The theory of *terroir* also applies to dairy farming. Milk type and quality are regional and, like their European predecessors, the new Australian specialist cheeses have developed on a limited regional basis. In cheese and wine, the riches of the soil and local climate are combined with human skill, endeavour and patience over a long maturation time. In view of these similarities, it is hardly surprising that cheeses and wines often provide an attractive combination of complementary flavours.

The classic combinations of cheese and drink arose originally in Europe, where regional cheese types were developed over centuries to be enjoyed with the local beverages. The south-west of England, for example, is famous for its cheddar and apple cider, and the Loire valley in western France for its chèvre and dry white wines, while classic ewe's milk roquefort from the south-west of France goes well with dry red Cahors or fortified sweet wines such as sauternes.

There is no easy guide to 'right' and 'wrong' wine and cheese combinations. Wine and cheese both vary seasonally and according to the maker's interpretation of a particular style, especially in Australia, where the restrictions of tradition do not apply. On the other hand, many of the classic European combinations still provide a reliable guide to matching cheese with today's modern wine types.

Usually cheese and wine matching is based on similarities rather than contrasts. The idea is to provide a complementary balance of flavours and textures. The traditional starting point is to approach the two on the basis of strength, matching the weight and flavour of the cheese to the wines in order of their taste strength. Fresh, mild, rindless cheeses balance well with light white wines; then you can work through the various categories until you reach hard, mature cheeses and older, full red wines. Blues and mature goat's milk cheeses are generally matched with sweet fortified wines or stickies.

There are intriguing parallels between certain cheese types and wine varieties. Goat's milk cheese and unwooded white wine, for example, both require delicate handling during the making process, and most goat's milk cheese is consumed quite young, as are many white wines. The character and flavour of both depend on a careful balance of refreshing acidity. Is it just a coincidence that they make a good marriage? Cow's milk, on the other hand, is far more resilient and makes longer-maturing, full-bodied cheeses. There are parallels with the handling and maturation of red wines, and a well-matured cow's milk cheese is probably going to make a good companion to that special bottle of older red.

Contrary to popular myth, however, white wines and stickies are far easier to match to most cheese types than full red wines. Red wines often contain a lot of tannin, which is a natural enemy to the taste of most cheeses and can produce bitter, metallic or mousy flavours. Having said that, when a red wine combines especially well with cheese it can be a true source of delight. This is often the case with older red wines where the tannins have disappeared.

Wine merchants have an old adage: 'Buy on apples and sell on cheese.' The idea was that, while apple cleanses and sharpens the palate, the fatty coating of cheese can easily hide imperfections in wine. By offering potential customers cheese when they were tasting wine, the merchant could make the wine seem smoother and richer than it really was.

Cheese and wine or wine and cheese? It might sound pedantic, but the order is important. While it is debatable whether good wine really needs a good cheese, there is no doubt that the pleasure of eating a good cheese is considerably enhanced by adding a good matching wine.

There are no definite rules when it comes to matching cheese and wine, and all individual palates vary. The best general guide is your own tastebuds and imagination. What follows is what I have observed rather than the last word on the matter, and you can have fun trying the myriad of possible combinations.

PORT AND STILTON

The Victorians developed the novel idea of scooping out the centre of stilton with a spoon and mixing it with port, presumably as a way of using up old, dry or imperfectly made cheese. This is wonderful if you want to sell more cheese, but it is a waste of good port and stilton, which are far better enjoyed separately as companions at the same table.

Perfect Matches

Fresh

By its nature, fresh young cheese is usually very simple but delicate in flavour, and often slightly acidic and herbaceous. These cheeses are best suited to light, refreshing wine styles that will not overpower the pure, subtle flavour of the young cheese. The most numerous and popular cheeses in this category are made from goat's milk, which is the most easily matched of all. Try simple, light, fruity white wines or young, refreshingly acid wines that have dominant varietal fruit flavour and have not been matured in oak.

Wines:	*Breads:*
Riesling	Baguettes
Gewurztraminer	Walnut bread
Chenin blanc	
Sauvignon blanc	
Young sparkling whites	

White

Young traditional white-mould cheeses are chalky and acidic and have little depth of flavour, but will match well with cider.

As traditional white-rind cheeses mature, their flavour becomes stronger and their texture turns to a buttery goo. The rind develops a strong brassica or sometimes ammoniac flavour that dominates the creamy inner paste. When matching such cheeses with wines, it is well worth trying the cheese with the rind on and off.

These cheeses are stronger than fresh varieties and so need wines with a bit more punch and a fuller bouquet. The wines required are more complex too, with a flavour that has been enhanced by the skill of the wine-maker, most commonly by maturation in oak casks (or, for cheaper wines, in vats with oak chips). Older chardonnays are the thing to drink with ripe, almost runny white moulds. Maturation adds concentration and nutty, toasty overtones to the fruit and changes the texture of the wine in the mouth so it becomes luscious and buttery.

Wines:	*Breads:*
Oak-matured chardonnay	Baguettes
Light pinot noir	White sourdough
Wooded semillon	

Washed

This diverse group ranges from very mild and delicate cheeses with a firm, moist texture to very strong, stinky, wild cheeses that tend to ooze everywhere. This makes it difficult to produce a single rule for matching them with wine. They often need robust, aromatic wines that will match the strength of the cheese.

Vintage sparkling wines can be a good match for the milder cheeses because the yeastiness of the cheese rind and the wine's crisp acidity act as a counter to the full, creamy character of the cheese. Wild, robust cheeses require full-bodied, spicy, fruity wines such as pinot and grenache, or sweet, concentrated wines that will not be dominated by these powerful cheeses. In Alsace and Germany, these cheeses are commonly matched with sparkling, yeasty beer or semi-sweet wines.

Wines:	*Breads:*
Heavy pinot or grenache	Spiced fruit bread
Vintage sparkling wines	
Late harvest riesling	

Blue

Matching blue cheese and wine is one of the great challenges, but a wonderful marriage when you get it right. Most blue cheeses are salty, and the moulds that enjoy this environment give a strong extra dimension to the flavour. The choice of wine depends on whether the blue has definite acidity or a long, rounded, creamy flavour.

The safest match for blue cheeses is a time-honoured one: sweet or sticky wines that can balance the immense flavour strength of the blue mould. These include rich, luscious dessert wines affected by noble rot or *Botrytis cinerea,* a mould that grows on the grapes in humid conditions at the end of a season. Botrytis-affected wines are sweet but not cloying because they have high levels of acidity as well as sugar.

Other classic partners for blue cheese are fortified wines such as tokay or muscat – powerful, very sweet wines that are strong enough to balance most blue cheeses.

Red wine and blue cheese can often be an unpleasant combination, because the moulds of the blue counteract the tannin and acidity to produce sensations that are like chewing on silver foil, or aromas reminiscent of sniffing a mouse or worse! There are exceptions, however: old Australian red wines matured in small barrels with a high alcohol level and inherent sweetness, especially those from warmer climates such as the Barossa, can match surprisingly well with some soft blue cheeses.

Wines:	*Breads:*
Tokay	Rye bread
Muscat	Walnut bread
Port	

Semi-hard

With age, natural-rind cheeses become more concentrated, stronger and rounded in flavour, with a texture that becomes increasingly dry and sometimes crumbly. For balance, they require fuller-bodied, robust red wines with ripe fruit and a slightly bitter tannin finish. Red wines are usually good companions to cow's milk cheese, but a glass of apple cider with a good cheddar can make an interesting change.

Wines:	*Breads:*
Cabernet sauvignon	Walnut bread
Shiraz	Wholemeal bread
	Oat cakes

Hard

The cooking of the curds to make hard cheeses caramelises and concentrates the natural milk sugars, producing a slightly sweet, nutty flavour. This type of cheese is quite versatile. It goes particularly well with old red wines or fortified sweet wines that match the sweetness and strength of the cheese.

Wines:	*Breads:*
Tokay and muscat	Fruit bread
Mature sweet sherry	
Old red wines	

MATCHING GOAT'S AND EWE'S MILK CHEESES

Goat's Milk

Goat's milk is extraordinarily versatile in matching with many wines. The lingering, creamy flavours of a fresh goat cheese go particularly well with sparkling wines or fresh, crisp whites with a dry finish, while mature goat cheeses are among the few cheeses that are at home with robust reds.

Ewe's Milk

When young, these very rich cheeses are often difficult to match. Sparkling chardonnay is good, but for a miraculous combination try a dry sherry to balance the milk's natural richness. More mature cheeses combine well with big, rounded reds or fortified wines.

ing

COOKING

Cooking

It would be easy to conclude that cheese is best enjoyed simply with a loaf of bread, a glass of wine and some good company. Yet cheese is a convenient and versatile ingredient for many cooked dishes, and provides an astonishing variety of options in the kitchen. The options are based not just on the range of cheeses available but also on the extraordinary range of ingredients that can be matched with different cheeses and the many alternative methods of cooking.

The principle of cooking with cheese is the same as cooking with most other foods: using high-quality raw ingredients is crucial to the flavour and texture of the finished dish.

Heating cheese adds yet another dimension to its individual flavour and character, and also changes its texture. At a low temperature cheese will simply melt. At higher temperatures the curd will shrink, releasing moisture and fats, while a still more intense heat will brown or caramelise the cheese. Heating also releases the aromas of the cheese. Different milk types produce different results under heat. Cow's milk has large fat globules that separate quite quickly from the curd, while goat's and ewe's milk are naturally homogenised and are slower to melt or coagulate.

Using Different Cheese Types

Fresh

The soft texture of fresh cheeses lends itself to melting but not to grating. In some cases, care must be taken to avoid curdling or separation with heat. Goat's milk cheeses provide a more dominant flavour and character than fresh cheeses made from cow's or ewe's milk. When matured slightly, goat's milk cheese is perfect for slow baking or grilling with a little olive oil, as its homogenous composition means it will hold its shape longer than cheeses made from other milks.

White

White-rind cheeses are seldom used in cooking, partly because much of their character lies in their texture, which is not improved by melting. There are, however, some classic French recipes for filled white-rind cheeses, as well as the infamous white-rind cheese coated in breadcrumbs and fried.

Washed

Washed-rind cheeses offer new and rich dimensions to many cooked dishes, in texture and particularly in aroma. They are normally melted or grilled, but are almost always stripped of their crusty rinds first.

Blue

Blue cheese is generally blended with other strong ingredients that balance out its spicy, rich flavour. Blue works well melted into savoury and sweet dishes, but is difficult to brown to a crust.

Semi-hard and Hard

Semi-hard and hard cheeses are the most concentrated types in terms of flavour and texture, and were originally designed for storage and for use in cooking. These are ideal for grating or as melted bases for many traditional cheese dishes. They are best freshly grated from a piece; pre-grated cheeses tend to be poor quality and rapidly lose any aroma they had to start with.

Recipes

Fresh

Goat's Cheese Croutons and Agresto Sauce

Maggie Beer

Agresto sauce

1 cup (150g) roasted almonds
1 cup (100g) roasted walnuts
2 cloves garlic
2 ³/₄ cups flat-leaf parsley
¹/₂ cup basil leaves
1¹/₂ teaspoons sea salt
Freshly ground black pepper
³/₄ cup extra virgin olive oil
³/₄ cup verjuice

Croutons

1 French stick
Olive oil (for croutons)
Rocket
Extra virgin olive oil
Red wine vinegar
Sea salt
Freshly ground black pepper
250g fresh goat's curd

Using a food processor, whiz all agresto ingredients except the oil and verjuice into a fine paste, using a little of the olive oil to make sure it is liquid enough. Add the balance of the olive oil and then, when amalgamated, add the verjuice. This will be the perfect consistency for using with croutons.

To make croutons, preheat oven to 180°C. Cut French stick diagonally into croutons, brush one side with olive oil and toast in hot oven till golden. Wash and trim the rocket, dress with extra virgin olive oil and red wine vinegar and arrange on plates. Pile the croutons with goat's curd and top with agresto sauce.

Serves 6

BASIC DOS AND DON'TS

- If you are grating cheese, chill it first.
- Avoid overcooking: it coagulates the casein and will make the cheese tough and rubbery.
- Don't reheat, overheat or burn dishes with cheese.
- Always add cheese to sauces at the last minute – just long enough to melt it.

Twice-baked Goat's Cheese Soufflés

Stephanie Alexander

from *The Cook's Companion* (Viking, 1996)

These soufflés are not served in their dishes, so it's possible to use aluminium moulds or even teacups of approximately 150ml capacity.

60g butter
60g plain flour
350ml warm milk
75g fresh goat's cheese
1 tbsp grated parmigiano reggiano
2 tbsp chopped fresh parsley (or parsley and other herbs)
3 egg yolks
Salt and freshly ground black pepper
4 egg whites
2 cups (500ml) cream

Preheat oven to 180°C. Melt 20g of the butter and grease 6–8 soufflé dishes. Melt remaining butter in a small heavy-based saucepan. Stir in flour and cook over a moderate heat, stirring, for 2 minutes. Gradually add the milk, stirring all the while. Bring to a boil, then reduce heat and simmer for 5 minutes. Mash goat's cheese until soft and add to hot sauce with parmigiano reggiano and parsley. Allow to cool for a few minutes. Fold egg yolks in thoroughly and taste for seasoning. Beat egg whites until creamy and fold quickly and lightly into cheese mixture. Divide mixture between prepared moulds and smooth surface of each. Stand moulds in a baking dish lined with a tea towel and pour in boiling water to come two-thirds up their sides. Bake for about 20 minutes until firm to touch and well puffed. Remove soufflés from oven – they will deflate and look wrinkled. Allow to rest for a minute or so, then gently ease them out of the moulds. Invert on a plate covered with plastic film and leave until needed.

To serve, preheat oven to 180°C. Place soufflés in a buttered ovenproof gratin dish, so that they are not touching. Pour over cream ($1/3$ cup per soufflé) to moisten them thoroughly. Return to oven for 15 minutes. The soufflés will look swollen and golden. Serve with cream from the dish or a fresh tomato sauce spooned around them and a small green salad.

Serves 6–8

Goat's Cheese Beignets

Andrew Blake

The ideal cheese for this recipe is chabichou (see p. 152), one of France's leading aged goat's cheeses. Alternatively, you could try a local cheese such as Meredith's Caprini or the Yarra Valley Dairy's Grabetto.

400g potatoes
200ml water
Salt and pepper
80g plain flour
60g butter
2 eggs
170g mature goat's cheese, grated

Peel potatoes and cover with cold water. Add a pinch of salt and bring to the boil. Simmer until soft, strain off all the water and mash the potatoes.

Place water, butter and pinch of salt and pepper into a saucepan. Bring gradually to the boil over a low heat. Once the mixture has come to the boil add the flour. Stir, still with the saucepan over a low heat, until the mixture comes away from the sides of the pan. Remove from the heat and add eggs one at a time, stirring continually. Allow to cool. Fold the mashed potatoes into this mix, and then fold in the goat's cheese.

Deep-fry tablespoon-size portions of the mix at 170°C until golden brown. Sprinkle with salt before serving.

Serves 6–8 as a nibble

Fresh Goat's Cheese and Capsicum Gateau

Serge Dansereau

Olive oil
1 large onion, peeled and sliced
6 large fleshy red capsicums, cut into large pieces
2 cloves garlic, whole
6 basil and 6 parsley stems
11 leaves gelatine
600g fresh goat's cheese, at room temperature
50g butter, softened
30g olive tapenade
1 tbsp chopped parsley
300ml cream

Preheat oven to 180°C. Heat the olive oil in a pan and sauté the onion until soft. Add the capsicums, garlic and herb stems, sauté for a further 10 minutes. Transfer to preheated oven for 15 minutes or until fully cooked. Allow to cool, discard the herb stems and purée in a food processor. Strain through a fine mesh sieve to remove the skin, then chill.

Soak 8 leaves of gelatine in cold water in one bowl. Repeat with remaining 3 in another bowl.

Mix goat's cheese with butter and spread firmly into the base of a 20-cm cake ring that is sitting on a tray lined with waxed paper. Brush with tapenade, sprinkle with parsley and refrigerate.

Whip the cream and gradually add three-quarters of the cold capsicum coulis. Strain the 8 sheets of gelatine and squeeze out water. Melt on low heat for 1 minute, pour into the capsicum cream mixture and combine delicately. Pour immediately into the cake ring and smooth the top. Return to the fridge. When set (approx. 30 minutes), melt the remaining 3 gelatine leaves and add to the remaining capsicum coulis. Pour on top of the cake to form the last layer – a beautiful red glaze. Refrigerate for 4 hours.

To serve, dip a small knife in hot water and cut carefully around the inside of the cake ring. Remove the ring slowly. Cut into 8 wedges, using a thin sharp knife dipped in hot water. Accompany with a crisp green salad of small mixed leaves and blanched asparagus.

Serves 8

Cream Cheese Cake

Jill Dupleix

A baked creamy tart with a hint of lemon, in the central European style.

200g caster sugar
3 eggs (65g)
750g soft cream cheese
300ml sour cream
1 tbsp lemon juice
1 tsp vanilla extract
2 level tbsp custard powder, sifted

Preheat oven to 180°C. Beat sugar and eggs together until smooth, using a hand-held or electric mixer. Add cream cheese and sour cream gradually, beating until smooth for up to 10 minutes.

Stir in the lemon juice and vanilla extract, and mix in the sifted custard powder. Pour into a lightly buttered 22 cm diameter springform cake tin and smooth the mixture evenly.

Bake in preheated oven for 50–60 minutes until the centre is firm and the top is slightly golden and looks as if it is about to split. Turn off the oven, leave the door ajar, and leave the cake in the oven to cool. Slice into wedges and serve the same day, accompanied with fresh berries, or poached cherries or plums.

Serves 6

Chabichou

Pan-fried Mozzarella

Geoff Jansz

Breadcrumbs
Buffalo milk mozzarella
Basil leaves
Proscuitto
Plain flour
1 egg, beaten
Olive oil

Prepare breadcrumbs by scooping the white of a sourdough loaf into a food processor and blending until fine crumbs form. Scatter onto a baking tray and place in a very low oven to dry.

Cut mozzarella into 1 cm slices. Place a basil leaf on each. Wrap tightly with a very moist, very thin, intact slice of prosciutto. Press flat. Dust with flour, dip in beaten egg and coat with freshly made breadcrumbs. For a thicker, crunchier coating, repeat the egg and breadcrumb dip. Place on a tray, making sure the pieces do not touch, and refrigerate.

When chilled, pan-fry in good olive oil over a medium heat, turning once. Serve immediately when golden and accompany with a Napolitano sauce, some tiny capers, grated parmigiano reggiano cheese and a glass of Chianti.

Tomato and Whitelaw Cheese Salad with Basil and Balsamic

Geoff Lindsay
from *Chow Down* (Allen & Unwin, 1997)

1 Whitelaw cheese
4 vine-ripened tomatoes
20 young basil leaves
Salt and pepper
80ml extra virgin olive oil
40ml balsamic vinegar

Slice each tomato horizontally 5 times. Spread slices on both sides with some cheese, a basil leaf, salt and pepper. Layer the tomato back to its original shape. Dress with oil and vinegar.

Serves 4

Eggplant, Goat's Cheese and Pesto Sandwich

Christine Manfield
from *Paramount Cooking* (Viking, 1995)

3 eggplants
Sea salt
Vegetable oil for deep-frying
30ml balsamic vinegar
90ml virgin olive oil
Extra pinch of sea salt
Pinch of freshly ground black pepper
300g fresh goat's cheese, at room temperature
2 roasted red capsicums, peeled and cut into strips lengthwise
9 tsp basil pinenut pesto
3 tbsp finely shredded rocket leaves

Cut each eggplant into 4 slices, each 2 cm thick. Sprinkle with salt and leave to sweat on a dry tray for 1 hour. Dry with paper towels to remove any excess moisture and salt.

Heat the vegetable oil in a deep-fryer or large saucepan to 180°C and fry the eggplant slices until golden brown on both sides. Drain, then pat dry with paper towels.

Make a vinaigrette by whisking together the balsamic vinegar, olive oil, the extra salt and the pepper.

To assemble the sandwiches, cut the goat's cheese into 6 slices 1 cm thick. Put a slice of eggplant on a plate and top with a slice of goat's cheese. Cover the cheese with a few strips of capsicum and a teaspoon of the pesto. Drizzle over some vinaigrette and then sprinkle rocket on. Cover with another slice of eggplant, pesto, vinaigrette and shredded rocket. Repeat this process using the remaining ingredients to make 6 sandwiches. Serve immediately, while the eggplant is still warm.

Serves 6

King Prawns and Goat's Cheese Tortellini

Neil Perry
from *Rockpool* (William Heinemann Australia, 1996)

Tortellini

*350g potatoes, unpeeled (kipflers, bintje, pink eye
and King Edwards are best)
Sea salt and freshly ground pepper
150g hard (baker's) flour
150g goat's milk fromage frais
Lemon juice*

Prawns

*Olive oil
12 large Yamba king prawns, or any large wild king prawn,
peeled and deveined
1/4 cup pinenuts, roasted until golden brown
1/2 cup raisins, soaked in hot English Breakfast tea
1/2 cup freshly grated parmigiano reggiano
200g unsalted butter*

To make tortellini, boil potatoes in salted water for about 20 minutes. When cooked, drain and leave until cool enough to handle, then peel and push through a potato ricer or food mill. Add sea salt and flour, and mix into a cohesive mass.

Season fromage frais with lemon juice, salt and pepper. Spoon mixture into a piping bag.

Take half the dough and cover with a tea towel to keep warm. Put the other half through the pasta machine at setting 10, dusting with a little flour each time if necessary. After about the third time through, the dough will start to come together, but don't expect it to look as smooth as normal pasta dough.

Lower machine to setting 5 and feed dough through. Fold dough into three and with a rolling pin roll out the seam and end to an even thickness. Open machine out to setting 10 again and roll dough through. It should become silkier and smoother with each passing. Continue down the scale until you reach setting 3. This dough is not as thin as normal ravioli, but it does have a sexy mouthfeel.

Lay the pasta sheet on the bench and trim the edges with a pizza cutter. Cut the sheet in half lengthwise, then cut the halves in perfect squares of about 3 cm. It is very important that you work in squares, as the sides roll over to make a triangle. This dough doesn't need water to stick together, but be careful not to use too much flour on the bench or in the last winding through, because the flour stops the tortellini from sticking together. The dough deteriorates as it grows cold, so try to work with it while it is hot.

With the dough directly in front of you, pipe a bit of goat's cheese towards the top left-hand corner of each square. Fold the bottom right-hand corner to the top to form a triangle enveloping the goat's cheese. You should have triangles on the bias with the point facing away from you to the left. Fold the base of the triangle up so it is level with the top point. You will have a long skinny piece of pasta with a bump in the middle. Pick up the pasta and wrap it around your index finger, with the top point of the triangle facing away from you. Squeeze the two ends together where they overlap. Place on a floured tray and repeat with the other pasta squares, then with the remaining dough. The filled pasta will keep in the refrigerator for a day and freezes well.

Place a heavy-based frying pan on high heat and add a little olive oil. When it starts to smoke, add half the prawns. Cook for 1–1½ minutes on each side. Be careful not to overcook; they should still be slightly translucent in the middle. Repeat with the other half of the prawns.

Bring a large pot of water to the boil. Salt the water and add 2 tbsp of olive oil. Place the tortellini in the boiling water, and remove them with a slotted spoon as soon as they float to the surface.

To serve, place 5 tortellini around the outside of each bowl and 2 king prawns in the middle. Sprinkle the prawns with pinenuts and raisins, and sprinkle the whole dish with parmigiano reggiano.

In the same pan used to cook the prawns, add the butter and burn it until it is nut-brown. Put a spoonful of hot butter over the tortellini and serve immediately.

Serves 6

Salad of Baby Spinach, Feta and Kalamata Olives

Jeremy Strode

This dish was inspired by a Greek salad and the quality of the young spinach leaves that the French call 'Pousse d'Epinards'.

½ fiscelle (small baguette), one day old
1 tbsp balsamic vinegar
40ml olive oil
40ml extra virgin olive oil
Sea salt
Freshly ground white pepper
100g baby spinach, picked, washed and drained
200g ewe's milk or mixed milk feta, cut into 0.5 cm squares
24 Australian kalamata olives, pitted
½ continental cucumber, peeled, cut in half,
seeded and finely sliced
2 ripe Roma tomatoes, cored and cut into 6 wedges

Cut fiscelle into thin slices, place on a baking sheet and bake at 180°C until golden brown. Make vinaigrette by whisking balsamic and oils together and season to taste. Toss salad ingredients together in a large bowl and dress with vinaigrette. Divide evenly between four entrée plates or salad bowls and serve.

Serves 4

Barbecued Asparagus and Feta

Richard Thomas

This recipe requires feta marinated in good olive oil and fresh herbs.

Paint tender asparagus spears with the oil marinade, plus some crushed garlic and a little chilli if desired, then char-grill. (If you don't have a charcoal grill, it can be fried, or cooked direct on the hotplate.) Serve on a warmed plate, with feta broken over the top and a little of the oil.

It is not necessary to overdo the cheese. Let the flavour of the asparagus show through.

Goat's Milk Feta with Roast Tomatoes, Herbs and Olive Oil

Martin Webb
from *Fusions* (Ebury Press, 1997)

The roast tomatoes are best made the same day you plan to eat them, but they may be made a day or two before and stored in the refrigerator. If you do this, remove them in plenty of time to allow them come to room temperature before serving.

Marinated feta

300g goat's milk feta
100ml olive oil
2 cloves garlic, sliced
2 sprigs rosemary
2 sprigs thyme
2 bay leaves
Loaf of crusty bread, to serve

Roast tomatoes

55g fresh mixed herbs, including stalks, such as basil,
thyme, parsley, oregano and sage
500g ripe Roma tomatoes
Salt and pepper

Several days ahead, cut the feta into 4 and place it in a bowl with the oil, garlic rosemary, thyme and bay leaves. Toss to coat and leave to marinate in the refrigerator until required.

Preheat oven to 250°C. Scatter half the herbs into a shallow roasting tray. Remove the stalk ends from the tomatoes with a small knife and cut each in half lengthwise. Place these halves on top of the herbs, cut side up. Sprinkle over ¼ teaspoon of salt and grind pepper over, then scatter with the remaining herbs. Roast at 250°C for 15 minutes, then turn the oven down to 150°C and cook for a further 2 hours. Allow to cool. Remove, leaving the herbs behind.

To serve, place 2–3 of the roasted tomatoes on each plate. Put a piece of feta next to them and drizzle over a little of the oil in which the cheese was marinated. Grind black pepper over and serve with crusty bread.

Serves 4

Top Paddock Washed Rind

White

Gnocchi with Cheese Sauce

Geoff Slattery

Gnocchi

1kg desiree or Toolangi delight potatoes
1 egg
300g plain flour
A little salt

Cheese sauce

50g brie (skin removed)
50g raclette
50g soft washed-rind cheese
15g creamy blue cheese
50ml cream, plus additional 100ml cream
2 spring onions, chopped roughly
A little grated parmigiano reggiano

Place potatoes, unpeeled, in cold water, and bring to the boil. Simmer until cooked. Drain and peel while still warm, then purée in a mouli. If you have no mouli, use a potato masher.

Place mashed potato on a clean work surface, and work in egg, flour and a little salt. Work together gently – overworking exercises the gluten in the flour and causes unwelcome elasticity – until you have a smooth texture in a long cigar-like shape. The texture should be airy, soft and delicate.

Cut into small pieces and cook in batches in boiling salted water until they rise to the surface.

To make the cheese sauce, bring all cheeses to room temperature, then blend in a food processor, adding some cream to ensure a smooth blend. Cook the cheese mixture over gentle heat with the rest of the cream and spring onions, gently stirring to blend. Add the cooked gnocchi, ensuring the cheese sauce 'grips' each piece of gnocchi.

Serve with only the sauce attached, and some pieces of spring onion. Season with black pepper and salt to taste. Sprinkle with parmigiano reggiano and chopped parsley if required.

Serves 4

Truffled Brie

Liam Tomlin

1.2kg ripe brie
250g mascarpone
2 leaves gelatine
3 tsp Madeira
3 tsp port
3 tsp truffle juice
50g chopped truffle

Cut the brie horizontally into two even rounds. Place the mascarpone in a bowl. Put the gelatine into cold water until softened, then remove and gently squeeze out the excess water.

Heat the Madeira, port and truffle juice until it boils. Remove from the heat and stir in the soaked gelatine until dissolved. Allow to cool slightly, then pour on to the mascarpone. Add the chopped truffle and gently fold through.

Spread the mixture smoothly over the cut surface of one round of brie, place the second round on top and press gently so the cheese is in its original shape. Cover and refrigerate overnight.

At Banc we cut the brie into long strips and then smaller bite-sized squares, place then on wheaten biscuits and serve them as a tasty canape, or simply sliced with a green salad.

Washed

Pepper Risotto with Washed-rind Cheese and Sage

Donna Hay

4 ½ cups (1125ml) vegetable or chicken stock
1 cup (250ml) dry white wine
2 tsp freshly ground black pepper
6 shallots, sliced
2 tbsp olive oil
2 cups arborio rice
¼ cup grated parmigiano reggiano
2 tbsp olive oil, additional
2 tbsp sage leaves, whole
150g washed-rind cheese, rind removed

Place stock and wine in a saucepan over medium heat and allow to simmer slowly. Place pepper, shallots and oil in a large saucepan over medium heat and cook for 2 minutes or until shallots are soft. Add rice and cook for 1 minute or until translucent. Add the hot stock mixture to the rice, a few cups at a time, stirring frequently so the rice doesn't stick and the risotto has a creamy texture. Continue adding stock until liquid has been absorbed and rice is tender. If the rice is not tender add a little boiling water. Stir the parmigiano reggiano through.

Place the oil in a small saucepan over medium heat. Add sage leaves and cook until sage is crisp and oil is golden. To serve, spoon risotto into bowls and top with a wedge of washed-rind cheese. Pour over the oil and sage mixture and top with lots of freshly ground black pepper.

Serves 4–6

Soft Polenta with Reblochon, Asparagus Spears, Poached Egg and Truffle Oil

Liam Tomlin

We sometimes serve this dish with parmigiano oil, which we make by placing the rinds from the parmigiano reggiano in a bowl with warm olive oil to cover and some cloves of garlic. We cover the mixture and allow it to infuse in the fridge for two days, then pass it through a fine sieve.

1 tbsp white wine vinegar
4 eggs
1 ½ cups (375ml) milk
190ml cream
190ml chicken or vegetable stock
1 clove garlic, crushed
2 sprigs thyme
150g polenta
Salt and freshly ground pepper
150g washed-rind cheese (e.g. Heidi Reblochon),
diced and with rind removed
16 spears asparagus, blanched
Truffle oil (optional)

Bring a large, deep pan of water to a rolling boil. Add the vinegar. Crack the eggs into the water and poach gently for 3–4 minutes until the whites have set. Remove with a slotted spoon and place in a bowl of iced water.

In another pan bring the milk, cream, stock, garlic and thyme to a simmer, remove from heat and allow the garlic and thyme to infuse for 10 minutes. Remove the garlic and thyme and return the liquid to a simmer. Whisk in the polenta and cook over a low heat for 10–15 minutes, whisking constantly until thick. Season with salt and freshly ground pepper. Fold the reblochon through the polenta so it begins to melt.

To serve, reheat the eggs and asparagus in boiling water, drain well and season lightly. Spoon the polenta on the warmed plates. Place the asparagus beside it and the poached egg on top, with a little truffle oil drizzled over and around the egg.

Serves 4

Taleggio Pizza

Geoff Jansz

Will and I developed this simple but impressive pizza together in our usual way – with an intensity as though the future of the human race depended on it! It was the triumph in an 'afternoon of a thousand pizzas' at my farm.

For each of the two quantities of dough, you will need:

750g plain flour
1/2 tbsp sugar
1/2 tbsp salt
7g dried yeast
50ml grassy-green olive oil
Warm water
Sea salt, black pepper
Taleggio cheese for topping (about 50g per person)
Rocket and cherry tomato salad to accompany

Warm the flour, sugar and salt in the oven, but don't let them get so hot that they burn to the touch. Mix the flour, sugar and salt with the yeast and oil and add enough warm water to form a smooth, spongy dough. Knead for 10 minutes, then leave in a warm spot for 2 hours to rise, covered with a damp cloth (not touching the dough). Cover with plastic and refrigerate overnight.

The following morning take the dough out and leave until it has risen completely, then collapsed. This will take hours, but is needed to develop the required sourness.

Make a second batch of dough and leave it aside to double in size. Knock back and knead the previous collapsed batch into it. Knead for about 5 minutes, let rest for 20 minutes, then tear off pizza quantities. Flatten and prepare pizza in the following way.

Place an unglazed terracotta tile (slightly larger than pizza size) into a hooded barbecue and turn on the heat. Brush the pizza dough with your best olive oil and put slices of taleggio cheese on top, leaving room for cheese to melt and spread.

Once the barbecue reaches about 230°C, open it up and scatter half a handful of semolina flour over the tile, then slide the pizza quickly and courageously on. Bring down the hood and prepare a rocket and cherry tomato salad dressed simply with olive oil, salt and pepper and some freshly squeezed lemon juice. The acids cut through the taleggio to refresh the palate and prepare for the next mouthful.

Have a good pepper grinder and some flaky sea salt ready. When the pizza emerges from the barbecue, sprinkle the molten surface immediately with the salt and pepper to taste. The perfume of the black pepper, released by the pizza's heat, is essential to the experience. With a huge knife slice through the pizza, taking time to appreciate the crunch as you pass through the crisp underside created by the tile. This pizza must be eaten hot. Serve with the salad and a good yeasty beverage, and listen to the angels sing!

Blue

Gippsland Blue and Walnut Potato Gratin with Witlof

Gabriel Gaté

400g medium-sized potatoes
Salt
1 medium-sized witlof
10g butter
½ tsp sugar
50ml milk
50ml cream
80g Gippsland Blue
Freshly ground black pepper
1 tbsp finely chopped walnuts
2 tbsp fresh breadcrumbs

Preheat oven to 180°C.

Peel and quarter potatoes. Cover with cold water and add a couple of pinches of salt. Bring to the boil and cook until just done. Meanwhile, wash witlof and halve lengthwise, then cut into small strips or julienne. Heat butter and sugar in a pan. Add witlof and cook on medium heat for 5–8 minutes or until soft.

Bring milk and cream to the boil in a saucepan. Turn off heat and add drained, cooked potatoes and blue cheese. Using a fork or potato masher, mash without making the mixture too smooth. Mix in witlof and season to taste with salt and pepper. Spoon preparation into a greased gratin dish. Sprinkle with walnuts and then with breadcrumbs and bake for about 15 minutes.

Serve this delicious dish with a salad of curly endive seasoned with a walnut and garlic dressing.

Serves 2, or 4 as a side dish

Herb Crumbed Lamb Cutlets with Blue Cheese Stuffing

Iain Hewitson

12 lamb cutlets, trimmed of all fat and sinew
Slivers of any good blue cheese
1 cup fresh breadcrumbs
2 tbsp chopped herbs (parsley, basil and mint)
Plain flour
Salt and freshly ground black pepper
2 eggs
¼ cup milk
Olive oil
Lemon wedges

Give the cutlets a whack with a meat mallet to flatten slightly. Place on a bench and make a cut into the cutlet parallel to the bench, almost to the bone. Place blue cheese slivers in cut and re-form.

Mix breadcrumbs and herbs together in one bowl, the flour with seasonings in a second bowl and whisk eggs and milk together in a third bowl. Dip cutlets into flour, then the egg wash and finally breadcrumbs.

Heat oil in a large heavy-bottomed pan and cook cutlets in batches until golden on both sides. Drain well and serve with lemon wedges.

Serves 4

Blue Cheese Sauce

Philippe Mouchel

You can make this sauce with any good-quality Australian blue cheese. It goes well with barbecued red meat such as a rib of beef or rump.

50g unsalted butter
1 shallot or 1/2 small onion, finely chopped
150ml dry white wine
1 cup (250ml) chicken stock
2 sage leaves
1 clove garlic, finely chopped
250g blue cheese, crumbled
1 tbsp tarragon mustard
Salt and pepper to taste

In a stainless-steel pan melt the butter, add shallot. Cover with a lid and cook over a low heat until soft without colouring. Add white wine and reduce completely. Add stock, sage and garlic and reduce by half.

Add the blue cheese and mustard with a wooden spoon and stir until cheese dissolves, taking care not to let the sauce boil. Remove from the heat and adjust seasoning. Be careful not to oversalt as the blue cheese is often salty, but use plenty of pepper.

Serves 4

Spinach Risotto with Gorgonzola

Damien Pignolet

A perfect risotto takes about 20–25 minutes to make and should be served immediately. Constant stirring is essential for an evenly cooked result.

2 large bunches of spinach
Salt
1 medium-sized onion, finely diced
100g unsalted butter
400g arborio rice
100ml dry vermouth such as Noilly Prat
1 1/2–1 3/4 litres light chicken stock, well seasoned
150g finely grated parmigiano reggiano
100ml extra virgin olive oil
150g piccante gorgonzola, broken into small pieces

Remove the spinach stalks and wash the leaves in several changes of water. Place the leaves in a pan with a small glass of water and some salt, and cover with a tight-fitting lid. Cook over medium heat, stirring from time to time, until the spinach has softened. Remove the lid and continue the cooking, stirring constantly, for about 5 minutes until the spinach is very soft and rather dry. Purée in a food processor and transfer to a bowl.

In a wide, shallow pan, cook the onion in the butter over moderate heat until transparent, add the rice and combine well. Add the vermouth and allow it to almost evaporate, then add sufficient hot stock to barely cover the rice. Continue to stir, adding more stock to keep the rice well moistened for the first 10 minutes. Taste a few grains for texture: it should be firm but not hard.

Stir in the spinach and a little more stock, and continue cooking until the right texture is reached. Adjust the seasoning and add half the parmigiano reggiano. Remove from heat and stir in the olive oil. Distribute between four deep pasta plates. Dot each serve with gorgonzola, pepper, and remaining parmigiano.

Serves 4

Fig and Aniseed Bread

Semi-hard and Hard

Cheese Fondue

Stephanie Alexander

To make a fondue you must have a table-sized fondue cooker with an adjustable flame and a heavy earthenware pot. Traditionally, long-handled forks are used to spear the bread and dip it into the communal pot.

1 clove garlic
1½ cups (375ml) dry white wine
1 tsp lemon juice
4 cups grated cheese (a mixture of gruyère and raclette)
1 tbsp cornflour or potato flour
3 tbsp kirsch
White pepper, grated nutmeg and paprika to taste

Accompaniments

Cubes of chewy white bread (sourdough for preference)
Cubes of rye bread
Pickled cornichons
Pickled vegetables
Boiled potatoes
Green leaf salad

Crush the garlic with the handle of a large knife and rub the inside of the pot. Tip in the wine and lemon juice. When it begins to simmer at the edges, it is time to add the cheese. Add the cheese gradually, stirring continuously in a figure-of-eight motion. Dissolve the cornflour in the kirsch. When the cheese mixture is bubbling, add the kirsch and cornflour mixture, still stirring. Cook 2–3 minutes more, stirring, and season to taste. Use your fork to dunk pieces of bread or potato in the fondue.

The pickles are there to nibble on while waiting and to refresh your palate during or after this delicious hit of cheese.

Serves 4–5

Parmigiano Reggiano, Fresh Pear and Green Oil

Maggie Beer

Nothing complicated is necessary to show off quality parmigiano reggiano and extra virgin olive oil. Wait till pears are next in season and serve as a luncheon dish with crusty bread or as a dish to finish a meal (though not necessarily accompanied by red wine).

1 bunch rocket
3 pears
300g parmigiano reggiano in a wedge
120ml extra virgin olive oil from an early-season crush

Wash rocket and spin dry. Halve pears and remove cores with a teaspoon or melon baller. Cut the parmigiano reggiano into shards. Place the rocket leaves around the serving plate. Either slice the halves of pear or position them on the plate cut side down. Divide the parmigiano reggiano and drizzle with extra virgin olive oil.

Serves 6

Baked Cheese Custard with Gruyère

Serge Dansereau

75ml milk
300ml cream
150g gruyère, grated
Salt and white pepper
4 medium eggs
3 egg yolks
50g gruyère, grated (for gratinée)
50g parmigiano reggiano, grated (for gratinée)

Combine the milk, cream and gruyère in the cooking pot and slowly heat until the cheese is melted and well combined. Add salt and pepper to taste and strain through a fine chinois (or sieve) and cheesecloth. Chill well.

Preheat oven to 170°C. Beat the eggs and yolks into the chilled mixture. Strain again. Pour mixture into 10 small cups lightly coated with an oil spray. Place cups in a bain marie (water bath) and bake for 55 minutes or until set. Remove and either allow to cool for 5 minutes before unmoulding or sprinkle with the gruyère and parmigiano, then place under a grill to gratinée the top of the custard. Carefully run a small knife down around the edge of the cup to unmould. If serving gratinée, place with the top side uppermost; if not, turn the custard over to serve.

To serve, place the custard on a plate and accompany with small leaves tossed in a mild vinaigrette, a slice of prosciutto, an oven-roasted tomato and a piece of roasted wood-fired bread.

Makes 10

As Good As It Gets Macaroni Cheese

Terry Durack

300g penne pasta (preferably Martelli)
Dash of extra virgin olive oil
3 tbsp butter
3 tbsp plain flour
3 cups (750ml) milk
½ tsp sea salt
½ tsp ground black pepper
1 cup grated parmigiano reggiano
1 cup grated gruyère
2 slices leg ham, 1 cm thick, diced
2 tsp Dijon mustard
Dash of Tabasco
½ tsp grated nutmeg
1 tsp truffle-scented olive oil
½ cup fine dry breadcrumbs
2 tbsp extra grated parmigiano reggiano

Preheat oven to 200°C. Cook the pasta in plenty of simmering, salted water with a dash of olive oil until tender. This should take about 11 minutes. Drain well.

To make the white sauce, melt the butter in a heavy-based saucepan and sprinkle the flour over the top. Blend the flour and butter together with a wooden spoon and cook over a low heat for 2–3 minutes, being careful not to let it brown.

Heat the milk to boiling point and pour half of it into the flour mixture, stirring well until the sauce thickens. Pour in the remaining milk a bit at a time, stirring, until it forms a thick but running sauce. Add sea salt, pepper, the two cheeses, ham, mustard, Tabasco and nutmeg and simmer for 5 minutes.

Oil the inside of a 30cm x 20cm baking dish or casserole with the truffle oil. Arrange a layer of pasta on the bottom, then spoon a generous layer of sauce over the top. Repeat until all ingredients are used up. With a couple of wooden spoons, gently mix the pasta and sauce. Combine the breadcrumbs and extra parmigiano and sprinkle evenly over the top. Bake for 30 minutes, or until the sauce is bubbling and the crust is golden brown.

Serves 4

Gruyère Fritters with Watercress Salad and Baked Green Tomatoes

Janni Kyritsis

Baked green tomatoes

5 large shallots, sliced
5 cloves garlic, sliced
2 bay leaves, crushed
500g green tomatoes, sliced
$1/2$ cup (125ml) white wine
$1/2$ cup (125ml) olive oil
Salt and pepper

Gruyère fritters

6–8 slices gruyère, 3 mm thick
Flour
1 egg, beaten
1 cup fresh breadcrumbs
Olive oil or clarified butter for frying

Preheat oven to 175°C.

To make the baked green tomatoes, place shallots, garlic and bay leaves in a non-aluminium baking dish. Lay tomatoes on top. Pour wine and oil over the top and sprinkle with salt and pepper. Bake for 30 minutes or until wine has evaporated.

To make the fritters, dip slices of gruyère in flour, egg and breadcrumbs. Shallow-fry in light olive oil or clarified butter.

Serve tomatoes and fritters with a simple wild rocket salad.

Serves 4

Spicy Cheddar Muffins

Siu Ling Hui

1 cup (250ml) milk
40g unsalted butter, melted and cooled
1 egg (60g), lightly beaten
Generous pinch cayenne pepper (or to taste)
200g plain flour
1 tbsp baking powder
1 tbsp caster sugar
$1/2$ tsp salt or to taste
1 cup grated sharp mature cheddar
100g walnuts, lightly roasted and chopped, or 1 grated apple

Preheat oven to 180°C. Combine milk, butter, egg and cayenne pepper in a large bowl. Sift together the flour, baking powder, sugar and salt. Toss cheddar with flour to mix well. Add cheese mixture to the milk mixture with either walnuts or apple. Stir until just combined.

Spoon into muffin tins and bake for 20–25 minutes or until muffins are golden and a skewer comes out clean.

Makes 6 large muffins

Fig and Aniseed Bread

Andrew O'Hara

This bread is an ideal companion for stronger washed-rind cheeses.

Day 1

250g strong flour
20g fresh yeast, or 10g dried yeast
150ml cold water

Mix all ingredients together to form a firm dough.
Place in sealed container in the refrigerator overnight.

Day 2

750g strong flour
20g salt
350ml warm water
400g figs, sliced
30g ground aniseed

Take the previous day's dough from the refrigerator and leave to come to room temperature. Combine it with flour, salt and water to make a fairly firm dough. Knead until it comes away cleanly from the bench, then add figs and aniseed. Knead again.

Cover and leave in a warm place until doubled in size, then knock the air out of the dough, cover and leave for a further 30 minutes.

Divide the dough into two equal portions. Round them up into tight balls, then flatten them out, using a rolling pin if you like. Roll up to make a Vienna shape. Cover and place in a warm place until doubled in size.

Turn the oven to 220°C and place a ceramic tile or a tray inside. When the loaves have doubled in size, slash the top of the bread with a sharp knife and place on the tile or tray.

For crusty bread, place a cover (for example, a meat dish) over each loaf, remembering to allow room for the bread to expand. Bake loaves for 20 minutes, then open the door. Remove the covers and leave the door ajar for 10 minutes (use a wooden spoon or peg to hold the door open). The bread should bake for 30 minutes all up. Then remove to a wire rack for cooling.

Makes 2 loaves

Burgundian Cheese Balls

Ian Parmenter

Bourguignonnes are small choux-pastry balls baked with cheese and served warm, popular as a pre-dinner appetiser in the Burgundy district of France. Delicious and easy to make.

125g unsalted butter
1 cup (250ml) water
½ tsp salt
125g plain flour
4 eggs (55g)
2 tbsp parmigiano reggiano, grated
100g gruyère, cut into 2-cm cubes

Preheat oven to 190°C. Cut butter into pieces and put in pan with water and salt. Bring to boil. Boil for 1 minute. Add flour all at once, stirring constantly. When mixture comes away from the side of the pan as a glossy mass, remove from heat. Stir in eggs, one at a time, stirring constantly. Stir in 1 tbsp parmigiano reggiano.

Put a generous heaped teaspoon of mixture on to a non-stick baking tray. (You could do this with a piping bag.) Press a cube of gruyère cheese into each mound of mixture. Sprinkle with remaining parmigiano. Bake for 15–20 minutes or until puffed up and brown.

Serves 10 as an appetiser

Afterword: The Raw and the Cooked

Making cheese from raw milk is a tradition practised for centuries in Europe, but in Australia it is currently illegal to make or sell cheese made from raw milk, although imports of certain European hard-cooked cheeses are permitted. Whether this policy should be changed is one of the most emotive issues facing specialist cheese-makers today. The largest dairy producers and policy-makers in Australia, New Zealand and America continue to debate the issue, many claiming that unpasteurised cheese is unsafe and should be banned. The General Agreement on Tariffs and Trade (GATT), which seeks to reduce both tariff and non-tariff barriers to international trade, has been seeking to establish an internationally accepted standard on the matter. This debate has important implications for the future of cheese-making in Australia.

Pasteurisation is a method of sterilising milk by heat treatment. Its primary aim is to apply sufficient heat to kill off potential pathogens and achieve an acceptable safety standard with as little damage as possible to the flavour and nutritional quality of milk. Australian national food standards require that milk or milk products used for cheese production should be subjected to pasteurisation or an equivalent heat treatment. The most widely used method is to heat milk to 71–74°C for 15–40 seconds, but 'batch processing' of milk for 30 minutes at 62–65°C is also accepted as adequate. Pasteurising milk to modern standards destroys 99 per cent of potential pathogens, reducing the risk of disease and allowing fresh milk and cheese to be kept for longer before they go 'off'.

The French scientist Louis Pasteur discovered this process during his experiments on wine fermentation during the 1850s, and his discovery was to have important implications for the development of many fermented food products, including cheese. At that time, almost all cheese was made in limited quantities, either on the farm or in small dairies, using raw milk. Milk hygiene was unreliable for a number of reasons: little was known about the sources of contamination in milking and storage, refrigeration was not commonly available and bovine diseases such as brucellosis and tuberculosis were not controlled.

From the 1880s onwards, the combination of new refrigeration techniques, pasteurisation and improved transport meant that for the first time fresh milk could be collected from a number of different farms with limited health risk as long as the milk was sterilised and stabilised after delivery to a central regional dairy. This process assured the rapid development of co-operative milk collection, which was the basis of many of the large industrial manufacturers that now dominate the Australian dairy industry.

The co-operative system today depends on taking vast quantities of milk from a large number of farms. Despite strict controls, milk quality inevitably varies from farm to farm, and there is always the remote possibility of contaminating the milk pool with a dangerous micro-organism from just one bad batch. Because of the scale of these operations and the risk involved, there is a very good reason to promote pasteurisation as a vital part of hygiene control for the mass production of milk, butter and cheese.

The question is whether small Australian specialist cheese-makers, who by definition work with a limited and controlled supply of very good quality milk, should be indiscriminately subjected to the same restrictions. There are several reasons for arguing that they should not.

First, pasteurisation alone does not absolutely guarantee a safe milk supply. The cleanest raw milk is far from sterile; once it leaves the udder, it contains bacteria that will sour and acidify it into curds and whey. These benign bacteria and microflora compete with pathogenic bacteria, and so help to protect raw milk from contamination. By killing 'good' and 'bad' bacteria alike, pasteurisation destroys this balance, so that milk for cheese-making actually becomes more open to subsequent contamination than its raw equivalent unless additional controls are implemented. In fact, almost all major health scares from cheese have arisen from contamination *after* pasteurisation or poor control of the pasteurisation process.

Secondly, traditional cheese-makers had developed their own methods of hygiene control long before pasteurisation was understood. These methods arose out of the basic fermentation principle. Homemade starter cultures, which relied on encouraging the production of lactic acid, not only had a preservative action, but were also a vital control measure to combat potentially pathogenic bacteria. This natural lactic acidification is a particularly effective form of control, and many harmful pathogens are unlikely to survive the actual cheese production process.

LISTERIA AND CHEESE

Listeria monocytogenes, or listeria as it is more commonly known, is an organism found in many foods, including pâté, cook-chill foods, smoked or pickled fish and some cheeses. It can cause listeriosis, an infection that is normally like a mild influenza but is more serious for certain groups of people – the very young, the very old, pregnant women and people with immune deficiencies. Those at risk should not eat white-mould, washed-rind or blue cheeses, *whether the milk has been pasteurised or not.*

Finally, the starting point for making any good cheese is the selection of good-tasting, clean, raw milk from healthy animals. If milk from an individual farm is clean in the first place, why pasteurise it for making cheese? The most important reason for not doing so is undoubtedly flavour. As Patrick Rance puts it, 'Most natural sources of aroma and flavour are destroyed by pasteurisation.' Pasteurisation kills off natural flora, yeasts, enzymes and essential esters that contribute to the complex and individual flavour of good cheese.

Many of the world's great benchmark cheeses owe their unique qualities to their origins or *terroir*: the combination of soil, climate, animal breeds and grazing patterns with the craft of the cheese-maker and the centuries-old methods of maturation. It stands to reason that a cheese made from natural raw milk will embody this *terroir* in a more immediate way, and will therefore have more individuality and interest, than a cheese made from pasteurised milk. The pleasure of eating specialist cheese is all about celebrating the differences in cheese, the excitement of a unique taste and flavour present on a particular day. Discovering the depth of flavours available in a well-made raw-milk cheese is rather like discovering colour television for the first time after years of watching black-and-white broadcasts.

Making traditional cheeses from raw milk also assists marginalised rural areas within the industrial nations. In Europe, many remote areas have benefited from maintaining traditional ways and old dairy breeds. Europe produces more than 400,000 tonnes of cheese from raw cow's milk annually, primarily in France and Italy. Many of these are classic hard cheeses such as parmigiano reggiano, grana padano, gruyère and emmental, which are made by large industrial producers, but small-scale production of raw-milk cheese on individual farms is enjoying a resurgence of interest, particularly among a new generation of cheesemakers in Britain and Ireland. These farmhouse cheeses are most commonly made from raw goat's and ewe's milk, because it has proved hard to organise milking these animals on a large industrial scale.

Raw milk can be indeed be dangerous from a poor, unregulated source, but with the correct monitoring raw-milk cheese is a natural and safe preserved food. Australia is a leader in disease-free herds, with clean, green pasture that is available almost all year and enviable milk quality. We could be exploiting this natural advantage by introducing a code of practice to allow cheese to be made from raw milk. The present legislation gives small Australian cheese-makers no choice on this issue, and there is no accepted code of practice for making cheese from raw milk.

PROBLEMS WITH POSSUMS

Australia and New Zealand have a common trade agreement known as the Closer Economic Regulations (CER), which includes an agreement to develop a joint approach to food regulations.

New Zealand has a problem accepting the principle of making cheese from raw milk, in part because of the danger that introduced feral possums might carry tuberculosis. Possums in New Zealand have no natural predators, and instead of living in trees they have become ground-dwellers. They pose a health risk because they mark their territory with urine spray, which might infect a paddock grazed by lactating animals.

Accurate testing and control of tuberculosis has to be conducted on individual animals rather than on milk or cheese, and is very time-consuming. The difficulties and added expense of trying to develop a system of more regular testing are among the many arguments put up by the New Zealand dairy authorities for insisting on the need to pasteurise all milk.

Small specialist Australian producers would benefit from a change in the law in several main ways:

- heightened awareness of the small producers and the virtues of their products, allowing them to take full competitive advantage of the regional character and flavour that make them different from the industrial producers

- increased margin and profit from premium raw-milk cheeses, and

- a growing respect and demand for local specialist cheese, both locally and in overseas markets.

Small artisan and farmhouse cheese-makers are niche players by definition, hand-making cheese with care and affection in small quantities from a limited supply of milk. They cannot compete with the large industrial producers on price. To remain economically viable, they need to be able to command a premium for their cheese, and the obvious way to do this is to offer customers cheese with more soul, more flavour – cheese that is distinctly different and interesting. For specialist cheese-making to continue to develop in Australia, there needs to be a 'real' quality and flavour difference between the small producers' offerings and those of the large industrial companies. The opportunity to make cheese with raw milk is a necessary part of this.

In Europe, centuries of experience have gone into making a diverse range of cheeses from raw milk, and urban gastronomes have widely supported the preservation of these traditional methods. As food has become more industrialised, there has been a countervailing consumer response from passionate foodies looking for more natural and interesting products with character and flavour. This development has occurred in specialist bread, wine, beer, eggs and now dairy products. The premium that people will pay for good cheese carefully crafted from raw milk may in the future mean economic survival for a small Australian cheese-maker.

Unless the current Australian legislation is changed, our new range of specialist cheeses will suffer from a sameness and will lack obvious competitive difference. Small artisan and farm-house producers will be forced out by larger producers with similar products. As consumer demand for specialist cheese develops, the market grows, and it is only a matter of time before the larger manufacturers will seek to enter this segment of the market too. The danger is that specialist cheese-making will come to be dominated by marketing dollars rather than a clear character and flavour difference. For small producers to compete, they need the opportunity to be different, and this should include the right to make raw-milk cheese.

Specialist Cheese-makers – A Visitor's Guide

New South Wales

Trading Name: Hobbitt Farm
Retail Address: Barry Way, Jindabyne 2627
Telephone: (02) 6457 8171
Hours: 7am–5pm daily, September–June only

Trading Name: Hunter Valley Cheese Company
Retail Address: McDonalds Road, Pokolbin 2320
Telephone: (02) 4998 7744
Hours: 9am–5pm daily; closed Christmas Day

Trading Name: Jannei Goat Dairy
Retail Address: 8 View Street, Lidsdale 2790
Telephone: (02) 6355 1107
Hours: Closed Wednesdays and Sundays;
10am–5pm all other days

Trading Name: Parmalat Foods Australia
Retail Address: 470–482 Hovell Street, Albury 2640
Telephone: (02) 6021 3455
Hours: 9am–5.30pm Monday–Friday; 9am–1pm Saturday;
closed Sundays and public holidays

South Australia

Trading Name: Island Pure
Retail Address: Gum Creek Road, Cygnet River,
Kangaroo Island 5223
Telephone: (08) 8553 9110
Hours: 1pm–5pm daily; closed Christmas Day

Trading Name: Woodside Cheesewrights
Retail Address: Hillstowe Wines, 104 Main Rd, Hahndorf 5245
Telephone: (08) 8388 1400
Hours: 10 am – 5pm daily

Tasmania

Trading Name: Ashgrove Farm Cheese
Retail Address: 6173 Bass Highway, Elizabeth Town 7304
Telephone: (03) 6368 1105
Hours: 9am–5pm daily; closed Christmas Day and Good Friday

Trading Name: Healey's Pyengana Cheese
Retail Address: St Columba Falls Road, Pyengana 7216
Telephone: (03) 6373 6157
Hours: July and August 10am–4pm daily;
September–June 9am–5pm daily; closed Christmas Day,
Boxing Day and Good Friday

Trading Name: Heidi Farm Cheese
Retail Address: 3784 Meander Valley Hwy, Exton 7303
Telephone: (03) 6362 2882
Hours: 9am–5.30pm daily, including public holidays;
closed Christmas Day

Trading Name: Lacrum (Cheese) Pty Ltd
Retail Address: 235 Hardmans Road via Mella, Smithton 7330
Telephone: (03) 6452 2653
Hours: 3pm–5.30pm daily; closed Christmas and New Year's Day

Trading Name: Lactos Pty Ltd
Retail Address: 145 Old Surrey Road, Burnie 7320
Telephone: (03) 6433 9200
Hours: 9am–4.30pm Monday–Friday;
10am–4pm Saturday, Sunday and public holidays;
closed Christmas Day and Good Friday

Trading Name: Westhaven Dairy
Retail Address: 89 Talbot Road, Launceston 7250
Telephone: (03) 6343 1559
Hours: 9am–5pm Monday–Friday;
closed weekends and public holidays

Victoria

Trading Name: Hellenic Cheese Farm
Retail Address: 55 Cotters Road, Epping 3076
Telephone: (03) 9408 1539
Hours: 10am–4pm Monday–Friday;
closed Saturday, Sunday and public holidays

Trading Name: Milawa Cheese
Retail Address: Factory Road, Milawa 3678
Telephone: (03) 5727 3589
Hours: 9am–5pm daily, including public holidays;
closed Christmas Day

Trading Name: Mountain Shepherd Cheese
Retail Address: Factory 3, 53 Sinclair Road, Dandenong 3175
Telephone: (03) 9793 3377
Hours: 9am–4pm Monday–Friday; 8am–midday Saturday;
closed Sundays and public holidays

Trading Name: Tarago River Cheese Co.
Retail Address: 2236 Main Neerim Road, Neerim South 3831
Telephone: (03) 5628 1569
Hours: 10am–5pm daily; closed Christmas Day and Good Friday

Trading Name: Timboon Farmhouse Cheese Pty Ltd
Retail Address: Ford and Fells Road, Timboon 3268
Telephone: (03) 5598 3387
Hours: 10am–4pm daily; closed Christmas Day and Good Friday

Trading Name: Top Paddock Cheeses Pty Ltd
Retail Address: Fitzgeralds Road, Bena 3946
Telephone: (03) 5657 2291
Hours: 10am–4pm Monday to Friday; closed Saturdays;
midday–4pm Sunday

Trading Name: Yarra Valley Dairy Pty Ltd
Retail Address: McMeikans Road, Yering 3770
Telephone: (03) 9739 1222
Hours: 10.30am–5pm daily, including public holidays

Western Australia

Trading Name: Kervella Cheese
Retail Address: Lot 52, Clenton Road, Gingegannup 6083
Telephone: (08) 9574 7160
Hours: By appointment only

Trading Name: Kytren Pure Goats Milk Cheese
Retail Address: Lot 99, McKnoe Drive, Gingegannup 6083
Telephone: (08) 9574 7147
Hours: Monday–Friday by appointment

Trading Name: Margaret River Cheese Company
Retail Address: Bussell Highway, Cowaramup 6282
Telephone: (08) 9446 3666
Hours: 10am–3pm Monday–Friday;
10am–4pm weekends and public holidays

Notes on Contributing Chefs

Stephanie Alexander is a Melbourne food writer and restaurateur (currently of Richmond Hill Café and Larder) and author of several books, including *The Cook's Companion* (Viking, 1996).

Maggie Beer is a South Australian food writer and producer of fine foods under the Maggie Beer label.

Andrew Blake is proprietor of Blake's restaurant in Melbourne and Events Warehouse by Blakes.

Serge Dansereau is chef and partner at Bathers' Pavilion, Sydney, and author of *Food & Friends* (Harper Collins, 1998).

Jill Dupleix is food editor of the *Sydney Morning Herald* and the Melbourne *Age,* and author of *New Food* (William Heinemann Australia, 1994) and *Old Food* (Allen & Unwin, 1998).

Terry Durack is a food columnist and author of *Yum* (William Heinemann Australia, 1996) and *Noodle* (Allen & Unwin, 1998).

Gabriel Gaté is a chef, food columnist and author of several books, most recently *Good Food for Men* (Heinemann, 1996) and co-author of *Anyone Can Cook,* a children's story book with recipes (Five Mile Press, 1999).

Donna Hay is food editor at *Marie Claire* magazine.

Iain Hewitson is a restaurateur and celebrity chef.

Siu Ling Hui is a freelance food writer and a regular contributor for *Good Weekend.*

Geoff Jansz is host of the Nine Network's *What's Cooking.*

Janni Kyritsis is chef and co-proprietor of MG Garage, Sydney.

Geoff Lindsay is a chef and author of *Chow Down* (Allen & Unwin, 1997).

Christine Manfield is a Sydney restaurateur of Paramount restaurant and author of *Paramount Cooking* (Viking, 1995), *Paramount Desserts* (Viking, 1997) and *Spice* (Viking 1999).

Philippe Mouchel is chef and director at Langton's in Melbourne.

Andrew O'Hara is the head baker at Phillippa's Bakery in Melbourne.

Ian Parmenter is presenter of *Consuming Passions* on ABC-TV and director of the Adelaide Tasting Australia Festival.

Neil Perry is chef and co-proprietor of Rockpool, Wockpool, MCA Cafe, Star Bar & Grill and Rockpool Catering in Sydney and author of *Rockpool* (William Heinemann Australia, 1996).

Damien Pignolet is executive chef and co-owner of Bistro Moncur and Bistro Deux, Sydney.

Geoff Slattery is the co-owner of D.O.M.O. in Melbourne.

Jeremy Strode is a restaurateur and chef at Pomme, Melbourne.

Richard Thomas owns Richard Thomas Cheese Company and Parma Cheese Company.

Liam Tomlin is chef at Banc and Wine Banc in Sydney.

Martin Webb is co-author of two books, *Quaglino's: The Cookbook* (Conrad Octopus, 1995) and *Fusions* (Ebury Press, 1997).

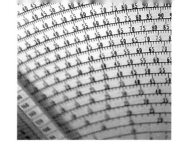

Bibliography

Adelaide College of TAFE, *Cheesemaking, Book I,* Department of Technical and Further Education, 1992.

Pierre Androuët, *Guide to Cheeses,* Aidan Ellis Publishing, 1993.

——————————, *Le Livre d'Or du Fromage,* Editions Atlas, 1984.

L. G. Ashton, *Dairy Farming in Australia,* Commonwealth Department of Commerce and Agriculture, 1954.

J. G. Davis, *Cheese,* Churchill Livingstone, 1965–76.

André Domine, *Organic & Wholefoods,* Konemann Verlagsgesellschaft, 1997.

K. T. H. Farrer, *A Settlement Amply Supplied: Food Technology in Nineteenth Century Australia,* Melbourne University Press, 1980.

Norman Godbold, *Victoria. Cream of the Country,* Griffin Press, 1989.

Juliet Harbutt, *The Specialist Cheesemakers' Association Guide to the Cheeses of Britain and Ireland,* The Specialist Cheesemakers' Association, 1994.

——————————, *The World Encyclopedia of Cheese,* Anness Publishing, 1998.

Randolph Hodgson, *Neal's Yard Dairy Cheese List,* Neal's Yard, 1996.

Steven Jenkins, *Cheese Primer,* Workman, 1996.

Frank V. Kosikowski, *Cheese and Fermented Milk Foods,* F. V. Kosikowski, 1997.

Max Lake, *Food on the Plate, Wine in the Glass,* Max Lake, 1994.

T. A. Layton, *Cheese and Cheese Cookery,* Wheaton & Co., 1971.

Kazuko Masui and Tomoko Yamada, *French Cheeses,* Dorling Kindersley Ltd, 1996.

Patrick Rance, T*he French Cheese Book,* Macmillan, 1989.

——————————, *The Great British Cheese Book,* Macmillan, 1982.

Cherry Ripe, *Goodbye Culinary Cringe,* Allen & Unwin, 1993

R. Scott, *Cheese-making Practice,* Elsevier Applied Science Publishers, 2nd edition, 1981.

André Simon, *A Concise Encyclopaedia of Food,* Collins, 1956 edition.

Michael Symons, *One Continuous Picnic,* Duck Press, 1982.

Maguelonne Toussaint-Samat, *The History of Food,* Blackwell, 1998.

Josef Vondra, *A Guide to Cheese in Australia,* Cavalier Press, 1992.

Index of Cheese Names

Subject Index